OUR GUMBALL RALLY

OUR GUMBALL RALLY

3000 Miles
3 Countries
65 Ferraris
Only 1 Volvo

Clement Wilson &
Richard Dunwoody

First published in Great Britain in 2005 by
Virgin Books Ltd
Thames Wharf Studios
Rainville Road
London
W6 9HA

A catalogue record for this book is available from the British Library.

ISBN 0 7535 0992 X

Typeset by TW Typesetting, Plymouth, Devon
Printed and bound in Great Britain by
Mackays of Chatham PLC

CONTENTS

With special thanks to
Olivia Galvin
who got our Gumball rolling
and
David Lehrer
for fuelling its momentum

AUTHORS' NOTE

You'll have heard the rumours, the stories from the past. The Gumball is both a delectable fact and tantalising fiction, truth and tales mixed into one.

This was no more than an intriguing statement on the Gumball rally press release; and one I initially dismissed as the mere hyperbole so common to press releases. Having done the Gumball rally we now know it to be something of an understatement. Firstly many of the apparently enticing promises behind the promotional literature such as 'breakfast with the Beckhams' and 'partying with the King of Morocco' are pure fantasy that more pedantic people might think ought to be examined by the Advertising Standards Authority. Secondly the tales, anecdotes and myths that abound on the rally itself are rapidly gaining legendary status amongst Gumballers accustomed to never being too sure what to believe.

For those people who have never heard of the Gumball rally it is essentially a motoring 'adventure'. Whilst marketed as 'it's not a race, it's a rally' in reality it is neither since the competitive element is basically defined by the individual entrants. Some like to race each other and others are more content with the touring nature of the event. While the organisers do not condone speeding or the mass flouting of traffic laws, and entrants undertake to abide by the terms that forbid speeding, it is readily accepted as an integral part of the 'fun' by all those involved.

The event was started in 1999 by Maximillion Cooper who organised '50 of his closest friends' for a road trip from London to Monte Carlo and has grown remarkably from there, spawning spin-offs from clothing to computers as well as many imitators. Since that first motley crew of fashion aficionados the Gumball has attracted an ever-increasing number and variety of entrants and has visited the United States as well of covering most of Europe at high speed. The basic premise of a 3,000-mile dash punctuated by prodigious partying has remained the same.

The nature of the rally attracts fans and criticism in equal numbers. Inevitably there are those who frown upon some of the wilder antics involving high-speed driving on the back of all-night partying. However, this book is not about criticising some of the more indefensible aspects of the event. While acknowledging that road safety and speed limits are not trivial matters we have taken a positive view of the Gumball rally, having thoroughly enjoyed the experience.

The following account of our Gumball adventure is predominantly fact, and not 'truth and tales' mixed into one. All the stories and anecdotes are real experiences, and for the most part the names have not been changed, except for in one or two cases in the interests of discretion. In keeping with the 'Spirit of the Gumball' there is one cheeky fib, ostensibly included for entertainment value, but in reality allowing us the opportunity to hide behind it should a girlfriend, mother, father, aged aunt or insurance company ever try and draw us into a 'Surely that's not true?' line of questioning. The other Gumballers mentioned in these pages might find it a useful defence also.

Among many, particular thanks are owed to Ali Gunn, Amanda Richards, Helen Barbara McAslan, Henrietta Magan, Mr and Mrs George Magan, Gordon Thomas, Noll Uloth of Cordings of Piccadilly, Sarah Atkins, James McNaught, Charlotte Hawes, Nicky Brownhill and Lucy Osborne. Apologies, as well as thanks, are due to Imogen Clist and all at Les Routiers, particularly Alex Chambers. Vanessa Daubney deserves a medal for stoically enduring some abusive and unwarranted telephone tirades from quarters best left unmentioned.

Above all I am indebted to Andrea Baker and David Lehrer, two people who showed enormous commitment and enthusiasm for our mad plans, and without whose assistance and support it would never have been possible.

CLEMENT WILSON

INTRODUCTION BY RICHARD DUNWOODY

Looking back I would still say the Gumball rally is the craziest, most dangerous, yet oddly one of the more enjoyable events I have ever participated in. It has some stiff competition amongst fourteen Grand Nationals and two Pardubice Velkas – a hair-brained cross-country race in the Czech Republic. I've also been on a 350-mile ski race to the Magnetic North Pole, coming face to face with a polar bear, and an endurance car rally, which took us deep into the foothills of the Alps for a hellish night. I spent most of that literally hanging out of the co-driver's window being violently carsick.

I cannot and do not condone much of what went on during the Gumball, but I must admit Clement and myself were as guilty as the rest of the drivers caught up in the madness of the whole thing. The book explains some of the occurrences in more detail, but bear in mind that if you are driving with a large white number on your car door, I have little doubt that the majority of people would allow their competitive instincts to take over, when yet another similar white number speeds past.

Notwithstanding the danger, I am happy to report that everyone survived to tell the tales, including, most importantly, many bemused – and some literally quite shaken – Moroccans, whose King had been most helpful in giving us the green light.

Maximillion Cooper, the Gumball founder, did warn us before the off that by the time we had completed 3,000 miles in six days with some epic partying along the way, we would experience fatigue like never before. I could not agree more. At the end of the first overnight leg to Marbella I was physically and mentally exhausted. From that point on, whenever there was a chance of rest over the next five days adrenaline, fear or just the idea of missing something made sleep virtually impossible. Under these circumstances it is hardly surprising that by the time we reached Barcelona I was somewhat disorientated and finding it difficult to remain steady on my feet!

Clement, my co-driver and co-author, would scandalously have you believe that this was due to some excessive partying. In the following pages he may convey that impression and, at the risk of being laid open to some pretty serious stick from friends and foe alike, I have encouraged him to tell it as he saw it. It is possible he may have used some artistic license and embellishment in the interests of humour, although it must be also be said there are other times when I am glad he has exercised some discretion! It is said it is good to laugh at yourself from time to time, and during the Gumball I found myself doing it far too often.

I will forever take him to task over his criticism of my navigational skills and my understanding of the local languages. Whatever he says, I did get us out of Madrid by the quickest route possible, and I find it difficult to agree with his criticism of my French in light of his D-grade A-level. As for my dancing? The less said the better.

This book is not meant to be taken too seriously and I apologise to anyone who may find any of it slightly offensive, but I hazard a guess that most will find it amusing and somewhat removed from the profession and pursuits that I am normally associated with.

RICHARD DUNWOODY

1. 'GENEVA – WHERE PEOPLE MEET'

'Geneva – where people meet' is the promising-sounding slogan of the Geneva Tourist Board. Thanks, but I think I'll be the judge of that. I had been in Geneva for a whole day and the place struck me as far from offering the sort of social excitement the slogan suggested. Looking around, I was not confident of meeting anyone at all, let alone anybody remotely interesting. As I nursed an empty glass, in an empty bar, having scoured the empty streets, I was thankful that I had not come in the low season.

'But, sir, it is the busiest week of the year. We cannot possibly find you a room at such late notice,' was the response from the thoroughly efficient Swiss type in the tourist office who could not believe I had decided to come to Geneva only 24 hours earlier, as such zany spontaneity was clearly unheard of in Switzerland.

After much persistence, I found a 'Chambre Demeure' in a building that was 'originally built as the accommodation for a religious order of women'. The bar I had found in the town centre seemed positively lively compared to the hotel.

'The busiest week of the year' is the Geneva Motor Show, one of the leading motor shows in the world. I was always puzzled as to why Geneva was the venue for such an important show, and now, having visited it, I was none the wiser. I had come to the press preview days, ostensibly as part of my work as a motoring journalist, but in reality I was there for the sole reason of blagging a car for the Gumball rally. Some preliminary attempts to secure a suitable car had ended in tears, suffering time and time again at the hands of the Gumball's reputation for fast living and faster driving. The trip to Geneva was a last-ditch attempt in the hope that, by meeting the press officers face to face, I might be able to convince them that we were sensible people not prone to the stereotypical Gumball excesses.

The 'we' element was myself and Richard Dunwoody, a former champion jockey. Though privately I suspected him of being a bit of a lunatic, I felt that his public persona of a record-breaking professional athlete turned motivational speaker was just the thing to get the PR people on side. Richard was not available to join me in Geneva because he was training for running the London Marathon to raise funds for Spinal Research and, on the back of this sort of talk, it was tempting to feel confident that first impressions would suggest we were not your typical Gumballers.

The reality was that Richard and I had made the decision to go on the Gumball after a bit of pub chat had got out of hand. We had met a couple of times socially and had agreed to meet to discuss my doing some sort of motoring feature on him as part of my day job. With the benefit of hindsight, since it was a 'day job' meeting, Richard's local pub was probably not the best venue we could have chosen. Towards the end of his horse-racing career, Richard had developed a keen interest in motor sport thanks to a girlfriend who moved in such circles and, as a self-confessed speed and adrenaline junkie, it was not long before he moved beyond a mere spectator's role and became actively involved by competing in a Formula First series and Porsche Super Cup races among others. From chatting to him in our previous meetings, it was apparent that he would be a more interesting interviewee than many who might tend to witter on about pistons, camshafts and their first Ford Capri.

This proved to be something of an understatement. After a few beers, we agreed that we would do two motoring features: one involving a race with Vicki Butler-Henderson, the racing driver and television presenter, and the other involving a 3000-mile, high-speed drive on the Gumball rally. Meeting

Richard for an interview had turned out to be similar to going to the dentist for a filling and subsequently agreeing to some extensive root canal work.

It has been conveniently forgotten exactly how we got on to the subject, but, after a discussion in which Richard claimed he reckoned he was faster in a car than Vicki, a plan was hatched that they would have a car race and a horse race, head to head. We were fairly confident that, as a double-barrelled, Home Counties sort of girl, she must have done a bit of riding in her youth and her abilities in a car were well documented, so this was a simple enough matter to arrange after Vicki sportingly agreed. The Gumball thing was a little trickier.

A suitable car was obviously a prerequisite. The Gumball is known for flash cars and beautiful people. We could not do a lot about the beautiful people angle and I was not too concerned about flash but we felt that a fast car was vital. I did not own a car less than thirty years old and Richard's convertible Jaguar was more used to cruising around Fulham. Again with the benefit of hindsight, the fact that we thought it would be 'more fun' to do it in a press car probably spoke volumes about the difficulties we experienced in securing one.

There are two press days at the motor show and the plan for the first was simply to engage in a bit of a recce; see what was what, have a look around and take a few notes, as well as taking advantage of the ample corporate hospitality on offer. The plan was to stop by a few stands, casually introducing myself, generally talking up my importance and promising to pop by again at some stage. After making an appointment I would then return the next day, flash the glossy magazine I worked for, talk a great game about the professionalism and achievement associated with Richard Dunwoody, and lay out the story of how myself and Richard were going on a 'road trip'. Only when the press officers had been mesmerised by visions of their latest model photographed in exotic locations such as Paris, Biarritz, Marbella and Cannes, and by the brand benefits of being involved in such highbrow pursuits, did I intend to slip in the Gumball chat. In theory this was a sound enough plan but in practice it was all too easy to get distracted by the liberal amounts of free drink and end up making inappropriate remarks about the quality of the eye candy hired to sit in the cars, and that was not the sort of talk to encourage the highbrow image. Not the right sort of talk at all.

Thankfully, it was not all bad news though, and as I sat in the bar after the first day I was secure in the feeling that some progress had been made. Cordial relations had been re-established with Jon at Rolls-Royce, who fortunately did not seem to be put out that I had described the Rolls-Royce Phantom as an automotive Prince Philip. There had been some slight concern on my part as I had recently written that, if you could liken a car to a person, surely the Duke of Edinburgh was 'Phantom Man'.

It might seem a little tenuous at first but there are similarities. Although personally he is sometimes known as 'Phil the Greek', the Royal Family has a touch of German parentage, just like Rolls-Royce after its recent acquisition by BMW, yet both are still seen as quintessentially British: noble; possessing a huge history and heritage; respected and revered in some quarters and resented in others; capable of arousing emotions of awe and envy in equal parts. It's a German regal car. It's a man's car, so that rules out Prince Edward. It is not really organic enough for the Prince of Wales, notwithstanding the free-range bulls that donate the hide. It has a little too much road presence for the low-key Prince William, and perhaps not enough street cred for his brother Harry. The Phantom is a cigar-smoking, fine-wine-drinking sort of car and Prince Harry's vices are known to differ somewhat. That only leaves Prince Philip who, as the Queen's husband, is often expected to be seen and not heard, although, rather like the Rolls-Royce, he manages this only part of the time. If the situation demands, both car and man can be relied upon to proceed inaudibly, lending a certain dignity to proceedings, and effortlessly keeping up with those around them. Put your foot down, however, or, in the Duke's case, his foot in it, and they both possess a natural ability to leave others floundering in their wake.

Jon's reaction was an encouraging start, but, although he had mentioned that 'in theory he had no objection' to me taking a Phantom abroad for a feature, I thought it best to wait until the following day before including any talk of three thousand miles in three countries and two continents in six days.

Appointments had also been confirmed with Audi, Porsche, Lamborghini, Bentley and Jaguar. A pretty neat haul by any blagger's standards and I would have been feeling rather pleased with myself had it not been for the terminal dullness of Geneva. Although the bar was dead, I had no real desire to go anywhere else since a) I had been for a wander and everywhere else was also empty and b) this particular bar had its cloud lined with silver in the form of its credit-card machine. It was one of those increasingly difficult to find establishments where they still swipe your card with the old-fashioned carbon-paper gadget. I was enjoying abusing my credit-card limit with short-term impunity. Of course, it would catch up with me eventually, and my bank manager would be asking some pretty probing questions about just why I felt the need to run up large bills in Geneva, but in the meantime I amused myself by doing just that and planning on telling him that I was in Switzerland to see my 'other bank manager'. That sort of chat ought to give him something to think about.

That is when the significance of 'where people meet' dawned on me. Normally I have no problems travelling alone since generally some sort of mischief will turn up, but in Geneva the concept of 'meeting' was not bumping into random kindred spirits, but strictly arranged affairs involving a suit and tie and sitting down to discuss money laundering or the price of gold. Abundant wealth is in evidence and Geneva is obviously a rich town and, with all this meeting malarkey, clearly somebody somewhere is yodelling all the way to the bank.

If I wasn't likely to meet anyone, was there anybody in Geneva I knew? I only knew two people in Geneva and both were unlikely to welcome a telephone call. The first was my cousin and his wife who had recently moved there, and sadly the last time I had spoken to them there was a lot of litigation talk. Previously I had been in the business of selling classic cars, and unfortunately awkward conversations concerning rust in the chassis and other such gremlins was something of an occupational hazard. It was a little more difficult to pull the old 'caveat emptor' gag on one's family and consequently the long-standing bonhomie had gone a bit tits up.

The second was Vicki Butler-Henderson, also in Geneva for the motor show. I had spotted her earlier and decided to stay out of her way. Having not even said hello at the show, when it would have been a simple professional encounter, I had no intention of ringing her and asking her out for a drink. Years ago, as an impressionable young car buff, I had developed a mild crush on Vicki after watching her doughnutting technique on BBC's *Top Gear*. As wild as her in-car antics are, her onscreen persona and giggles don't really prepare you for the fact that she is actually an exceptionally engaging and lively character in the flesh. Since meeting her the previous week for the car and horse feature, that mild crush had developed into a stronger attraction that could hardly be described as mutual, or healthy. And I think she suspected it. Perhaps it was the text messages I had sent her that gave it away.

I had given her a lift to the racetrack on the day of the shoot, and arranged for Richard to give the photographer a lift. The motivation, and injustices, of this arrangement did not escape Richard when I called him the night before to check that all was in order.

'Hi, Richard, all set for tomorrow? Can you pick up Nina at around 9 a.m.?'

'Sure, no problem, I've spoken to her and it's all arranged,' he replied.

'Excellent, I'll see you at Bedford at about 10.30 then.'

'Great. How is Vicki getting there?'

'Well, you see, it's like this . . . well, actually I'm giving her a lift,' I mumbled.

'I'll bet you are. Cheers, mate, thanks for the married photographer!'

It was during this car journey that Vicki had told me she was off to Geneva for the motor show, and I had expressly said I was not going. Having seen me turn up at the show, and on the back of my text messages, if she received an invitation to meet for a drink she understandably might have raised the full-on stalker alarm.

With no prospect of drinking buddies I decided to get some work done, since I needed to write up the piece about Vicki and Richard and I had my notebook with me. I got stuck in with the introduction.

On Grand National Day, it is something of a racing certainty that many people reading this will recall indulging teenage daughters in pony paraphernalia. No doubt, some will have endured long-suffering trips to gymkhanas and three-day events, and in some instances it is possible that concerned parents endured the above secure in the knowledge that a daughter without such wholesome interests could be engaged in some altogether less worthwhile pursuits.

Spare a thought then for Mr Butler-Henderson, a Hertfordshire farmer, whose daughter's horse-riding hobby distracted her from her karting. The son of a racing driver, and a member of the British Karting Team, he could be forgiven for preferring the idea of tinkering with the throttle cable than the bridle at the weekend. At one stage of his daughter's formative years he was fighting such a losing battle that he was forced to advertise her kart for sale with the rueful explanation 'daughter prefers four legs'.

7

I reread it. 'Mr Butler-Henderson?' That didn't sound great. Not the right tone at all. I needed his Christian name. Perhaps I should text Vicki and ask for it? That was a purely professional enquiry and as such was perfectly appropriate. I reached for my phone but then thankfully realised just in time that text messages along the lines of 'Who's your Daddy?' or 'How's your Father?' were liable to result in restraining orders.

At this stage, mercifully, the bar was beginning to fill up, with people who were obviously visiting the motor show in a professional capacity. Journalists are notorious pissheads and I could not work out why the bars were empty. While keeping one eye on the gathering crowd, and scribbling in my notebook with more flourish and pomposity than was strictly necessary, I decided that the people arriving did not look terribly like journalists. For a start they were sober, a rare condition for a journalist at the best of times but unheard of when on a press junket to a motor show. The real giveaway was the uber trendy stylish dress sense and look. A touch of eavesdropping confirmed that they were not journalists at all, but, in fact, were car designers. I had unwittingly stumbled on some sort of car-designing convention or shindig. While scruffy journalists might be expected to have unkempt hair, this lot all had a similar close-cropped or shaven, rather camp look. Perhaps this hairstyle, or lack of it, was some sort of car designer's union requirement or else they were simply balding from spending too much time in the wind tunnel.

A big cheer went up as someone entered the bar, clearly a guest of honour. Straining my neck, I saw that it was Chris Bangle, BMW's controversial Chief of Design. Since his appointment, media and public alike have condemned some of his work as being ugly, although clearly, among his peers, he is revered as being at the cutting edge of car design. Ironically enough the acute angular nature of some of his designs has prompted criticisms that he is taking the cutting-edge approach a little too literally. Being one of those who had publicly panned his work, I decided not to join his little gathering and retreated to the rear of the bar where a large group of girls had congregated. I noticed that they had cheered Bangle as enthusiastically as the rest and was curious about their presence among such baldness.

They turned out to be a Volvo design team who had proudly unveiled a concept car at the show. Called YCC it was a car designed solely by women for women, which basically seems to have involved them throwing their brothers' toys out of the pram, and replacing them with a few feminine ones of their own. One particularly girly touch was changeable seat covers, or seat pads as they called them, in different hues and fabrics, which could be swapped to suit the driver's mood. These Swedish girls, like most Scandinavians, spoke impeccable English but thankfully they were blissfully unaware of the humour value arising from their own comments that women motorists will appreciate being able to 'change their pads regularly'. Sadly, though, a similar language barrier prevented my joke about the car's bum looking big with that bumper from being the hit I anticipated.

Predictably, there was something of a hangover in evidence the following morning. After the first day's recce I decided that the most obvious place to start was with Rolls-Royce. Jon saw me coming a mile off and wasted no time in politely declining, saying that Rolls were not in the business of lending £250,000-worth of car flippantly, no matter how flippant the request. However, realising that the car PR world is a small one, and knowing that he was a fan of the magazine I worked for, I reckoned he would have a few pointers. Sure enough, with a nod and a wink, and a 'you didn't hear it from me', he suggested I try Al Clarke, a friend of his at Ferrari and Maserati. Ferrari and Maserati? Now you're talking.

'Hi, Al Clarke, is it? My name is Clement Wilson and I am the Motoring Correspondent for *The European Magazine*.' I handed him a copy of the magazine and waited for the Louis Vuitton and Chanel adverts to sink in.

'Good to meet you. What can I do for you?'

'I'm planning a road trip through Europe for a magazine feature and potentially a book. Myself and Richard Dunwoody, former champion jockey, will be doing 3000 miles through France, Spain and North Africa.'

'What's the angle?'

'Sort of Dunwoody and cars: a consummate professional who is a keen motoring enthusiast. Since retiring from horse racing, he has done a bit of motor racing, always striving to be the best, that sort of thing. The story will be a serious look at how he spends his holiday time combining a love of travel and cars. His name is synonymous with achieving the highest standards, and really it's just the sort of thing your brand should be associated with,' I said, thinking I should let him have it with both barrels of bullshit.

'Couldn't agree more, Clement,' he replied enthusiastically. 'I think it's a Maserati piece. 'The GT, the Grand Tourer, substance with style and less in your face than the Ferrari. It's a good fit and the kind of thing we go for. It would be different if it was just two lads on the wheeze.'

I gulped. On the 'wheeze' perfectly encapsulated our approach to a week-long party, despite the nonsense that I had fed him just a moment ago. He seemed to be a good guy doing his job, thinking he was helping me to do mine. I couldn't do it, although it would have been tempting simply to accept the car, hope that he did not get suspicious that our dates and routes were coincidentally close to those of the Gumball, and just let him read about it later. It was these sorts of morals and ethics that made me such an appalling car salesman, no matter what my cousins or customers might say.

'When you say on the "wheeze", would that include the Gumball?'

'The Gumball? No bloody way, that's not what we're about. There is a thing called the "Supercar Run", which is for charity and that's a whole different ball game, which we would gladly support. The Gumball could be seen as for idiots with more money than sense, sticking two fingers up to authority and that's not us.'

This anti-Gumball sentiment was a depressingly repetitive theme, no matter how I pitched it. Lamborghini didn't like my line that Richard was more 'raging bull' than 'prancing horse'. Aston Martin firmly said that they did not loan cars for more than one day to the likes of me, and then got in a huff when I suggested that was because they invariably broke on day two. I did not even get through the doors at Mercedes and everyone else I tried delivered a variation on 'Oh, yes, the Gumball, we've been stung by that one before'. Clearly, the Gumball had something of a reputation that defied the PR industry's mantra of 'all publicity is good publicity'.

The difficulties involved in blagging a Gumball car was summed up in Jaguar's attitude. I had saved them for last, thinking they would be a formality as Richard is one of their 'celebrity drivers'. Basically, this involves them leasing a Jaguar at favourable rates to the great and the good, and then reaping the rewards of the positive publicity generated. I quite fancied doing the Gumball in their monster XJR, a fat-cat saloon capable of frightening all but the quickest supercars, and approached the stand with confidence. I even had an appointment.

Sadly, it was an appointment that lasted all of five minutes before I was fobbed off with the insurance excuse. 'We'd help you and Richard if we could, honestly, but we just can't get insurance.' That old chestnut. I subsequently discovered that their other 'celebrity drivers' include Tim Henman and Sir Clive Woodward. Men of achievement undoubtedly, as Sir Clive has been knighted for winning the World Cup and Tiger Tim had a hill named after him for winning nothing, but you couldn't really picture them on the Gumball. On further reflection, I reasoned Tiger Tim is an appropriate Jaguar driver as is he a national institution, rather like Jaguar was before it was sold to the Americans. He is an essential part of a British summer. Like the A-level results getting easier and the mind-numbing antics of the *Big Brother* housemates, Henman's annual progress at Wimbledon follows a predictably familiar, and thereby comforting, pattern to the Great British public. The newspapers in summer might as well be a calendar. Oh look, Henman got into the second week at Wimbledon, full of talk that this was his year, but got knocked out in quarters/semis (delete as applicable) – it must be the end of June. Goodness me, the boring character won *Big Brother*; how come all the interesting people got voted out earlier – it must be the end of July. Wow, it says here in the papers that A-levels are getting easier – it must be the end of August. I live in hope that one year there will be a big shake-up. Wimbledon should be run along the lines of *Big Brother*, whereby the public have a telephone vote to knock out Henman's opponents thereby ensuring that nice guys finish first. *Big Brother* conversely should be a knock-out; three rounds in the boxing ring, male versus female, ensuring that the final is between the token meathead and token transsexual restoring faith in nice guys and girls finishing last; and the A-level exam should be made more difficult to restore faith in the education system, where the intelligent finish at the top of pile with the thick at the bottom, and niceness doesn't come into it.

With no luck at Jaguar, and feeling fairly dejected, I went back to the free drink courtesy of Toyota and didn't even bother to ask them for a car as, in the unlikely event of them offering one, I did not fancy telling Richard, 'Great, we have a Toyota.' Their advertising slogan is 'The car in front is a Toyota' and, while that might have some relevance on the suburban supermarket circuit, I could not it see working on the Gumball.

That night I went back to the bar where I had met the Swedish girls on the previous night. Sadly, there was no sign of them, but I thought the best strategy was to sit tight and wait. Christina, one of the blonde ones, had told me that they had a Volvo corporate shindig on, and would try and pop along later. It was an irritating development, but they were here to work after all. It is not often that you meet a pack of fifteen Swedish girls out on a spree, and I decided that, when the story came to be retold on my return to London, Swedish girls they would remain rather than Volvo employees. For some reason, as Volvo employees, they sounded a little more grey than blonde.

2. RICHARD DUNWOODY

'So, how did you get on in Geneva, then?' asked Richard.

'Well, I didn't blag us a car, if that's what you mean.'

'I know you didn't get a car, but what other mischief did you get up to?'

So I was back in London, in a pub with Richard. Back where we started, having a drink and talking nonsense. Not only was that how the whole Gumball plan kicked off, but it was also in these circumstances that I first got to know Richard.

Some people assume, perhaps because we are both Irish, that we met through an association with horses. Although I have a lot of horsey friends, which is a bit of a geographical hazard living in Ireland, I don't have much time for the animals, and their devotees are little better. My good friends know this and consequently waste little time discussing equestrian matters with me, since not only will I not be interested, but also my ignorance is such that I will not have anything interesting to add.

One friend, a girl whom I have known for years, recently delivered the shocking news that she had a pony in her youth. I had always considered this particular girl to be the queen of her species, largely because she seemed to have such intelligent and reasonable opinions on most matters. It was quite a devastating blow to discover that she had a murky past and a misspent youth, similar to realising Santa Claus is not the man you thought he was.

Horsey people are capable of boring you to death about the trials and tribulations of their horsey life, be it racing, breeding, hunting or just looking after their daughter's pony. Briefly as a child I went to a riding school, since presumably my parents thought it would be a useful skill to have, and I must admit I enjoyed careering around on horseback. My problem with it was the ancillary rubbish like mucking out. I could not get over the glee with which some of these kids sponged a horse's arse, and delighted in getting a hearty pat on the back from some woman who invariably smelled like a wet dog, and barked like a vicious one if your shit-shovelling technique was substandard.

Unfortunately, as an adult, I was saddled with manners, which made it difficult to control the urge to simply scream, 'I just don't care,' whenever someone kicked off the horse chat. Difficult but not impossible. On one occasion, I was sitting next to a quite well-known trainer at a dinner party. Inevitably, they spent the guts of the meal telling me that Hill Billy Plant Pot by Candlemaker's Whippet out of Some Other Such Nonsense (Dobbin to you and me) had developed some sort of funny breathing problem, and that was a disaster since he was much fancied in the second 'bumper' at Navan. Gobbledygook, of course, but I feigned interest and realised that whatever they were talking about was not good, so offered some sympathy to their plight.

'Oh, that must be terrible for you. I am sorry.'

'Well, that's just horses, don't you know. Always a problem somewhere. They're not machines and, when you've worked with horses, you come to take these things in your stride.'

Well, good for you and your stride. It appears to me, if you've worked with horses, you will come to pray for these setbacks so you can all engage in some collective sympathy regarding the latest astronomical vet bill, and all offer each other congratulations on how much money you piss down the drain because you just love horses. As I chatted on through all the masochistic excitement about the latest lame horse, which he was once again taking in his stride, though presumably the poor animal was having a little more difficulty doing so, it occurred to me that it was all rather similar to classic-car enthusiasts who just can't wait for their 1968 Ford Anglia to break so that they can whip their spanners out and get oiled up, in a bid to match the best hard-luck story and relate how their mechanical ingenuity kept their old dear on the road. This classic-car driver syndrome blatantly ignores the sound advice of 'if it is not broke, don't fix it', as they are never happier than when 'fettling', a process whereby they poke around a lot looking for something to break. I find this sort of chat equally boring, but at least I was on familiar ground and could not resist having a bit of fun.

'I have a 1973 MGB; that's a chrome bumper one,' I started, as I spotted a rare conversational gap. 'After 1975, the Americans insisted they had rubber bumpers for safety reasons, but those ones are not "real" MGBs. I was in mine the other day and suddenly, without any warning at all, the brakes went. The brakes, by the way, are discs all round, which is rare because a lot of MGs are on drums. Anyway as you can imagine, no brakes, traffic heavy, it's a miracle I wasn't killed.'

I continued in this vein for some time, elaborating on my near-death experience, and offering him an infinite variety of ridiculous scenarios that might have caused such potentially fatal brake failure, before summing up that, although I was lucky to be alive, I would not give you tuppence for some new-fangled machine with ABS, because such incidents were all part of the 'experience'.

'Hmm, I'm not really into cars actually, and to be honest you might find all that a bit boring if you weren't,' he said, as I eventually drew breath.

'Rather like horses, perhaps?'

To his credit, he smiled knowingly to confirm he had got the point.

There was a coincidental horsey association when I first met Richard, because it was at a fashion show organised to raise money for The Injured Jockeys' Fund. Richard was there in a professional capacity as he was modelling, ignoring the normal height requirements associated with the job description. I met him briefly in a bar after the show, and my first impressions were that he seemed a decent sort, though undoubtedly fond of a drink, and the social opportunities that result, when off duty.

Some months later we met again, as a mutual friend called Caroline, who had been involved in running the show, had invited us both to dinner with two of her girlfriends. I had been told that the girls were running late but I would find Richard Dunwoody there already, waiting at the bar. I arrived at the restaurant and a rather enormous evening kicked off, with Richard, three girls and myself, culminating in all five of us returning to the girls' house. More drink was provided and it was not long before we had our first casualty; the highbrow barrister, more used to judges than jockeys, found the pace difficult to live with and retired to bed in a heap. And then there were four. At this point, approximately three o'clock in the morning, I was beginning to wish Richard would make himself scarce. Not that I did not like the guy; on the contrary, I thought he was excellent fun and had contributed enormously to the enjoyable evening. It was just that, as both girls left awake lived in this house, one of whom was married, and the other had been romantically involved with me when we had last met, it seemed appropriate that Richard should be leaving to go home.

I got up to go to the loo, misguidedly thinking my absence might create a bit of a lull in the conversation and Richard would get the point. I gave him about five minutes to say his goodbyes, and when I returned I was pleased to see no sign of him. I did not immediately notice that there was no sign of Caroline either.

'Richard's gone home, then?' I asked Sasha, our married hostess.

'Don't be ridiculous; he's gone upstairs with Caroline.'

'The cheeky bastard!'

The next morning I awoke around eleven o'clock and, while there was a full complement of girls in the kitchen, once again there was no sign of Richard.

'Where's he gone now?'

'Oh, he got up early to go to The Church.'

'That fellow is some nutter. I know it's Sunday but after his performance last night I am surprised he is in any fit state to go to church this morning. I suppose he needs to pray for his sins.'

The girls giggled. 'No, you pillock, he's gone to *The* Church; it's an early-morning Sunday nightclub in King's Cross! He left at nine.'

'Christ, he really is crackers.'

After getting to know him better, I discovered that Richard is typical of the 'work hard, play hard' mentality. Of course, he is famous for his riding achievements, but he is clearly intensely driven and focused on whatever he does, whether it is in a professional capacity or getting his round in at the bar. After witnessing how seriously he took what was supposed to be a fun 'celebrity guest appearance' in the Ginetta race at Donington, I not only understood how and why he reached the pinnacle of his sport, but also why most people do not reach such heights, no matter how talented.

The Ginetta race in Donington was the final instalment of the whole Vicki Butler-Henderson horse and car piece. Between the jigs and the reels, they had wound up in the 'celebrity cars' on the Grid at Donington. This all took place on Grand National Day, the tenth anniversary of Richard's 1994 win on Minnehoma, and, while the rest of the cars were making their way to the grid, Richard was in a motor home watching a horse race. This might suggest that he was not taking it seriously but nothing could be further from the truth. Although his first priority was to be quicker than Vicki, he quite obviously wanted to make a bit of an impression on the rest of the field as well. He certainly made an impression on Vicki. He put quite a dent in her rear bumper as he punted her off the track in the first race. In the second race, they disappeared from view, around a bend, with Vicki leading, but with Richard catching fast. When, on the next lap, Richard came back into view with no sign of Vicki, the smart money was on him having nudged her out of the way again. It was definitely his innate competitiveness that drove him in that race, as this all unfolded before he had the chance to read Vicki's comment that it would be 'embarrassing to be beaten by a pint-sized jockey'.

So he is a serious guy, but, on the other hand, meeting him socially, I also got the impression that he had mellowed quite a lot since he had retired from being a professional jockey. I asked him what he'd been up to since retiring.

This and that apparently.

Like what?

You know, the usual, enduring frostbite while trekking to the magnetic North Pole, that sort of thing.

Fine, is that usual? Who else does that sort of thing? Hardened commandos and ex-SAS types. Great, he clearly has not mellowed that much; it's just that I only saw his social side, which I guessed is as strong as it has always been.

As a fair-weather race-goer, I knew who he was when he was riding, and realised that he was one of the more successful jockeys purely on the grounds that I had actually heard of him. Apart from that, I did not know a lot about him. My best friend, Edward, who is about as horsey as they come, was more enlightened and could not get his head around the fact that I was doing the Gumball with Richard.

For a start, Ed was my regular rallying co-driver, and we had endured many madcap Monte Carlo Rallies and also a thousand-mile drive in a Model T Ford. The Model T Ford journey was a particular endurance test since it had taken place during the World Trade Center attacks of September 2001. As suicidal terrorists were flying planes into the Twin Towers, we were meandering around the Gaeltacht in the west of Ireland. The Gaeltacht is an Irish-speaking region in Ireland, more Irish than a shamrock, and not known for their fondness for mod cons such as television. Every summer legions of kids from Dublin are sent to the Gaeltacht to learn Irish, and spend a miserable couple of months wishing they were anywhere else but there. Except pony camp, of course.

As I am something of a news junkie, it was particularly frustrating to be travelling at 15 mph in search of a television or a radio. The only other people were fellow competitors on the Irish Centenary Rally who did not seem to know any more than we did, not that they cared when there was some fettling to be done.

'Have you heard that someone has flown a plane into the Pentagon?' I would ask.

'Really how interesting, but have you heard this rattle? Listen carefully, perhaps, it's a wheel bearing,' came the reply.

Ed had always refused to entertain the idea of entering the Gumball on the grounds that it was an event for idiots with more money than sense. With that sort of point of view, you would wonder why he insists on playing with racehorses.

'So, Ed, I've given up on you. I'm going ahead on the Gumball without you,' I informed him the next time he came to London.

'Good for you, with whom?'

'Richard Dunwoody.'

'As in the jockey?'

'Yes, that's him. I think he used to ride horses,' I jested, knowing it would get up his sizeable nose.

He ignored my attempts to bait him. 'Well, good luck is all I can say,' he said in a tone laden with meaning.

'What are you getting at?'

'Well, I don't know Dunwoody, but I know about him. And I certainly know enough about being stuck in a car with you to have some worries that your trip might not be a roaring success. For a start, he's highly motivated and very professional, whereas you're about as bone idle and as disorganised as it's possible to be.'

'Go on,' I said, sensing he was just warming up.

'He's a fitness freak, so I don't think your twenty-an-hour in-car smoking habits will be too popular, and I can't see him listening to you on your soapbox rant entitled "Things I Hate About Horses and their Riders". How on earth did you come up with this plan anyway?'

'Pub chat.'

'Pub chat!' Ed scoffed. He knew only too well the dangers of pub chat if left unsupervised. Our Monte Carlo rallying careers had started on the back of a beer mat, and one particularly ill-judged session culminated in us driving a huge bus around Iceland. 'I'll tell you one thing,' he continued, 'if you think I'm uptight –' which I did '– wait until you get in a car with Richard Dunwoody. I've heard he's a bit intense.'

This was a recurring theme. Quite a few people, when they heard I was embarking on 3000 miles in a car with Richard, cryptically said, 'He's a bit intense, read his autobiography.'

I read it and it struck me as a brutally honest account of his career, but I also noticed that, while the will to win remained as strong as ever, towards the end of his career he realised that there were more important things to life. To me, as a person he seemed fairly laid-back, more from a sense of having things in perspective than actually being genuinely carefree. I thought it foolish to get anxious that he was going to be a nightmare travelling companion based on this book, or hearsay from racing fans.

The internet is a wonderful research tool for journalists, writers and high-minded academic types, but equally useful for gathering a bit of information about a potential loose cannon. 'Googling' somebody has become relatively commonplace and it seemed a wise move to 'google' Richard Dunwoody. There was inevitably a lot of guff about his riding career, page after page of the sort of information that gets racing folk giddy with excitement. For instance, did you know that Game Trust provided his first winner in 1983 at Cheltenham or that Yorkshire Edition at Wincanton in 1999 was his record-breaking 1679th? No? Well, me neither, and it was all fascinating stuff, but it did not give me much insight into whether or not he'd get his round in on the Gumball.

It was time to narrow the search, and try and find if anyone thought he was truly unstable. The next search was 'RICHARD DUNWOODY' and 'NUTS'. This brought some interesting results, and one in particular caught my eye.

> **Richard Dunwoody** has, as far as the Diary is concerned, been much better copy since he retired than when he was riding. His next exploit starts in a fortnight, when he sets off to Argentina with nine other hard **nuts** . . .

This linked to the *Daily Telegraph* website, specifically to the 'Racing Diary' written by Marcus Armytage. Browsing the Diary I was left in no doubt that Richard was a bit hard core to say the least. One report concerned a second-place finish in an Arctic Polar Race:

> Richard Dunwoody is back and giving the impression that the Arctic is, to be perfectly blunt, lacking a bit in scenery.
>
> The Diary has kept a vague eye on Richard's progress, which was hampered during the early stages, you might recall, by a polar bear, who lay down in their path and went to sleep. As it was in the middle of a 'rubble field', there was no way round it.
>
> 'We shot at it and it didn't blink,' says Richard, who now has a souvenir furry white hearth rug, which is very 'Fulham'.
>
> If you weren't already full of admiration for him, you should be now. In 11 days, he and Tony trudged to the North Pole, 330 miles as the penguin waddles but about 350 as two disorientated humans go, pulling a sled. The view, as you can imagine, doesn't change much – take a

blank piece of paper and it could easily be a postcard from Richard – and you don't meet people as you might were you walking, say, the Ridgeway. During those 11 days, he fell and dislocated his shoulder twice.

'Luckily, Tony was trained to put it back in,' he says, as if it were like extricating a small splinter. Trained Tony may be, but it took him four attempts to put the second dislocation back and Richard will now require an operation to tie it in properly. They might take a look at his brain when they do it.

Bloody hell, why was I worried about him as a travelling companion? This put things into perspective a bit; normally the company he keeps includes polar bears and people who 'luckily' happen to be capable of repairing dislocated shoulders. He might find my medical training a little below par, and I made a note to suggest he take out travel insurance.

A little further browsing of the site uncovered some more injury tales.

Polar explorer Richard Dunwoody, rider of 1,699 winners and survivor of a thousand falls, dislocated his shoulder last Sunday. Funny at first, he says, but by the time A & E in Crawley had kept him waiting for 90 minutes, without so much as an aspirin let alone morphine, it had become the most painful thing he's ever done.

Richard fell off while giving an after-lunch 'dressage demonstration'. His mount, called The Assassin, 'didn't do a lot' and dropped him. He swears he hadn't been drinking but, if that's the case, the communion wine in those parts must have some kick to it.

In a vain attempt to hang on to the horse (Pony Club lesson 1: Though it may be heroic, especially if you're on a million-dollar yearling, don't) he remained on the floor while his arm, disconnected at the socket, went with the horse. Upside kids with saucepans stuck on their heads, it was the ex-champion who was crying in the waiting room. 'I was on my hands and knees begging for a painkiller,' he recalls.

This was slightly better news, and more in keeping with the Richard I had met, and I didn't believe for one moment that he had not been drinking, and from the tone of the piece neither did the diarist.

In keeping with my thoroughness, perhaps I should ask someone who knew him when he was racing. The person who immediately sprang to mind was Jessie Harrington, the Kildare-based Irish trainer. I frequently used to stay as a guest of her daughter Emma at Commonstown Stud, generally in a house party for a nearby wedding or hunt ball. I hadn't seen her for a while, basically because I had not seen her daughter for a while. I was at a New Year's party where I'd hoped to see Emma, and then I spotted Jessie.

'Hi, Jessie, Happy New Year,' I said, dispensing the usual pleasantries.

'Hello, Clement, how come we haven't seen you at Commonstown for so long?'

'Well, there didn't seem a lot of point after Ritchie turned up.' Ritchie was Emma's boyfriend, a good horsey type who was the racecourse manager at Punchestown. Jessie looked rather shocked. It seemed a good time to change the subject. 'Tell me, do you know Richard Dunwoody?' I asked.

'Not terribly well, but he did ride for me a couple of times. Why do you ask? It's unlike you to show an equestrian interest.'

'I am doing a thing called the Gumball rally with him. We shall be cooped up in a car for a week and people keep telling me he's bonkers. I'm a bit apprehensive. What's he like?'

'Nonsense, he's not bonkers,' Jessie scoffed, 'he was very driven to succeed but at the same time he seemed to have an enormous sense of fun.'

'Still, being stuck in a car, it can be quite a stressful environment.'

'Try riding a Grand National.'

'Will he bore me about horses all the time?'

'Not at all. He's a jockey. They could be riding a bike; it's the winning that's important to them.'

'Great, and will he keep cool if things go wrong, say we break down or get lost?'

'Of course he will. Things go wrong; he'll know that better than most. When you have experienced and worked with horses as much as he has, he'll have seen it all. You'd never believe what can go wrong with –'

'Right, thanks, you've been a great help,' I said, quickly changing the subject.

After that, the better I got to know Richard I began to realise that there is often a huge gulf between the public perception of someone and the reality. In addition to this, I also believe that Richard is one of those people who have the rare ability genuinely to get on with anybody. For instance, he knew my interest in horses was limited and I was unlikely to be swapping frostbite stories, so I just saw a different side of his character. It probably says as much about me as it does about him that it was a fairly frivolous side that I saw.

'So, I'll ask you once more – what trouble were you causing in Geneva?' Richard asked again.

'Oh not much, I met some nice Swedish girls.'

'Swedish girls, eh? What was the story there?'

Predictably, as soon as I confessed they were Volvo designers, Richard hooted with laughter.

3. OBTAINING THE CAR AND LAST-MINUTE PREPARATIONS

Richard's amusement at the Volvo designers was not terribly surprising. Volvo has something of an image problem, and always has had. That a group of Scandinavian females can suddenly become boring because they are Volvo employees confirms this problem. The brand is seen as solid, reliable and above all safe.

My affections for Volvo are a little bit unusual but for a number of reasons I have always been a bit of a fan. Firstly, when I was an impressionable youngster, my father purchased a new car, and this Volvo 340 GL was the sleekest, sportiest thing that I had ever been in. Admittedly, these things are relative, but anyone who describes Volvos as boxy and square does not remember the Renault 20, which looked like an ocean-going bus. My father made sure I travelled in a Renault 20 until I was eight.

Secondly, I learned to drive in another supposedly boring 340 GL, but it was safe and slow. After learning to drive in it, I trashed it by taking it auto testing one Boxing Day. Auto testing is a form of motor sport where nimble little cars, such as Minis, complete a tight and twisty obstacle course, pirouetting around cones and handbrake turning into stables and barns. The course I took the Volvo on was a particularly muddy farmyard, and the rear-wheel drive was just fabulous fun, sliding this tank around and knocking walls down along the way. The Minis were shitting themselves. To this day, it remains some of the best fun that I've had in a car.

Finally, I am of the generation that Volvo targeted with the T-5. In the early to mid-90s Volvo turned up with a couple of estate cars at the British Touring Car Championship. Inevitably, there were sniggers, as if they had turned up to a posh wedding ignoring the dress code. In estate trim, they did not win much, but they did enough to make the established order sit up and take notice. The next year they returned with a brace of saloons, comprehensively beating their rivals on a number of occasions.

This ultimate aim of the on-track success was to get Joe Public driving Volvos. Soon the advertising campaigns were less of the 2.4-kids variety. Suddenly Volvo driver was making the Milk Tray Man look like the nancy-boy BMW driver that we had always suspected hid behind the polo neck. While BMW Man was delivering flowers to his grandmother, Volvo Lad was a stuntman busying himself dodging packing crates falling from moving aeroplanes, while driving through the eye of a hurricane. The advertisements unmistakeably suggested Mr Volvo was getting laid, and it was no longer the dogs that were drooling in the back of his car. While it all made a lasting impression on me, it had only shifted the 'boxy but safe' image slightly.

Reflecting on the injustice of the whole thing, I had a revelation. Bingo. Volvo! Why hadn't I thought of them? Surely nobody had approached them before? They would not have been stung in the past. Us Volvo aficionados are a rare breed, and I imagined that they would have been rarer still among Gumballers. Some doubters would think that this was all very well; yes, they might give you a car but it will still be a Volvo estate. Richard sprung to mind for instance. He had told me he'd driven a Volvo once. 'The one that looked like a wedge,' he'd said. That will be the 480 then.

'A garage and racehorse owner very kindly let me have it for the odd tip I could give him. I told him to put my name very discreetly on the side together with the name of his garage and it came back with just my name in foot-high block capitals. There were no secret liaisons in that one. In the end, rather fortunately, it was taken back after I advised him a 20–1 shot wouldn't win and it hacked up at Chepstow in a big handicap hurdle!'

Richard's blinkered Volvo views didn't bother me; surprisingly few car enthusiasts appreciate the full extent of Volvo's stealth car, but I did, and the more I thought about it the more I realised that it was the perfect Gumball car.

The 850 T-5 evolved into the R, and now the latest model is the V70R. With all the 'R for radical' trimmings, it is quite a mean-looking car, particularly in dark colours like graphite or gunmetal grey. You just know these colours sound fast.

The V70R is a 300 bhp monster, accelerating from 0 to 60 in under 6 seconds and limited to a top speed of 155 mph. It is the technical gizmos and gadgetry that make it sort of special. Having cracked a few cheap jokes at the expense of horse bores, I am not about to explain the full tedious side of the technology here. Plus, I don't really understand it. Suffice it to say it gives the car a bit of a schizophrenic character. Inevitably, on an event like the Gumball, there would be times when we would want to unleash the boy racers within, and put a few manners on the Maseratis and such like. Equally so, there would be times when we would be tired, fed up with the event, the route and each other and simply want to cruise. However, it was unlikely that we would be fed up with the car, as it would be able to match our moods. The driver of a V70R is confronted with three small push-buttons above the stereo. Labelled 'Comfort', 'Sport' and 'Advanced', they allow the driver to select the setting most appropriate for the conditions and his/her driving style. Press them and you change the stiffness of the ride as you drive, which is actually more fun than it sounds. 'Comfort' is just the thing for a relaxing wind down at the end of a long drive; 'Sport' firms things up a bit; and 'Advanced' encourages you to throw the thing through the corners as if it is on rails. For all the sense the techno-babble about electronic suspension changing 500 times a minute made to me, it might well be on rails. But I do know that it is very effective. It has a similarly effective dynamic stability and traction control with the obligatory natty and cryptic abbreviated name DSTC something or other. Basically, that makes you out to be a better driver than you are, and lets you bomb around in the wet with impunity, while the car hangs on to its ample rear so you don't have to. It might not have the cachet of some supercars, but, if you forgot your blinkered views of the badge, and concentrate on the combination of speed, comfort and space, it was nigh on unbeatable in the suitability stakes.

I thought I would keep my Volvo fetishes to myself, and try and progress the idea before Richard nipped it in the bud. If it was a fait accompli he could hardly complain, plus at that stage I would just need to let him loose in it for a spin and point out that it was actually quicker than his Jag. I knew that particular piece of information would bother him, so I looked forward to delivering it with some glee. No one who drives a convertible Jaguar XK8 wants to be told that it is a bit sluggish compared to a Volvo. He would have been even angrier if he knew that I planned to pimp his name for the cause, closely associating him with Volvo brand values, stressing his love for horseboxes and point-to-points.

A point-to-point is a sort of ersatz horse race in a muddy field, whereby horses who are generally hunters play at being racehorses for the day. The owners bring the horses point-to-pointing whenever they can get time off from telling you that hunting is not cruel or snobby, and indeed you will find plenty of plumbers that hunt. It is probably a bit more complicated than that if you listen to the stewards but basically that is the vibe in a nutshell. If it was not for all the mud, you could probably describe it as 'grass-roots' racing. The other defining characteristic is that, apart from the obligatory throng of horseboxes, 4X4s and horses, the field is full of Volvos with car stickers telling you that hunting is not cruel or snobby, with a picture of a plumber. Or it might be Lord Bufton-Tufton; it is difficult to tell because they are all wear funny red coats that match their cheeks.

My familiarity with point-to-points stems from the fact that my aforementioned friend Edward used to be a 'permit-holder', which in racing speak appears to be some sort of ersatz trainer. His horses regularly ran in point-to-points and one horse named Stag Party developed a bit of a fan club. As he was trained by one good friend and regularly ridden by another, I could see the sense in joining this fan club and toasting Stag Party's conspicuous lack of success with lashings of hot port, even though I did not really understand what was going on. 'Staggie' was a good mate by extension, and, to be fair, horse and jockey did once combine to show Richard Dunwoody and steed a clean pair of heels, or hooves, or whatever the terminology might be.

The last time I went to a point-to-point was in Gloucestershire. My friend had given up holding his permit and had become a mature student in Cirencester. When most students go to college they bring a fresh line of credit, and a healthy disregard for lecture schedules but Edward brought his horse. After Easter, I was giving him a lift back from Ireland, and we had to visit some point-to-point on the way. I had taken a Ferrari press car to Ireland, and was en route to returning it. With my experience of Irish point-to-points, where the day invariably ends with the car park field clogged up by beaten-up old Land Rovers pulling Volvo estates out of the mud, I understandably refused to take a car of this ilk anywhere near the place.

'Nonsense!' Ed retorted. 'This is Gloucestershire. It will not be the first time they have seen a Ferrari.'

I did not actually park in the field but, sure enough, there were three Ferraris already parked there. I was impressed with the Gloucestershire point-to-point scene. There were a few wealthy plumbers in these parts.

With the 'Dunwoody – he's a sensible horsey type, salt of the earth, don't you know' strategy perfected, the first thing to do was to ring the press office and see how far I got there. I had never had any dealings with Volvo and had no particular contact, so I just had to wait and see who answered the phone.

'Hello, Volvo press office, Andrea Baker speaking.'

Andrea was quite the most helpful press officer I had encountered. Yes, she knew about the Gumball, and was not overly concerned about the reputation since she liked the idea of the responsible 'more sense than money, point-to-point one weekend, Gumball the next' approach. Joking aside, the argument stacked up that the quick version of the Volvo estate would acquit itself just as well flooring it with the Ferraris as it would pulling the horsebox. Andrea promised to look into the idea, discuss it with some relevant people and she would get back to me. It was an encouraging start and I was quietly confident.

In the meantime, while I waited for Andrea's response, spurious offers of cars were suddenly coming out of the woodwork, like the proverbial buses that all come at once. I had touted myself around so many places looking for a car that I had forgotten exactly whom I had spammed. Now they were coming back. An Alfa Romeo dealer in Nottingham offered the pick of his range if we could provide our own insurance. Gibbs Aquada, who sell a seafaring car cum speedboat, were vaguely interested in the idea, but slightly concerned we might kill ourselves trying to cross the Straits of Gibraltar and they already had their hands full because Sir Richard Branson was making a lot of noise about crossing the English Channel in one. MG offered an MGF but even their own press officer thought it might be a 'bit girly for the Gumball', and discussions were under way with Vauxhall about using an Australian beast called a Monaro.

The most interesting call came from a PR company representing Extreme Music, or – to give them their full title – 'Extreme Music, the BAD BOYS of music production'. These people were modifying a Rolls-Royce to give it all sorts of bling accessories and fat wings. Luggage room would be a bit tight because of the vast in-car entertainment system, but at least we would make a lot of noise. The idea had tickled their fancy since a) they were 'BAD BOYS' and hence not bothered by the Gumball's underground reputation and b) they wanted the car in Cannes for the Film Festival anyway. As the Gumball was due to finish in Cannes the night before the Film Festival, it seemed like the perfect match all round.

It was certainly an interesting idea and so began a lengthy dialogue with Nicky, their PR representative. There were a few problems to start with, such as nobody being quite sure whether the car would be ready in time, as it was still sprouting its fat wings in a body shop in Oxfordshire. With less than a month to go, it did not seem likely. However, the biggest problem was that the bad boys at Extreme Music turned out to be extremely anal and paranoid. Their list of requests and requirements were seemingly endless, and they wanted to know if we could bring their clients as passengers, and also if four of their directors could join us for the parties. They would have been fairly dull parties since there was also some suggestion that perhaps we should not drink for the week if we had their car. Although neither Richard nor I is so shallow that we feel the need to drink to have a good time, we certainly were not going on the Gumball for a few shandies.

The final straw came when, before they had even agreed to give us the car, they sent a contract to be signed that included the following:

4. – Clement Wilson/Richard Dunwoody will not drive the car recklessly, or under the influence of alcohol or drugs, and will do everything possible to prevent any damage being caused to the car.

Infuriated, I rang Nicky, who, in all fairness, did not seem quite so pedantic as her clients. Although she did not actually say anything, I got the distinct impression that she thought they were making mountains out of molehills.

'Nicky, it's Clement. That's a nonsense. We're not signing that. We're doing your bad boys a favour by bringing the car to Cannes.'

'I thought you might freak when you read it,' she said sheepishly.

'How long is a piece of string? Reckless could mean speeding, and I'm fairly sure there will be more than a hint of that. Has the irony of this struck you at all?'

'What do you mean?'

'Well, I've told you how tempted I am by the Volvo.'

'Yes, but it's a Volvo. You can't do the Gumball in a Volvo. That is so uncool.'

'Rubbish, that's the point. It might be uncool, and the Extreme Rolls might be the biggest, baddest, meanest machine to hit the streets of Cannes, but the Volvo is quicker, safer, more reliable and in one piece. Plus it is a simple yes or no answer.'

'Yeah, but it's a Volvo,' she repeated.

'And the irony is Volvo will say, "There's our car, take it away and have a good time," whereas your bad boys want to make sure we don't drink and want us to bring their gimp directors with us. I don't hear Volvo getting concerned we might be a little bit reckless. If, touch wood, we damage their car, Volvo will look after us. Your guys will sue us for taking an aspirin and driving.'

After our conversation, Andrea made a timely call with the good news that Volvo would definitely give us the car, so all that was required was a polite email to indicate the Extreme Rolls would not be required, and nor would the company of their directors.

There were only a few more car problems to overcome. Firstly, Andrea was concerned about Richard's occupation. Apparently, jockeys are extremely high risk for insurance purposes, suggesting that there is an amount of statistical evidence to confirm that they are indeed mad lunatics.

'He's no longer a jockey, Andrea, he gave it up years ago,' I reassured her. She was then confused as to what to put down instead. 'Just put him down as retired,' I said, thinking he was sounding more like a Volvo driver every minute.

The last problem was that I still had not told Richard.

'You're kidding me?!' he said, when I broke the news. 'A Volvo? We'll be the laughing stock. The bloody Gumball rally, synonymous with supercars, and we're bringing a Volvo. Marvellous.'

'Listen, mate, would you be happy with a Porsche Boxster?'

'Oh yes.'

'Well, it's quicker than that,' I said, adding quietly, 'and with a lot more space.'

He had not missed it. 'Now, you're going to tell me it's an estate car?'

'Absolutely, and with integrated child seats.'

'An estate car? Integrated child seats? You're something else!'

'It's quicker than your Jag, Richard.'

It registered but he did not respond.

And there was still time for one final problem. I had to tell the Gumball rally people that we were changing the car. At that stage, we had put a Jaguar XJR down on our entry form, as it was looking the most likely. Since then I had asked whether it would be a hassle to change the car and was told, 'No problem, it does not matter, as long as it is cool.'

'Hi, Nick, we want to change our car. We'll be going in a different one.'

'It's not a Volvo, by any chance?' he asked.

I was taken aback. 'Yes, actually, it is. How on earth did you know that?'

'We asked Volvo for some crew cars, and they said no, because they were already giving an entrant a car. We've been looking at the list to figure out who might have been trying to sneak a Volvo in.'

After securing the car from Volvo we were set. Entry fee paid. Car confirmed. No more problems. Well, except one minor one. From the moment that we hatched the Gumball plan, Richard had told me he could not be one hundred per cent sure of being able to commit as he was being considered for a television show called *Hell's Kitchen*, due to be filmed at some stage in May. In January, when we first discussed the idea, it seemed reasonable to press ahead regardless and deal with the problem if and when it arose. In April, with less than three weeks to go, and Richard none the wiser regarding *Hell's Kitchen*, it was far from reasonable. Substantial sums of money had been coughed up for the entry fee, and I had a few professional commitments of my own riding on the Gumball. If Richard could not do it, I was rightly banjaxed and needed a Plan B, for insurance purposes.

I asked an ex-girlfriend if she was up for it, but she said no, and then, when I asked her if she would do the Gumball, she refused that offer as well, no doubt sensing the umpteenth attempt to worm my way back into her affections. I pitched it that, as a car enthusiast, I wanted to do the Gumball purely for the fun of it, but, as a writer, I needed a story to tell, and didn't she think that the story of our relationship in the pressure-cooker environment of a marathon motoring journey would make rather an amusing one? Once again, no was the short answer. After being pressed for the long answer, she told me she could not get the time off school. I should point out that she is, in fact, a schoolteacher.

Practising the pitch to the ex had convinced me that, if Richard needed to be replaced, it should be by a female, which would make for much hilarity along the 'men don't listen, women can't read maps' lines. That was at least some progress but delivering the pitch had simply convinced me that no girl who knew me well was going to agree to the idea. As I pondered the implications of this, it struck me that the obvious solution was to ask a perfect stranger. It would make a great story and surely, as long as they were satisfied that you were not an axe murderer, no girl of spirit and adventure would turn down an all-expenses-paid trip on the Gumball. It was a tenuous theory that did not really stack up, but it was all I had.

A few days later, I was in a London pub, doing my best stereotypical alcoholic journalist impression, furiously scribbling to a deadline while simultaneously skulling pints of Guinness. With only one eye on my work, I noticed a simply stunning girl enter the pub, who turned the heads on the pints as well as the punters. She sat down with some friends at the table beside me, and, after some spirited earwigging, it was clear that she had the banter to match the beauty. Most girls of this calibre tend to be somewhat limited in their conversational abilities, never having had to rely on their chat to engage a person's interest, but as this girl held court at the table it was clear that she had the full range.

Inevitably, as I drank more pints and continued to eavesdrop, my theory became significantly less tenuous. After only three pints it was actually perfectly sound, and not in the slightest bit weird to accost someone in a bar and say, 'Hi, do you fancy driving to Morocco with me? At high speed, and getting raucously drunk at parties along the way.' After five pints, I could not believe my ears, nor my luck, when I heard her discussing 'some sort of rally called the Gumball' with her friends. The theory instantly graduated from a tenuous Plan B to a 'bugger Dunwoody, if he wants to prance around Gordon Ramsay's hellish kitchen in an apron, I'm going Gumballing with this Plan A babe'.

Now for the difficult bit, I just had to ask her. Emboldened by the thought of a 'faint heart never won fair lady' and a considerable serving of Guinness, I sidled over to her table.

'Excuse me, I'm terribly sorry to interrupt, but did I just hear you mention the Gumball rally?' I slurred.

'Only if you were listening very carefully.'

'Ah, yes, well, I can't argue with that, I'm a journalist,' I stammered, as if in some way this gave me carte blanche to listen in on private conversations. She merely raised an eyebrow. Luckily, I had a copy of the magazine I work for and my business card with me. Pulling myself together, I produced them and reminded myself that I had a perfectly reasonable request. 'The reason I'm interested is I am doing the Gumball.

I'm a writer, look, see.' I shoved my credentials under her nose. 'I am supposed to be doing it with Richard Dunwoody, the jockey, do you know who I mean?'

She nodded.

'Well, to cut a long story short, we're hoping to write a book on it, and now Richard says he might not be able to make it so I am looking for Plan B. I reckoned that asking a stranger would make a good story, so how about it, all expenses paid?'

To my surprise, she did not look that surprised.

'Well, there is a bit of a problem. My boyfriend is doing the Gumball,' she said.

Lesser men, or less pissed men, might have been stymied at this development. My first reaction was that this could not be any better. Her boyfriend was clearly off on the mess for a week chasing skirt on the Gumball, and then I turn up with his girlfriend. What a story!

'Boyfriend, eh? Doesn't bother me!'

She raised an eyebrow again, this time a little higher. 'Well, it might bother him. Another problem is work, and these sorts of requests usually go through my agent.'

Oops! Work? Requests? Agent? I did not like the sound of this. 'Work? You can always get time off work. What do you do?'

'Do you not know who I am?'

Hmm. I definitely did not like the sound of that. I shook my head.

'My name is Georgie Thompson. I'm a presenter on *Sky Sports News*. I thought you realised that.'

I had certainly not realised that, whereas she was under the impression that I was looking for another famous face to replace Richard. My only impression of her face was that it was considerably better looking than Richard's was; famous did not come into it. I had never seen *Sky Sports News*; the simple mainstream *Sky News* is repetitive enough, and I had always assumed the sports variant was the height of tediousness. Having met the presenter, I now understood its attractions.

Retreating, and adopting a more professional demeanour, I asked her who her agent was. I was in for one more massive shock, unwittingly delivered when she told me that she was represented by Kate Elliot of Princess Management. Oh dear, in the small world of media darlings, her agent just happened to be Vicki Butler-Henderson's agent. No doubt, I would soon get an email from Kate commending me on the restraint shown in not recently texting Vicki, but please would I refrain from drunkenly inviting her other clients to Morocco, and to share my hotel rooms as well as the driving.

The difference in the aesthetic qualities of Richard and Miss Thompson reminded me that we were not scoring too heavily on the 'flash car, beautiful people' stakes. After we rejected the Extreme Rolls, the bling-bling factor was fairly thin on the ground as well. The Gumball brand is quite deliberately bling-bling, with an emphasis on gaudy jewellery and clothing, or stylish accessories depending on your point of view. Our point of view, particularly from the driving seat of a family estate car, was rather more understated than underground. Where others had customised ice buckets, we had integrated child seats, and a roof rack instead of a roll cage. I wondered whether we needed to look the part. Not really, as I could not envisage Richard, myself or the car carrying off the urban gangster rap look with any great success. I needed to find a more appropriate clothing supplier.

First call was to a shop in Cirencester, outfitters to the shires, tweedy types and apparently Prince William's choice of sock supplier. The marketing girl had heard of the Gumball and I explained that we were abandoning the bling-bling vibe, and needed a wardrobe more in keeping with the 'dogs in the back of the car' image of the Volvo. While she claimed to be amused by our approach, she was unable to offer assistance but she had some valuable advice. Her suggestion was to try Cordings, a clothing company in London, who might be more willing to oblige as Chris Rea had just bought a controlling share and hence they had lots of money. Chris Rea, you say? Perfect, you can keep your 50 Cent; that is my kind of music.

Cordings of Piccadilly is an old-fashioned firm, despite the rock-star ownership. Fabulously, they did not have anything quite as nouveau riche as a press officer or a PR firm, and I was told that the man to talk to was the managing director. He quickly confirmed that he would be delighted to assist us, and without hesitation offered us a tweed suit each. As diplomatically as possible, since I did not want to appear ungrateful, I explained that this was probably taking the theme a little too far. A full-on three-piece 'Sir Godfrey Huffington-Puffington, I'm at my happiest in a grouse moor' tweed suit was unlikely to be terribly practical in Morocco. Thankfully, Cordings do a natty line in lightweight linen or cotton suits, and invited us to come in for a shopping trip.

Going clothes shopping with Richard Dunwoody was undoubtedly an amusing experience, though not one I would like to repeat in a hurry, as it is just not possible to rush it. For someone so closely associated with a hunger for speed and adrenaline, the style of expanding his wardrobe is quite astonishing. From the moment we entered Cordings, having marched down Piccadilly at an exhausting pace, he treated myself and Arthur, our shop assistant, to a metrosexual mix and match approach to shopping that was staggering in its meticulous detail and delay.

After a relatively quick decision that only swarthy Italians could pull off the linen-suit look, Richard set about examining everything the shop had to offer. In addition to the suits and trousers, we had been offered two shirts and ties each. While I accept Cordings have an extensive range, picking a couple of shirts is a fairly straightforward matter. I was exhausted simply watching Richard playing the Great Gatsby, mesmerised by the combinations of colours like a kid in a toy shop. I suspected that Arthur might have been as well, notwithstanding the fact that surely he had seen his fair share of dandies in his time, but during a marathon shirt shopping session his professionalism did not let him down once.

It was only when we got downstairs to choose the trousers that our shop assistant could no longer resist. Once again there was a daunting array to choose from and, after briefly flirting with a pair of tangerine cords, more to pass the time than anything else, I had settled on a choice of either tan or blue chinos. I looked to Arthur for assistance.

'Do you have these in a 32-inch long?' I asked.

Before Arthur could even think about checking, Richard clocked the colour and said, 'I think you'll find the tan is only available in long from 34-inch upwards. I've been through that rack.'

Like an experienced and faithful old butler, Arthur stifled his giggles, and simply said, 'I think we should offer Richard a job here. He knows his way around the stock better than I do.' That was an understatement, and I decided to go for the blue, then a cigarette while I waited for Richard to run out of fabrics to fondle.

There was now not a lot left to organise before the departure. Richard had a marathon to run, but that was his own business and not something I saw the sense in. All the administrative details had been largely taken care of, and those that we had not sorted were in the capable hands of the staff at Gumball HQ.

Gumball HQ emailed us regularly with updates and snippets of information, most of which I missed because it got caught in my spam filter. I do not really understand why, even with a spam filter, I still have the chance to be out of debt, have a bigger penis and breasts, be working from home making $50,000 per week, while watching Britney Spears masturbate but I cannot read emails telling me which hotel I'm checked into in Paris.

When I eventually found the relevant emails, I would efficiently forward them to Richard to keep him informed as to what was going on. He seemed satisfied that all was in capable hands, rarely replying with any sort of intelligent insights, just forwarding things he had received that reflected his sense of humour.

FROM: Richard Dunwoody
TO: Clement Wilson
SUBJECT: FW: CHAIN LETTER

Read this mate, it's very funny . . .

INSTRUCTIONS

Anaesthetise your wife or girlfriend, put her in a large carton (don't forget some ventilation holes) and send it to the person who is at the top of your list. Soon, your name will be at the top of the list, and you will receive 823,542 women through the post.

Statistically, among those women, will be at least:

0.5 Miss Worlds
2.5 Models
463 Wild nymphos
3,234 Good-looking nymphos
20,198 Who enjoy multiple orgasms
40,198 Bi-sexual women.

In total, that is 64,294 women who are simply hornier, less inhibited, and tastier than the grumpy old bag you posted off. And, best of all, your original package is guaranteed not to be one of those that come back to you.

DO NOT BREAK THIS CHAIN LETTER.

One bloke for example who sent the letter to only 5 instead of 9 of his friends got his original bird back, still in the old dressing gown he sent her off in, with the same old migraine attack, and the accusatorial expression on her face. On the same day, the international supermodel he'd been living with since he sent off his old girlfriend moved out to live with his best friend (to whom he had not sent the chain letter).

While I am sending this letter, the bloke that is in 6th place above me has already received 837 women and is lying in hospital suffering from exhaustion. Outside his ward are 452 more packages.

YOU MUST BELIEVE THIS E-MAIL.

This is a unique opportunity to achieve a totally satisfying sex life. No expensive meals out, no lengthy conversations about trivialities (that only interest women). No obligations, no grumpy mother-in-law, and no unpleasant surprises like marriage or engagement. Do not hesitate . . . send this letter today to 9 of your best friends.

I read it, and then obviously deleted it because it was degrading to women.

4. LONDON TO PARIS

Despite all the complaints you hear about the congestion, driving in London is not so bad at 5 a.m., when there is little traffic to worry about, and you have a press car at your disposal to slide around Marble Arch. I got into Gumball mode with a fairly liberal interpretation of traffic lights and speed limits. Apart from being far too overexcited, I was already late and this was not a good start. I was sure Richard had a sneaking suspicion that my general organisational skills might not be up to scratch, and he would inevitably discover just how shocking they were. That discovery was destined to be sooner rather than later.

Predictably enough, Richard was waiting when I got to his house, bags packed, racked, stacked and ready to go. Hardly travelling light, but then again we had an estate car for our belongings. An estate car that made Richard give an involuntary shudder when he saw it again, shimmering rather unsexily outside his house. The shimmer effect came from the paint job – flash green metallic. Although I had convinced him that the car looked quite mean in black, Volvo had supplied our car in a limited edition lime-green flavour, a colour that is difficult to describe but Richard reckoned he had seen similar urinal cakes. There was a bigger shock in store when he came close and digested the colour of the interior leather. A sort of orangey-brown; it looked like the product of something that had not been digested as well as it might have been. Richard commented that this sort of colour of leather was all well and good for an Italian pimp's footwear but it was really a bit much for a car to be swathed in it.

Five minutes into our journey and Richard started shouting 'speed camera' with much gusto, just before we saw a big flash.

'I know for a fact there is film in that one. Look, when I say "Speed Camera", it means slow down, not check your hair, floor it and try and flash a winning smile for the camera.'

We had covered less than five miles and already had picked up our first speeding infringement. It did not bode well for our speeding-fines budget or our levels of in-car communication.

'The ticket will be sent to Volvo,' I countered.

'And then sent to you! They know you have the car.'

'Well, we both have the car.'

I had heard that Neil and Christine Hamilton had managed to wriggle out of a speeding conviction by claiming that they did not know who was driving the car at the time, and, while they did not dispute that the car itself was speeding, there was no proof of who was at the wheel. They got off scot-free. I was discussing this with Richard and he sportingly announced that he would find it very difficult indeed to remember who exactly was driving the car on the A43 at 5.43 a.m. that day. In fact, he doubted if he would be able to recall who was driving at any point over the following six days. I thought it unlikely that my memory would be up to it either.

Clearly inspired by the camera action, Richard produced his all-singing, all-dancing new mobile phone, with digital camera. I was watching him play with it excitedly like a kid with a new toy, and could not help thinking that he was a most unsuitable person to be let loose with such technology.

A camera phone is a particularly needless piece of equipment, though undoubtedly fun. I had bought one for myself purely to send pictures to a friend of mine who was a stockbroker. I was road-testing a Ferrari 575M, on a lengthy drive through Wales and I sent my pal pictures at thirty-minute intervals with the captions 'My job is better than your job' and 'Are you wearing a tie?' I suspected Richard had invested in one for similarly puerile albeit friskier reasons.

My suspicions were confirmed when I saw the screensaver picture revealing a rather attractive girl's finely toned midriff.

'New phone, Richard? Let's see. You didn't waste much time collecting photos, then? Who's the girl?'

'Oh, her, nobody. That picture was on it courtesy of Vodafone. Honestly, what do you take me for? I'm not that type.'

Nonsense, I thought. He just had not had time. I took the phone from him. Menu – Photos – Select. Hmm. Interesting.

'Oh, yeah, what about that girl then, who's she?' I said, laughing.

He grabbed the phone, and looked at the screen sheepishly. 'Shag off, you nosy sod. That's Milly,' he said guiltily, 'you've met her.'

Indeed, I had, and I am proud of the fact that I rarely forget a face, but I couldn't possibly have been expected to recognise her from that angle.

I had heard him talk fondly of her and could be forgiven for thinking that she was his girlfriend; I had met her about a week earlier in a bar in Fulham, out for a few pints with Richard. Appearances can be deceptive, however, and the motive behind meeting for drinks was not so I could get to know Richard's girlfriend. He had told me it was worthwhile putting in an appearance at the Fulham Mitre since he was meeting 'two girls who are going on the Gumball, sisters apparently'. The sisters were Sonia and Mandy, two blonde girls of independent, indeterminate and evidently substantial means. God knows where Richard had unearthed them but I was well impressed with his resourcefulness.

I got the distinct impression that this was equally clear to Milly, and obviously no surprise. Milly struck me as being well able for him, clearly suffering from no delusions of her status in Richard's romantic life. She showed a touching concern for my well-being, giving an involuntary shudder and a sympathetic look when she heard that I had never been in a car with him before. Clearly, she was experienced in this department.

After the speed-camera incident, the rest of the drive to Folkestone was incident free, and we actually arrived in pretty good time. Richard went to buy a paper and I watched with interest. I have always thought that you can tell a lot about a person from what newspaper they read and, given that I was about to spend six days in close quarters with this individual, I was curious to see what he returned with. For instance, if it was the *Guardian* I may have had grounds for concern that he would spend the week being irritatingly PC, worrying about fuel consumption and the hazardous environmental damage we were causing, and resolutely worrying about the illegalities of breaking speed limits. On the other hand, the *Telegraph* may have indicated a propensity for a high-handed 'get off my land, you don't understand about hunting, you thick townie' sort of approach to matters. I was most worried he would return with the *Daily Mail*, and thus stink of small-minded self-importance.

Thankfully, I needn't have concerned myself since he returned with a copy of the *Sun*, which confirmed my suspicion that much of the chat would be tits and bums, with a smattering of current affairs, albeit with very little understanding. Perfect. Leslie Grantham, aka *EastEnders*' Dirty Den, was on the cover. Apparently, he had been caught in an online chat room. In this day and age of deviants populating the subculture of internet chat rooms, some would see that as crime enough, but the appropriately named Dirty Den had gone one better and pulled out his webcam among a few other things. You would think that, of all the available fetishes on the internet, a TV star would choose something more imaginative to play with than his camera. Talk about taking your work home with you.

Predictably enough, we had a good chuckle at his expense, and my view was that whatever his sexual tastes he must be either a halfwit or suicidal to think that no one would recognise his face, no matter how impressive the rest of the show might be. One wonders why tabloid editors in the mould of Piers Morgan (or in his case former tabloid editors) go to such lengths to snare celebrities, duping them with fake sheiks for example, when clearly there are more than enough idiots like Grantham who will make fools of themselves of their own volition. I was pontificating along these lines when Richard confessed that he had strayed on to the front pages of tabloids himself on occasion.

Apparently, he had got friendly with a lap dancer, as you do, who 'stayed the night a couple of times'. Somewhat unsurprisingly, after their brief acquaintance had petered out, as he was unwinding in the weighing room at Newbury after riding three winners, Richard got a call from the *News of the World*, something he described with perfect understatement as 'not an introduction that puts you completely at ease'. He declined to comment suspecting that they had plenty to go on, and sure enough an account of their fling duly appeared written in the 'newspaper's inimitable style'. I got the distinct impression that, once he realised his parents and family were not too upset, he really was not that bothered about the whole thing, possibly viewing it as an occupational hazard. Further discussion revealed that the real reason he was not overly concerned was that the paper made him out to be the 'world's greatest Casanova'. Seeing his obvious satisfaction at the recollection, I could not resist the opportunity to point out that the newspaper's inimitable style was one of gross exaggeration and embellishment.

Queuing to board the Eurotunnel shuttle, we spotted two likely lads in a Mercedes 500SL with a skull-and-crossbones motif on the side. Gumballers? Hard to tell. They didn't look monied enough for a start, the car was a ten-year-old SL and a bit shabby, and they themselves looked a little more like amateur smugglers embarking on an illicit cross-Channel booze-and-fags run. We did not realise it at the time, but all this was a bit rich coming from two guys patiently queuing in a lime-green Volvo estate, with tangerine leather. I am sure we looked more like two antique dealers on a 'business' trip to Provence than hard and fast, rock 'n' roll Gumballers.

Coincidentally, we met the drivers of the SL at our first fuel stop in France, and the tell-tale Gumball logo on their jackets reminded us for the first, but not the last, time that Gumballers are a varied and diverse bunch. Also for the first, but not the last, time, I discovered how genuinely friendly and sociable Richard is. He will literally talk to anyone and, while I was still entertaining my blinkered stereotypes of these guys, Richard bounded into conversation.

'Gumballers, eh?' he said, nodding at the logo. 'We're on our way to Paris as well.'

Mike, the driver, had done a few Gumballs before in the States and was looking forward to being back in Europe. He was full of advice, and at pains to stress that it was quite hard work, particularly the first endurance stage. Richard was the chatty one; I was listening, but rather at the periphery of the conversation as I ordered the coffees. The conversation moved on to cars.

'So what are you driving?' asked Mike, innocently enough.

Suddenly, without any warning at all, Richard left me to take up the conversational baton and wandered off, immediately becoming engrossed in the football – a replay of the Chelsea versus Monaco Champions League match that I know full well he watched live.

'A Volvo V70R,' I announced, and proudly pointed at the car on the forecourt.

This was our first, or I should say my first, as Richard was long gone, experience of being the butt of the Volvo jokes. For some reason, among Ferraris, Porsches and Lamborghinis, a Volvo estate was destined to become a source of much hilarity. This guy did not so much snigger as totally convulse while he recycled his coffee through his nose.

'So where are the wife and two kids, then?'

I could see Richard grinning while he pretended to watch the football. I joined in the laughter, in that inexplicable way that you sometimes do, as you share a complete stranger's hilarity in taking the piss out of you. It's an odd phenomenon, especially when you're really thinking, Fuck off, you cretin. Nice Merc, I believe the new one is quite quick but, if you think that ten-year-old banger is going to come anywhere close to our stealth Volvo, you're as dumb as you look.

After a hearty laugh, I made my excuses and sat down to join Richard, who was still grinning.

'Don't look at me,' he said. 'It's your car.'

'It's not my car; it's a Volvo press car.'

'Ah, whatever, you're responsible for it.'

This line in childish bickering came to an abrupt halt when Joe French came to discuss the football. I am a great believer in attempting to speak the language of a country, in a 'when in Rome' sort of way. It shows great respect for the people and culture, and marks you out from the legion of ignorant tourists who would never dream of ordering a plate of *oeuf et frites*, because they're not having any of that foreign muck. The French, in particular, are fiercely proud of their language and, as such, you can understand why they might get a little annoyed with English-speaking types who, if they make any effort at all, tend to engage in a little Franglais.

Not Richard though. As noted above, he will talk to anyone, and he won't mess about with Franglais, even though they might have more chance of understanding it.

Joe French opened the conversation. '*Bonjeur Monsier, le futbol, oui? Qu'est que c'est?*'

'*Ah, si, Chelsea y Monaco, la liga Champions. Danke, gagne, aujord'hui semaine, auf wiedersehen, gracias.*'

To his immense credit, Monsieur did not laugh and merely looked at him quizzically with a '*Pardon?*'

'*Oui, football, non. Habla le French, ya?*' Richard continued his nonsense talk.

'Who is winning?' enunciated Joe with extreme care, not because he was struggling with a second language, but I think he was yet to work out what language Richard spoke, if any at all.

'Oh, it's a replay. Monaco won it last week.'

'Thanks.' Joe French wandered off.

Richard looked at me as if the man was mad. 'What language was he speaking?'

For the second time in as many minutes I could not believe my ears. 'Richard, what language were you speaking? I think I heard a bit of everything bar Chinese.'

'Well, he's European, isn't he,' he replied, clearly extending the boundaries of the 'when in Rome' school of languages.

I made a mental note to try and do the bulk of the talking during our time in France, notwithstanding my dismal D-grade performance in A-levels. I had a grasp of the basics and thus clearly a lot more than my co-driver.

I got up to leave. 'On y va, Richard?' I said.

'Cheers, mate, I take mine black.'

Having met a couple of other Gumballers, we anticipated seeing a few more as we continued the journey towards Paris, presumably a hard-core bunch of mentallers, speeding past us. We were now in Gumball mode and talk turned to strategy and how we intended to approach the drive, our 'riding orders', as it were. The 'connections', as in the Volvo press office, would have been proud had they witnessed such a mature and sensible discussion. No matter what everyone else was doing, we adamantly agreed that there was no point in driving like a lunatic and we should concentrate on making haste not speed. Although not strictly a law-abiding approach, as we intended to break the speed limit, we felt that if we cruised along at around 90 mph we would be both safe and swift. The logic behind such a grown-up point of view was that we were ill equipped to be shelling out thousands of euros in speeding fines, and ultimately that this was a fun event and we had no desire to show a blatant disregard for the law nor the safety of other road users. This might sound a little dull but the 'tortoise and hare strategy' was something that was set in stone.

Thus, we felt very responsible as we sped towards Paris at a steady 80–90 mph, arriving at the Four Seasons George V Hotel with our sensible hats on but in high spirits nonetheless.

5. PARIS

You will not find details of the George V in the *Lonely Planet French Edition* or *The Rough Guide to Paris*. These are travellers' guidebooks, whereas this hotel is at the high end of the tourist market. There are distinct differences between travellers and tourists, not least the £500 gulf in their nightly accommodation spend. Judging from the luggage that weighed down the numerous concierges, this was not a hotel that the *Lonely Planet* might refer to as 'backpacker friendly' and, after drinking in the atmosphere and surroundings, I considered the place to be all the better for it, though drinking the €10 cup of coffee in the sumptuous bar reminded me I was touring on a travelling budget.

After making enquiries about checking in there, I discovered that we were not staying here at all, and were booked into the hotel next door. Right, cheers pal, I thought, thanks for the cheap seats. This was a considerable blow to my new-found status, and I quickly consulted the *Rough Guide*. Mercifully, the Hotel Prince de Galles did not feature, not even in the 'High End' pages. I am sure the *Rough Guide* writers could bore you rigid with tales of the amazing places where they have been, but if their idea of 'luxury' is anything to go by they need to get out more.

A quick look around the Hotel Prince de Galles confirmed that it was cut from the same expensive cloth. There is a theory, which I think is an urban myth, that supermarkets circulate odours conducive to shopping. For example, every now and again you hear some scientist/consultant type say that the smell of freshly baked bread triggers all sorts of subconscious sensory reactions that make us spend more, hence these exotics are artificially created by big bad corporate types to increase profit margins. Utter bollocks. The supermarket smells of freshly baked bread because there are ovens with bread in them, baking. We buy the bread because it smells nice, and it's that simple. Similarly, a swanky Parisian hotel cannot recreate the smell of money so the residents feel wealthy; it just sort of smells that way because there are expensive perfumes and colognes, leather suites and rich food in the air. The Hotel Prince de Galles had a distinct whiff of money about the place, which I imagine was normal, but today, crammed full of Gumballers tossing the keys of £100,000 cars to the valet parking attendants, the place positively stank.

However, there were definitely strange stirrings in my subconscious, since as I approached the check-in desk I felt undeniably wealthy. No matter what I felt, my scruffy attire could not have looked the part but it did not matter, as the staff knew that we were Gumballers and reacted with the highest standards of courtesy and brown-nosing expected of them. These impeccable employees had undoubtedly trained meticulously in the art of dealing with their typical clientele and, as our check-in fiasco unfolded, I realised that such training achieves similar results as you might expect from a McDonald's employee. The scenarios that are thrown up in their jobs would, of course, be different but, if they are faced with a tried and tested system that suddenly breaks down, all hell breaks loose. For instance, there is some light, if brief, amusement to be had by asking the McWaitron for chips instead of fries. Without fail, they do a double-take because they are confused; chips are not on the menu, you see, and thus they are technically not available in McDonald's. On some occasions, you can be lucky enough to unearth the real thickies who actually follow through and inform you that chips are, indeed, not available, which makes the joke so much more enjoyable. It is probably rather cruel and pointless to engage in such pedantic behaviour, but I am ashamed to admit that these little interactions with the staff put the happy in my Happy Meal.

On one occasion, I witnessed a customer try to retrieve his wallet from the bin, which had got there after a McWaitron had emptied his tray into it, lock, stock and personal possessions. He understandably asked her to open the locked bin but she claimed that she was unable to until it was full. This, of course, would have made the task of finding the wallet considerably more difficult and unpleasant, but, since that was never covered in Refuse McModule B, it was a non-starter. It was an unusual scenario, and not one that she had been trained for so there was nothing she could do but consult the manual, which told her she could do nothing.

An unusual, if not similar, scenario of my own occurred checking in to the hotel. Just as the McDonald's employee has not been trained to deal with the inconveniences of opening bins, the courteous staff of the world's five-star hotels do not expect their guests' credit cards to be declined. The immediate assumption on their part is that it is the machine that is faulty, and not the customer's credit rating.

'Alors, monsieur, sorry for the delay. I don't understand. This has never happened before. The machine must be broken.'

I, on the other hand, understood only too well, as it had happened many times before. 'Don't worry, honestly it's fine,' I said, as I looked around for Richard.

'We will try again, monsieur,' she said, as she swiped the useless plastic.

'Richard!' I hissed through my teeth in a cry for help.

He sauntered over and enquired casually, 'What's up? Is there a problem?'

To aggravate my embarrassment, the receptionist reiterated the problem for Richard's benefit. 'The card machine appears to be broken, sir.'

This is all we need, I thought, Richard entering into some European dialogue to clarify the situation.

'Give me your credit card, Richard.'

'Sure,' he said, and reached for his wallet, 'but what's the point if the machine is broken?'

'It's not the machine; it's my fucking credit card that's broken.'

Richard handed over his card, and the receptionist recognised its distinctive golden hue immediately. Back on familiar territory, she swiped the card and registered no surprise at the machine's seemingly miraculous recovery. With the €50.00 deposit taken care of, she handed the card back to Richard, as he gave me a look clearly expressing his concern for my credit card's health and wishing it a speedy recovery. The receptionist on the other hand gave me a look that clearly suggested I leave the mini-bar well alone.

'Sorry, mate, I lodged money yesterday; it will have cleared by midnight.'

'I sincerely hope so or this is going to be an expensive week.'

Later that evening, we made our way back to the George V for our first Gumball party – a 'Welcome Cocktail Reception', which was very welcome indeed. As new Gumballers, we had no friends from previous rallies and spent the first ten minutes or so sizing up the competition. I had seen *Gumball – the Movie* and was pointing out characters who had featured. Look at him, same suit, same car, new girl.

A character called Torquenstein arrived in full costume, with an army of hangers-on cum staff. We had spotted this guy make his official arrival earlier in an ambulance. Somehow, presumably at great cost, he had procured a genuine French ambulance, and had had himself delivered to the hotel. Amid much fanfare, he was brought to life and introduced to the assembled throng of Gumballers, press and generally bemused locals as Torquenstein, half-man, half-machine and ardent proponent of something called 'Vehicular Lunacy'. Such lunacy was warmly applauded by the Gumballers and the press, but the locals were of the distinct impression that he looked a little old to be playing doctors and nurses, and that Parisian ambulances could be put to much better uses. Some of them went as far as to express the view that such hubris was utter ignorance, and they rather hoped that it would not be the last time his fondness for 'Vehicular Lunacy' landed him in an ambulance.

An infamous Gumball character and equally larger than life, though a little more literally, was a German of gargantuan girth and ego called Kim Schmitz. At the very thick end of twenty stone, the sheer size of his black suits meant his pockets were deeper than most, and apparently he put this depth to good use, as I had heard numerous anecdotes of Kim setting the standards for bribes and speeding fines. No one seemed to know what he did, and rumours abounded that he was a former hacker who had gone on to be a poacher turned gamekeeper, and then did a spell in prison for insider trading. One thing everyone agreed on was that he was something of a psycho on the road, driving flat out wherever he went, and had been involved in numerous bumps and shunts. Although we agreed that the presence of such larger-than-life characters was an essential part of the Gumball experience, we resolved to give Fat Boy Kim a wide berth on the road.

The room was filling up, but, even so, the striking height of an Eastern Europeanesque blonde was impossible to miss. Naturally over six feet, plus VAT in her heels, she towered over most of the Gumballers as she swaggered in. It was only when she got to the middle of the room, where the crowd was thinner, that we noticed the swagger of her companion. He was a funny little man who was closer to five feet tall than her six, with a curiously coloured suntan that might have been the inspiration for the Volvo's leather interior. You could sense the collective sniggers that rippled around the room, but equally so you could sense his own self-confidence in the grin that said 'I don't care what you're looking at; I've got bags of money and a blonde babe.' And a Ferrari Enzo, as it turned out.

Somebody pointed out Tony Hawk, the skateboard legend. Not being into skateboarding, the only thing I knew about him was he was a mere consonant removed from the author and comedian Tony Hawks. I once visited the author's website and found it a great source of amusement, not because of the excerpts from his books, but the 'Skate Mail' page. It seems that some of the skateboarder's younger fans mistakenly email Hawks requesting that he comes round to catch pipes in their playground. To his immense credit, Hawks does not do the decent thing and send them a stock reply explaining their mistake. He takes the time to send each one an individual reply and then posts their correspondence on his site for the rest of us to have a good laugh at.

FROM: Fabian
TO: Tony Hawks
SUBJECT: Peace

peace tony
you are a werry good skateboarder. I come from Switzerländ.
I play your game every day. I hope you can rhite a e- mail to me. i am 14 years. (sorry i can not good English)

bye bye Fabian
Fabian

FROM: Tony Hawks
TO: Fabian
SUBJECT: RE: Peace

Your English is werry good.
I'm not surprised you play my game every day. I'm told that in Switzerland, unless you ski or launder money, there's fuck all else to do.

Tony Hawks

Tony Hawk, the skateboarder, is a legend among his fans for his boarding skills, and specifically because he was the first boarder to complete something known as a 900-degree whizz bang loop something or other and he was understandably pretty 'stoked' about the significant achievement. I had always assumed that these radical types that got so stoked were of the 'baggy trouser, prepubescent bum fluff' school of fashion and deportment, but seeing Hawk in the flesh I was surprised that a) he was about 35 and b) he looked like a barrister. Tall and respectable looking, clean shaven and with a conservative hair cut and dress sense, he looked like just the sort of guy who would gain automatic parental approval should he begin courting their 'thirty-something, about to be left on the shelf' daughter. After registering my surprise at his appearance, somebody told me that, while he still holds 'legend' status in the skateboarding world, he is officially retired, and now devotes more time to his second wife and three kids. That would explain the radical look.

Appearances can be deceptive. Hawk was about as unlikely looking a champion skateboarder as Sebastian Coe was, and the same can be said for Emma, the alleged porn star, who was straight out of the middle-England, middle-class 'please Daddy can I have a pony' brigade. I have always thought that porn stars were more likely to look like a combination of the blonde/midget couple I mentioned earlier, a tall number with her breasts and his tan. On the first night of the Gumball, rumours were already rife that there was a famous porn actress in a Bentley Continental GT, on account of the fact that she was travelling with a guy who had his fingers in many pies, one of them being a pay-per-view porn channel. We agreed to investigate the porn-star story.

After being thoroughly pass remarkable about the other Gumballers, we finally started talking to some. First up was a group of lads who were driving a Hummer, and by happy coincidence they turned out to be Irish. I had noticed the Hummer, with the Dublin registration, outside the hotel and meant to introduce myself, thinking it might take a little effort to find them. I certainly had not expected that we would all end up congregating in the same area of the immense ballroom, and was pondering the coincidence when I noticed that we were all propping up the bar lashing into the free drink.

One of them, Bob, introduced himself to Richard. He had recognised him and, as his father was a keen horse racing enthusiast, had asked if he could have his picture taken with him. Richard happily agreed and afterwards we all got chatting, as Bob introduced us to the rest of his three co-drivers, John, Mark and Steven. I was thinking that both Bob and John looked vaguely familiar and, as we were doing the 'sniffing bums, what do you do and where do you come from' thing, the penny dropped.

'I am mainly into property now but for a while I was the only guy in Dublin hiring out sports cars,' said Bob.

At around the same time, I had run an ill-fated venture hiring out classic cars and, although we had never been formally introduced, I knew who he was and was fairly sure he knew me too.

'I think we've come across each other before,' I said. 'I used to hire classic cars based in Wicklow.'

'Oh, yes, I remember. You had that Rachel girl doing some work for you, didn't you? I knew her socially and I seem to recall her taking a very keen interest in the logistics of my business.'

Enough said. I too remembered exactly what he was talking about since she was working with me at the time, and had deliberately engaged in a little more detailed 'sniffing bums, what do you do and where do you come from' than could be considered purely social. I tried to move the conversation on.

Richard was most amused. 'Making friends, eh? Have you just been busted for a little light industrial espionage?' he said, chuckling.

Moving on swiftly, I mentioned to John that he looked familiar and quick as a flash Bob piped up, 'Oh, you've probably seen John in the papers. He got into bed with a famous Formula 1 driver, but their relationship went tits up and they have had an acrimonious parting.'

'Ah, of course, Eddie Irvine. Now I know why I recognise you,' I said. John clearly did not want to pursue this avenue of conversation so I dropped it, but Richard was agog, wondering if he could have heard the conversation correctly. 'I'll tell you later,' I whispered.

The party progressed, even though the free drink did not. At €30.00 for two beers, drinking in swanky hotels was an expensive pastime. When the pay per pint ran out, the assembled Gumballers began to drift across the street to La Suite nightclub where the real hi-jinks were due to begin.

As we were leaving, Bob turned to me and said, 'That Richard Dunwoody seems like a good guy, down to earth and up for a bit of a laugh.'

'Bob, trust me, you've seen nothing yet.'

La Suite is a fearsomely trendy Parisian nightclub with prices to match. Anticipating this I had gone to the cash machine, and when I returned I found Richard nursing his wallet after buying a round. He was also planning some strategic work, and he mapped out his thoughts.

'Right, Clement, there's Sonia and Mandy and I reckon our best approach with these two is to play hard to get,' he said with a straight face.

After laughing so hard that I choked on a €20.00 mouthful of beer, I recovered and said, 'Sorry, Richard, but the idea of you playing "hard to get" has a certain comic value.'

Before he could dispute this logic, we were interrupted by someone we had noticed earlier. She was a camerawoman covering the rally, and had a rather fetching and exotic look about her. Brazilian, as it turned out.

She introduced herself. 'Hi, guys, I'm Sarah. I've read about you two.'

This sounded a little strange. She could have read any number of things about Richard, but I could not think of anything about me.

Richard thought it odd as well. 'Really, Sarah, where did you read about us?' he asked.

'On the website.'

'Website?' asked Richard, now thoroughly confused.

Things were making a little more sense to me though.

'Nice photo, Clement,' she continued, 'but yours didn't really show your good side, Richard.'

She wandered off, leaving Richard none the wiser.

'Website? What's she on about? Are we on the Gumball website?'

'No, I don't think it's that website she means.'

'Hang on a second,' he said, as things began to dawn on him. 'Did you put a website up about us on the Gumball?'

'Well, sort of, there's nothing really on it apart from the fact we're doing the rally in a Volvo.'

'There's obviously a bloody photo of you, and of me. And it appears that you found your most flattering picture and went to work with the airbrush, while sticking up some crap photo of me,' he thundered, hitting the nail on the head.

'That's not strictly true, Richard,' I lied. 'It's that photo of you in your Irish rugby shirt, twiddling a pen. I suppose you might look a bit geeky, but it was the only one I could find. Relax, have another drink.'

We needed no encouragement as the party began to swing. Soul diva Kym Mazelle was attempting a solo, but being drowned out rather inexpertly by Steve from the Hummer. Chris Eubank appeared to be trying his hand at DJing. The tall blonde we had noticed in the Four Seasons was enjoying an intimate chat with her man, who was standing on a chair to whisper sweet nothings into her ear, while all sorts of groupies and Gumballers were getting acquainted.

After a couple hours of this merriment, I could neither stand nor stay awake any longer, so I left Richard in the capable hands of a Scandinavian and stumbled across the road to the hotel.

I awoke at around nine o'clock the next morning, in our twin room, alone. It was impossible to work out whether Richard was an early riser or simply had not returned yet. As I left the room, I bumped into him returning.

'I have been to bed. I've just come from breakfast,' he said, reading my mind. He had got in sometime around six o'clock and awoken at eight o'clock, which was great news. Particularly considering we had an all-night drive ahead of us. He was definitely full of energy though.

'Hurry up and have breakfast; we've got a lot to do today,' he enthused. 'Not least we have to sex that car up a bit.' He still had not come around to the Volvo.

'Sex it up? What do you mean?'

'We can chat about it after your breakfast.'

Some half an hour later, I found him packed up and planning the day. He was reading the itinerary that we had been given the previous day, scouring it for details.

'*One to seven p.m. – Registration* – done. *Eight to ten p.m. "Welcome Cocktail Reception"* – done. *Ten p.m. till late "Fuck Me – I'm Famous" at La Suite* – well, that hasn't happened yet.'

'That's the name of the DJ act, Richard.'

'Right, well, whatever, there's a bit of false advertising involved there. I wonder what the Trading Standards authority would have to say. *Seven to eleven a.m. Breakfast* – done. *Eleven a.m. – Hotel checkout and be in your car at midday ready to parade drive to the start line* – midday? That doesn't give us much time to do the car. Come on, let's go.'

Richard's plan was to source a few 'accessories' for the car. He was starting to get a bit fed up with the barrage of Volvo jokes and we desperately needed a substitute for the wife and kids. Like a rubber doll. He maintained that you could not swing a cat in Paris without hitting a sex shop so it wouldn't take long. Luckily, when we checked out, we discovered that the schedule had been changed, and our next engagement was the driver's briefing at 3 p.m. That gave us plenty of time to find a sex shop. Hooray! Having shopped with Richard before and recalling his delight in fondling the stock, I was not looking forward to letting him loose in a sex shop.

I insisted that our first stop should be a toy shop where we could buy a stuffed dog. As all the jokes had been about the dogs in the back of the car, it seemed a tad more relevant to me than the rubber doll. We must have looked like a right pair of weirdoes, holding up and scrutinising an assortment of soft toys. Our thoroughness paid off, however, when we discovered a dopey-looking basset hound with a long drooling tongue. He had the perfect look about him, and we agreed that he was just the right size to sit snugly in the back and stare goofily at all the cars we were planning to overtake.

With that achieved, it was time to find the sex shop. Oddly enough, it was not as simple as swinging a cat, or even the dog we had just purchased. I mentioned to Richard that we probably would not find a sex shop and a toy shop in close proximity.

'Of course not,' he replied, 'we'll have to get a taxi to Pigalle.'

'Pigalle?'

'It's the red-light district in Paris; there will be hundreds of good shops there.'

'Are you sure? How do you know where the red-light district is?'

'I haven't a clue but any taxi will have us there in a couple of minutes.'

After a short taxi ride, a suitable shop was sourced. We explained to the assistant that we were in the market for a blow-up doll, and why. We felt it was just too weird to be two blokes wandering into a sex shop with a stuffed dog looking for an inflatable doll. The woman did not seem to buy our story that they were vital passengers on our road trip to Cannes, and gave us a look that you might receive from a doctor in A & E if you said, 'I swear I just tripped and fell on the hoover while it was on full suction power.' Whatever she thought of our motives, she was definitely impressed with our choice of dog. Unwittingly, we had bought the toy version of a famous French cartoon character who she explained was much loved by adults and children alike. She cooed and fussed over him like a live puppy, but at the same time did not seem terribly concerned that he might be about to be put in a compromising position with two adult males and a rubber female. In fact, she seemed adamant that we required the top-of-the-range doll to complement our dog, and even arranged a discount for the all-singing, all-dancing model with three orifices. We paid and left hurriedly.

'Christ, Richard, don't put me through that again.'

'Yeah, that was a bit strange, all right. She loved the dog. We better give him a name.'

'We'll call him Pigalle,' I said, pointing to a large neon sign proclaiming Pigalle and its highlights.

'Good idea,' Richard replied, looking at his watch. 'Let's have a drink; we've got plenty of time. We'll try that place over there.'

The significance of the name hadn't dawned on me, and we've established that Richard's language skills were not really up to much, but 'Les Trois Roses' turned out to be a little more meaningful than, say, 'The Prince of Wales Tavern'. On first impressions, the pub seemed like any other, a bit small and rather quiet. We were the only customers. No sooner had we sat down at the bar and ordered a bottle of beer each than 'The Three Roses' appeared from upstairs to join us. Suddenly the €350.00 bottle of Veuve Elizabeth on the champagne menu was making a little more sense.

'Richard, this is a bloody brothel,' I hissed at him.

'It would appear so. Calm down. Just drink your beer and we'll leave. They won't bite.'

Once they realised that we were not 'looking for business', Pigalle the dog again became the centre of attention. The barmaid, or 'Madam' as would be the more appropriate job description, was pleading flirtatiously for us to leave him behind. Richard began negotiations to swap him for one of the 'roses' suggesting that they could be our mascot instead.

'Richard, drink up, we've got to leave now. We have a drivers' briefing to go to.'

'I was only joking,' he said with a grin, as we left.

The drivers' briefing was back in the Four Seasons George V, and Maximillion Cooper, the Gumball founder, addressed us all for the first time. He started off with a few administrative details. At registration we had all been supplied with specially designed Gumball race suits, but apparently there were not enough to go round and some of the latecomers had to do without. It seemed that they had got most annoyed, kicked up a bit of a fuss and taken out their anger on the Gumball crew members. Max's response was 'Just go with it, guys.' This was a marvellous way of dealing with disgruntled customers – telling them just to chill out – and I got the impression that it was one he used regularly.

'We don't want to be too corporate on the Gumball, we're a bit rock 'n' roll, and I know that things can get frustrating at times, but just go with it, guys,' he said in laid-back tones.

I do not know if it actually appeased them but it probably cut down on any more complaints, making people embarrassed to admit to being uptight.

It is not all rock 'n' roll though, as Max then proceeded to remind the Gumballers to behave themselves in the hotels. He took the opportunity to point out that the person who had defaced a painting with graffiti on the way home from the nightclub was not going to get away with it. The hotel had the benefit of closed-circuit television coverage and the guests' credit cards. Richard looked at me in horror, as he remembered that the hotel had his credit card and not mine. I shook my head to reassure him that I was not guilty.

The guilty party turned out to be the chief executive of a well-known bank. Presumably, in his day-to-day job and life, he was a person of great responsibility and respectability, and dare I say perhaps a little boring, yet put him on the Gumball and after a few beers and a party he starts trashing hotels. Great stuff. Maybe this was the 'Spirit of the Gumball' I had heard so much about. Or maybe it was just human nature or, more accurately, bloke nature. Feminists, academics, psychologists, wives and girlfriends often say that men are just big kids in reality. Whereas females grow up to be adults with mature thoughts, emotions and actions, the theory is that men only superficially grow up, and never really mature in the same adult and responsible manner. There are all sorts of theses, learned empirical evidence and intellectual suppositions, but, if you really needed any convincing, it would be far more effective to go to a Gumball party. There is a little less jelly and ice cream than your average kids' party, but the mentality and behaviour is not far removed. And you would have a lot more fun than reading an essay on the 'Inner Child'.

Max confirmed that the 'Spirit of the Gumball' was not about trashing hotels. It was the big award that everyone should aim to win, and went to great lengths to point out that the Gumball was emphatically *not* a race. There were no prizes for first place, whereas the 'Spirit' embodied a camaraderie and a Gumballer's sense of fun, while realising that it was not all about finishing first. The 2003 winner was Alex Roy for 'the effort he made in making everyone smile', and as he received the applause in his Royal Canadian Mounted Police uniform it was clear that he was intent on making everyone smile again this year.

In the briefing, Max put particular emphasis on the Moroccan leg. Apparently, the King had been quite helpful and we were 'valued guests'. Whatever this meant, it was surely encouraging since there were rumours that a rival road rally, The Cannonball Run, had faced armed roadblocks in Morocco. There was a significant plea not 'to take the piss' in Morocco, and specifically not to try and bribe the cops. Max was quite serious as he said, 'Please don't give them crazy sums of money like $10,000 and ask them to hold the rest of the cars up. It is a real pain for people behind you as they will just then want it from everyone else.' He was not exaggerating as we had heard that a number of Gumballers had paid frightening amounts of money to the Russian Police a couple of years earlier. It was an effective means of staying out of trouble, while getting others into it. Max was adamant that bribes would be unnecessary and advised us to keep a good stock of Gumball stickers and Top Trumps, which would be more than sufficient to keep a Moroccan cop on side. He followed up by telling us to prepare for a massive 'culture shock'. There had been mumblings of discontent as evidently some Gumballers were worried about the roads but Max reassured us that the roads were in perfect condition. As far as we were concerned, I was hoping that they would not be great as I felt the Volvo might look like a pretty good choice of car in Morocco.

The final item on the agenda of the drivers' briefing was a showing of a French film called *Rendezvous*, featuring a racing driver speeding through the streets of Paris. Our parade lap had been designed to follow his exact route. Before turning on the film, Max said, 'He did the route in seven minutes. It will take you guys three-quarters of an hour.'

The chorus of 'Oh really?' suggested this was a dangerous thing to say to a group of Gumballers.

6. PARIS TO MAS DU CLOS

After the briefing, we were told to go straight to the car park for the start of the parade. This was unfortunate as I had left my luggage in the hotel, and was feeling a little too lazy to transport it. The Hummer was sitting outside the hotel, as it would not fit in the car park. Perfect, they had loads of room so I would just throw it in there. I knocked on one of the tinted rear windows, which came down to reveal they had far from loads of room. Somewhere along the line, they had found four new passengers in the shape and form of four rather pretty Belgian girls.

'Hi, Clement, what's up? Meet our new friends. Luggage, eh? Things are bit tight in here, but don't worry we'll find the space.'

On my arrival back at the car park, Richard had inflated the doll and was dressing it in a Gumball race suit.

A little rubber-looking guy appeared, who had more of the 'stoked extreme skateboard' look about him than Tony Hawk, and was carrying a vast box.

'What's in there?' I asked him.

'Skateboards, man. We were told you guys had room.'

'Yeah, we've got room for a couple of skateboards; you look like you're moving house.'

'Sorry, man, it's all the team's gear,' he said, and surely would have performed some exaggerated hand movements had he not been weighed down so comprehensively. The box was full of helmets, kneepads and boards, and would have rivalled the paraphernalia of a teenager on the way to a gymkhana. With some effort we managed to fit it all in and keep the rear seats free for our passengers.

'Stoked, dude,' he cheered, and it was now time for the exaggerated hand movements. He held out his hand and, a little bemused, I reached to shake it. As soon as I touched it he withdrew his hand at pace, twisted his wrist and dropped his arm by his side, and, just as I thought he was about to walk like an Egyptian, he shot his arm up vertically and at chest height waggled his fingers at me. 'Go, Gumball man, see yo' in Marbella.'

'Hey, Richard, did you see that?' I called to the front of the car wondering whether he had witnessed the peculiar handshake.

'What? The skateboard guy?'

'Yeah, but did you notice he's a *freemason* skateboard guy?'

Eventually, it was time to leave and we pulled into what was to be the first of many car queues. Sitting in the car park, in the midst of a £15 million traffic jam, Richard had a bemused look on his face. I wondered if he was calculating that our contribution to the traffic was about 0.1 per cent of the total. The organisers had advised in the briefing not to start engines until the last minute, for fear of asphyxiating those at the back. The guts of two hundred cars in an underground car park can be a pretty lethal cocktail. Inevitably, two-hundred-odd petrol heads, childish with excitement about caning it to Cannes, were revving their engines like crazy. We, of course, were at the back.

As the cars inched slowly forward, we eventually made it to the ramp that would take us above ground to the streets of Paris; light was streaming in though a shaft but that was the extent of our view. We did not know what would be waiting but we could hear excited French people, all '*Oh la la*' and '*Mon dieu*'. The car in front of us was a Porsche 911 Cabriolet, as in convertible. The Cabriolet is often disparagingly referred to as 'the hairdresser's Porsche'. They were deliberately delaying, taking some minutes to take the roof down, and eventually we realised what was going on – they were waiting a minute or two, for a clear run up the ramp, no doubt so they could show the impressive turn of speed in a 911, and while they waited for that opportunity they used the time to check their hair for the photographers. After some time they sped off up the ramp, tyres squealing and billowing smoke. Good for them, I thought, gave them a little time in case they stuffed it into the locals and proceeded up the ramp after them.

We emerged into daylight, but only just. I have never see rain like it – it was lashing down. 'Wipers!' screamed Richard. They came on full pelt just in time to see the quaffed hairdos getting properly pissed on in the Porsche. It was an older model, pre-electric-roof days, so the agitated passenger was struggling desperately with the roof trying to raise it, much to the hilarity of the assembled onlookers. And ourselves I must admit. Hardly very 'Spirit of the Gumball' but vastly entertaining nonetheless.

The traffic was unreal. Five-thirty is rush-hour central in Paris, and the Gumball had mixed things up a bit by unleashing 200 cars and crew, and attempting a parade lap around the city. Cars were heading all over the place with no real sense of direction. Of course, we had already lost the town plan, which was floating around the car somewhere, though not quite as literally as those in the drop-top Porsche, I daresay.

We spotted the Black Hummer, where the Irish lads were having a contretemps with the gendarmes. Christ, I thought, they're only on the road ten minutes. In this traffic, what can they have done? Later they explained what happened. Apparently, the gendarme had taken issue with the element of overcrowding in the Hummer, as with the addition of four Belgian girls it had become a bit of a tight squeeze. But, when he had come over to give them a piece of his mind, Mark had complicated matters by rolling the Hummer over his foot. A Hummer is a beast of car at the best of times and, especially with eight occupants, it is sure to make a bit of dent in a gendarme's toes. Matters were complicated somewhat since Steve, bearing in mind Max's instructions in the drivers' briefing, had tried to buy the gendarme off with some Gumball Top Trumps. It was only when they were indignantly refused and threatened with arrest that he realised we were some way from Morocco.

Amid the chaos, we decided to abandon the parade on the grounds that we hadn't a clue where it was going, and for all intents and purposes neither did anyone else. We knew that we had to get to the Eiffel Tower which should not be too difficult to find. So we just followed a car. The car led us and a number of other Gumballers to L'Arc de Triomphe. Driving around this monument is pretty scary at the best of times since the French regard road-traffic laws as merely helpful suggestions, and they are not keen on indicating to suggest what they might do next. If Gumballers are liberally applied to this mixture, it becomes a recipe for disaster. Cars were shooting across one another like mad men and, while the Gumballers were treating the whole exercise as a true Gumball experience of zany driving, Joe French appeared not to notice as if it were all in a day's work for him.

Bursting for a cigarette in the traffic, I asked Richard about his in-car smoking views. Up until this stage, I had just waited until we stopped somewhere to have a fag, but it was clear that we were going nowhere fast so I thought it best to broach the subject. Richard's preparation for the Gumball included running the Belfast marathon the day before we left, whereas mine had concentrated more on getting my cigarette habit down to less than thirty a day. A constant question I was asked was how I thought Richard would cope with my in-car smoking routine. It was about time I asked him, since I obviously would not last the distance. Surprisingly enough, he readily agreed, saying that it did not really bother him, but he did point out the small print on Volvo's terms and conditions. Actually, it was not small print at all; it was in large block capitals spelling out the authoritarian message – DO NOT SMOKE.

With Richard's agreement obtained, the only problem was the lack of lighters. I am a terrible man for losing lighters at the best of times, but stick me in a car full of seat pockets and glove boxes and I am completely witless. Predictably, the car had more than its fair share of storage compartments and cubby holes, and then Volvo had complicated matters further by unhelpfully removing the in-car cigarette lighter in accordance with their anti-smoking press car policies. Bugger that, I thought, my humour will not last in this car by obeying that policy. The Maserati in front of us had an arm leaning out of the window, with a cigarette. The arm was long and svelte, and languishing in a most attractive way, clearly enjoying the nicotine's capability of providing some light relief from tense traffic. It seemed reasonable to pull up alongside and get a lighter from the arm's owner. We lane-hopped alongside and, as I pulled down the window, the arm's owner turned round to reveal herself as none other than Jodie Kidd, international supermodel and thankfully committed smoker. Before I could congratulate myself for getting my cigarettes lit on Parisian streets by leggy blondes, I was startled by a car coming straight at me. Damn French drivers, all over the road. They would just have to wait a moment. Jodie passed me the lighter and casually mentioned I was on the wrong side of the road. She called to the lady, who by now was gesticulating Frenchly, 'Don't worry, he's English.'

Indignantly I corrected her. 'Irish,' I said.

'Oh, of course you are, that explains it.'

We proceeded with some level of arrogance to disguise our blatant wrongdoing, cutting in front of Jodie and her Maserati, and narrowly missing the Frenchwoman who was becoming as inflamed as my cigarette.

The Eiffel Tower was just sheer traffic chaos. There were long lines of cars and locals, and girls handing out promotional goodies. Max had been keen to stage a 'noise off' where all cars shut their engines down, enjoyed the silence and then fired them again. This was never going to happen. Apart from the logistical difficulties, it would have been impossible to coerce such overgrown kids into sitting quietly in their cars. In Paris, the Gumball had attracted a noticeably large amount of 'hangers-on', many of whom had made their way to the Eiffel Tower. Stuck in the traffic and going nowhere fast, with our estate car and ample rear seats, we were sitting ducks. Some guy came up to the car and knocked on the window; an American kid with dodgy pink sunglasses and an irritating teenage Yankee bravado.

'Hey, man, my ride for the first leg has fallen through. I'm media. I'm official, I promise. Can I jump in with you guys?' he squealed.

All that extra space was beginning to look less attractive. Richard, ever the nice affable guy, said, 'Sure, why not?' The lad ran around the car to hop in the back. Luckily, the rubber doll was in the seat behind mine so he had to go to the far side of the car, which gave me time in one swift movement to whack on the central locking, wind up the windows, turn to Richard and glare.

'No bloody way!' I stated firmly.

'Why not? We've got loads of room. It's only for the first leg?'

'Richard, the first leg is sixteen hours-plus. We're in Paris and we are driving to Marbella. It will be a long night. Look at that kid with his pink sunglasses, and his jewellery; we can't have him yakking on incessantly throughout the night.'

Meanwhile, said kid was peering through the windows, knocking furiously and complaining that the door was locked.

'OK,' said Richard, and by now the kid was at Richard's window. 'But you deal with him.'

I called him over, while Richard looked out of the window innocently, and wound down my window. 'Listen, mate, sorry, this is not my car. It actually belongs to Volvo. You're media, yeah? You'll understand then, it is a press car and we are not insured to take passengers. I would if I could but I can't. I hope you understand?'

'Yeah, sure, thanks for nothing,' he mumbled in a tone that clearly suggested he far from understood.

I felt a bit sorry for him, but he took the whole thing rather badly I thought. I put the window up, with a 'shag off then, your rose-tinted spectacles are no good to you round here' glance. Richard was feeling bad, guilty for having so much space and refusing what he saw as a perfectly reasonable request. We had discussed the humour value in picking up passengers, thinking it would be a shame to waste the opportunity, but, to my recollection, they did not include Americans with verbal diarrhoea.

'That's bloody typical,' said Richard, pointing. I looked to see what he was pointing at and saw the Hummer with the Belgians hanging out of the window, all having a fine old time. 'Where did they find those girls?' he asked, with a touch of envy.

'Oh, yeah, I forgot to tell you about that. They're Belgian apparently,' I said, as if this in some way clarified matters as to how they had wound up in the Hummer.

'Belgian? What are you on about? That doesn't matter. What matters is you and your bloody Volvo. My point is their hitchhikers are attractive girls whereas ours are gobby lads.'

'Settle down. You've changed your tune all of sudden; you wanted to give him a lift.'

We inched our way towards the start, where each car was flagged off with much fanfare.

Richard was busying himself looking at the map of Paris. 'OK, we're definitely going to be heading south of Paris, so, when we leave, turn right and follow the river. Don't worry what anyone else is doing; just stick to my directions. Then I'll work out where to go once we get out of the city,' he said with confidence.

Early warning signs were encouraging. Richard seemed comfortable with the maps and confident in his abilities. It was reassuring to think that our in-car communications would be reasonably smooth, notwithstanding the fiasco concerning the Putney speed camera, nor the recent hitchhiker misunderstandings. The speed-camera incident was purely my fault and could be attributed to lack of concentration. Now the Gumball was about to start proper, we were both mentally alert.

As it came to our turn, Max stuck his head in the window, gave us a route card, wished us good luck and flagged us away. We were off! I spun the wheels on the wet cobbles, and our ample rear slewed from side to side, to much amusement and applause from the spectators. I indicated right, to follow the river. The NYPD car was turning left.

'Follow that car!' screamed Richard.

'You said turn right!'

'Forget what I said, just follow that car.'

Getting out of Paris was nearly as tedious as going into it, only with the added comfort that soon we would put all this hideousness of traffic behind us. We were headed for a place called Mas du Clos, with an address in a village called Les Pluids. It was a race circuit and sounded terribly exciting when Richard read the route card.

> Your first destination is at the magnificent private home
> and race circuit of Pierre Bardinon, one of the most
> beautiful circuits in the world. The track was created in
> 1963, and over the years just about every racing team and
> champion driver has driven the circuit. So tonight's
> checkpoint and supper at Pierre's house is a real privilege.
> Please respect that this is a private home.

This was great stuff and we instantly had a real respect for Pierre. How refreshing to hear that, while most public motor-racing circuits suffer from the local 'not in my backyard' nonsense, as mealy-mouthed people complain about a bit of noise, some chap had actually built a circuit in his own backyard. No doubt his wife wanted something useful like a pool or a conservatory or a new kitchen, but you have to admire a man who builds a world-class racetrack at home.

Although the route card was full of these nuggets of information, they did not actually provide the correct address. After much scrutiny and searching Richard declared there was no such place as 'Les Pluids', but there was a 'Les Puids'. People without maps and relying on hi-tech sat-nav systems were going to struggle.

Finally out of Paris and on the open road, we were surprised that we did not see too many Gumball cars. Richard was adamant that we were on the right road and, somewhat sceptically, I proceeded. A quick look in the mirror confirmed that we were on the right road, and things were about to start hotting up. A car was approaching at a terrifying pace, and within seconds a Lamborghini Gallardo shot past us, making our attempts at speeding look a little novice. Our car shook as the Lambo passed, and Richard was convinced I was rubbernecking.

'Keep your eyes on the road, mate,' he stressed.

'Never mind my eyes, I'm struggling to keep the car on the road. That was turbulence!'

Moments later, it was a Ferrari at breakneck speed and then Jodie Kidd's Maserati. We had been sticking with our sensible hats and comfortable shoes, and were certainly somewhat taken aback by the pace of the whole thing.

So our first proper Gumball impressions were that the pace was a little lively. We were in France, where the cops are not known for their friendliness, and, while we'd expected there to be a small hardcore group of quick boys, neither of us was prepared for the fact that the entire field seemed to be lighting it up.

As car after car flew past us, I had a change of heart. I had been waiting for an opportunity to open up the Volvo and show Richard and the other Gumballers what it could do. Balls to the 'sensible hats, nice guys finish last' approach: it was time to put the foot down. The mpg indicator plummeted as the speedo rose, and Richard got thrown back in his seat. Richard was by no means complaining. His competitive streak is as strong as it ever was and, as soon as we realised that we were in the thick of it, he was in no mood to sit back and simply watch everyone chuckle at the slow boys in the family estate car.

The first Italian supercar we picked off was a Ferrari 360 Spider. It's a marvellous feeling to overtake a Ferrari in a fully loaded Volvo estate, particularly one that has been the butt of all the jokes for a couple of days. It appeared that the Lambo and the Maserati were long gone, but we kept up the pace nonetheless. After a few miles, we came across a truck overtaking another truck at 50 mph in the irritating way that trucks do. We were unavoidably slowed for a minute; the Ferrari caught up, as did the Maserati who must have stopped for petrol, and the three of us were jostling for position behind the trucks. I looked across at Richard to gauge his sense of adventure.

'What about the Gumball Lane?'

'OK, go for it, take it easy though.'

The 'Gumball Lane' was discussed with reverence by old-school Gumballers and something I had initially dismissed as an urban myth. I dismissed Gumball veterans recounting driving feats of derring-do and bravado as about as likely as the seniors at my boarding school swearing blind that the biology teacher's wife who cut the pupils hair habitually slept with her customers. All talk and no trousers, designed to impress and unsettle the new boys in the same breath. Gumballers had told us that the Gumball Lane was the hard shoulder, admittedly used sparingly, but now and again whenever there was troublesome traffic that was not keeping good lane discipline – for example, some slow truck hogging the fast lane. I heard many tales of intrepid Gumballers using the Gumball Lane to good effect but the only time I knew it was for real was when I had seen a 911 GT2 on the Gumball DVD.

Well, if it is good enough for a GT2, the Volvo would make it with no problems. I pulled into the slow lane and let the Ferrari overtake us in the grown-up's lane, but still behind the truck. Jodie Kidd was in her Maserati, behind us in the slow lane. Mirrors, signal, mirrors, as the best driving instructors say, and as I looked in the mirror after signalling I noticed Jodie filming with a video camera, and looking a little confused as to why we were signalling right instead of left. I dropped to third, and with the horn blaring we shot up the hard shoulder, much to the bemusement of the French trucker.

It was a staggeringly ignorant manoeuvre but surprisingly good fun. I would never in a month of Sundays dream of driving like that normally, so what made me do it? Richard had a theory that, in the absence of anything else, seemed to fit the bill. He believes that all human beings are instinctively competitive, and particularly if you have a number on your car, any reasonable individual will get the bit between his/her teeth and try to beat as many of his competitors as he/she can.

'But, Richard, it's not a race, it's a rally; there are no competitors, only participants.'

'Bugger that, look at the way people are driving, yourself included. It's not an official race, but it's not far off it. Look, I'm not saying I condone speeding or reckless driving, I'm just saying I can understand the psyche that goes behind it.'

'It's not a race, it's a rally' is a great Gumball catchphrase, adorning posters and T-shirts. Apparently, it had been coined during the previous year's rally, when a chap in a feisty 911 blew away some youngsters in a heavily tuned car. Illegal street racing has quite a large, underground following in the States and no doubt these aficionados were mightily impressed with the big-balled display they had just witnessed. He eventually slowed from speeds in excess of 190 mph, and the kids pulled alongside to congratulate him on some pretty mental street racing. Their pimp mobile could not have been more different from the Porsche, whose only concession to individual customisation was a large Union Jack on the roof. As the street racers whooped and hollered, 'Mean racing, dude, way to go, yo' the man, brother!' the Gumballer simply replied, 'It's not a race, it's a rally,' and sped off. The phrase caught on and is often quoted with as much irony, if not the panache, as originally intended.

With our sensible hats well and truly out the window, and Pigalle suffering an extreme dose of motion sickness, we made it to the outskirts of Clermont Ferrand in excellent time. After the initial flurry of excitement, we saw very few Gumballers, largely because we had been proceeding pretty rapidly. Something else we had not seen was any police, but there were a few cameras. Richard's speed-camera-spotting ability had let him down since the A43 out of Putney and it was not until we saw 'OV03 TVD – TROP VITE' lit up in front of us that we realised we had been flashed.

'Did you see that? You know what that means, don't you?' asked Richard, pronouncing it oddly and thereby indicating that his peculiar brand of European had not reached these parts.

'It means we were going a little too quickly,' I replied.

'A little? You were doing 130 mph!'

'Really? Imagine that – 130 mph in a Volvo. I tell you one thing, its very stable – it certainly doesn't feel like 130 mph.'

Richard gave a little chuckle. 'It will in court, mate!'

After the debacle of leaving Paris, which actually turned out rather well in hindsight, Richard had turned out to be a most accomplished map reader. Issuing instructions with utter confidence, he was keeping me left and right at all the appropriate junctions leaving the autoroute. After the autoroute, the minor road junctions became Gumball central with all manner of supercars shooting off in opposite directions. We found Aubusson, which was the nearest town to Les Puids, and it appeared that the chaps with the sat-navs complete with bells and whistles were playing silly buggers. After their hi-tech navigational systems understandably could not find Les Pluids, they had headed for Aubusson, which was also given on the route card. At Aubusson they hadn't a clue where to go or what to do about it. A Porsche would stop at a junction for, say, five seconds, tear off down a road with something approaching authority and then five or six cars would fly off after him. Richard, with eminent sense, said, 'Hold it right there,' studied the map and said, 'That way.' We departed the scene in completely the opposite direction and sure enough within a few miles found a sign for Le Mas du Clos. It was only when we arrived that we realised why we had seen relatively few Gumballers; after our impressive pace and map work we had made excellent time and arrived in the top ten.

7. MAS DU CLOS TO MARBELLA

Mas du Clos – The Racetrack

'Watch it there, mate. It's a bit slippy; quite a few people have spun off,' the Gumball crew man warned.

Yeah? Pants to them. I'm in all-wheel-drive Volvo, I thought, as I sped off. First corner was a bit tight and I felt the back end twitch, but then the track opened up to a good long straight, or so I thought. The only criticism I would have of the Volvo – well apart from the colour – was that its turning circle was not great. On this occasion, as I spotted the cones ahead, I discovered that it was not great at turning in either. At the last minute I tried to turn it and lost the back end, which went this way, then that, before the DTSC traction-control gizmos thought bugger this and ploughed straight through the cones, bringing us out the far side, having cut off a bit of the track. Richard, navigating at this point, though clearly without pace notes, was at a loss to know whether to turn left or right. It wasn't on the maps; he was hanging on for dear life plus it was pitch dark. I punted for left and proceeded with caution.

'You're going the wrong way!' screamed the mad marshal who had come out of nowhere. Suitably chastened, we spun around and the rest of the lap was completed without incident, and with much more due care and attention.

At the end of the lap, it was Richard's turn. 'Wicked, I'll have a go.'

'Right, you are. I'll wait here.'

'You will not! Hop in the passenger seat, you fool.'

Now, I had seen Richard spin a car on a dry track in broad daylight but, after my efforts, I was not in any position to bring this up. I needn't have worried; his lap was considerably smoother than mine was, which would not have been a difficult thing to pull off.

At the restaurant, Tish, the girl whom we'd met at registration, was signing in Gumballers and muttering that we had arrived too early. Apparently, she had set off long before the field in Paris and arrived at her set time, long before she was told the first car would arrive. Imagine her surprise when she found ten or so Gumballers waiting and twiddling their thumbs. A number of gendarmes arrived and appeared to share Tish's view that we had arrived a bit early as well.

I went outside to keep an eye on the pesky gendarmes and ascertain what the story was. They were proceeding down the line of cars, which were neatly parked in what was obviously the order in which they had arrived. As they passed Porsches, Ferraris and Lamborghinis, they duly noted down each registration. I waited nervously as they approached our car, which we had proudly parked in tenth place, nose out just in case any of the hecklers missed it as they drove in.

The gendarme went to take down the number and then looked at the badge. Puzzled, he called his colleague, and they had a quick chat. His colleague shook his head and then put his notebook away, deciding for whatever reason not to take our registration. Bingo, I thought, go Volvo stealth vehicle. With that, a couple of other cars pulled in, a Ferrari Enzo tailed by a Lamborghini Murcielago.

The gendarme looked shocked and he got his book out again, chewed his pencil with intent, and started to take down the number. Time for action.

'Monsieur, monsieur, parlez vous l'anglais?'

'Oui, bien sur . . .'

'What's the problem, then? Why are you taking our number down?'

'Well, we have reports that some people are driving a little – how do you say – fast, non?'

'Non.'

'Oui . . . you are here now. Is too fast,' he said, while tapping his watch.

'Monsieur, you are mistaken. Look, we are in a Volvo. See, look at all the luggage; it's an estate car. We are a media crew. We left hours before anyone else because we knew we would be slow.'

With that, a look of understanding crept over his Gallic features and he called something out to his colleague. He laughed, nodded and said something along the lines of 'That explains it. No way would someone bring a Volvo and try and race with all these other cars.' The cop moved on to the Enzo, and I patted the trusty Volvo affectionately on the bonnet.

I found Richard inside the clubhouse, eating and chatting with some Ferrari drivers.

'Trouble?' he asked.

'Apparently some of the Ferraris etc. were going too quickly. Cops are taking registrations of all cars who got here too soon. Except us.'

'Why not us? What did we do right?'

'We're driving a Volvo.'

A Ferrari driver choked on his bread.

Although we had seen no police at all until we actually stopped at the checkpoint, as the rest of the cars arrived, it became clear that there had been a flurry of police activity and a number of €750.00 fines. We spoke to three drivers who had their licences taken away on the spot, so now were technically unable to drive. I naïvely assumed that this might be a problem but very few of them seemed terribly concerned about the lack of licences. One guy I spoke to had a back-up plan.

'It is the first stop, and I've already lost my licence and been fined a whole heap of euros. But, hey, no worries, that's Gumball,' he stated confidently.

'What do you mean no worries? Would a driving licence not be a useful thing to have?'

'Of course, it would, that's why I have three more in the glove box.'

We had agreed that Richard would drive the next stint and, after he finished his meal, he announced that he was going for a quick power nap. I reckoned I had some time to relax over food before taking a look at the maps for the next leg. I managed to fit in some amateur flirting with Tish while I collected the new route card, and then proceeded to the car expecting to find Richard asleep. Not a bit of it, he was poring over the maps. Although I had noticed that he was a competent navigator, it was the first indication I had of Richard's map fetish and his inability to leave them alone.

'What are you doing? You're supposed to be asleep.'

'I'm just having a quick look at the maps.'

'What on earth for? You're driving now. I'm navigating, and besides you don't even know where the hell we're going yet!' I said, waving the route card at him.

'We're going to Spain, so south,' he retorted, which I had to concede was a fair point.

I took the maps from him, and as I did so he continued, 'It's OK. I've looked at them. I'm turning left out of the gate. Have you done this before by the way?'

'Yes, many times, Richard. I'm on the maps; you'll go where I'll tell you to go.'

'I'm turning left.' Grinning, Richard shut his eyes and reclined the seat.

I looked at the maps for about five minutes, gave him a shove and said, 'Come on. Cars are leaving; go out this gate and turn left.'

Richard and I had arrived at the same conclusion from looking at the maps, that sometimes what appears to be the most sensible route might not always be the quickest. We knew the cops were about, having discovered that there was a band of lunatics careering about their country, and it was a safe bet that they would be keeping a watchful vigil on the obvious road the rally would take. It was clear to anyone who put a bit of thought into the route that, while turning left would take you along a twistier and slightly longer route to the motorway, there was far less likelihood of police activity or associated congestion.

We departed Mas du Clos, swung left out of the gate and watched the others turn right like Lambos to the slaughter.

Les Puids to Madrid

'Right, stay on this road all the way to the motorway, its about 28 clicks, take care, it's a bit twisty.'

There was no response from Richard, who was deep in concentration as he drove. He was giving it a bit of welly, and I could tell that he was secretly reassessing his hitherto blinkered views on Volvo performance cars.

'Jesus, it can fairly shift this thing, eh?' was his ringing endorsement after ten miles or so. After twenty he was waxing lyrical about its handling, and after thirty we were deep in conversation about whether you'd buy one or not. I could tell that he was tempted. Richard, whose daily drive is a convertible Jaguar XK8, thought he might get mistaken in his native Fulham for a dad on the school run, but apart from that he agreed that, if he was ever in the market for an estate car, the Volvo would certainly be on the shopping list. Since my quip he had been waiting to put me right about the speed of his Jag but, after driving the Volvo, he was having second thoughts.

I have to confess that is what I like about it. It is a Volvo. It is an estate car. They are not meant to go that fast. Strictly speaking, they are only meant for transporting Labradors and child sick. In V70R trim, it is so stonkingly fast it is no wonder the children get carsick, and the dogs in the back of the car must be absolutely petrified.

The image suffers because invariably Volvo are associated with estate cars run by middle-Englanders to transport their children and animals, and there is a lot of truth in this stereotype. At any posh public school, you will see Volvo after Volvo unloading trunks at the beginning of term time, and returning at the end of term when the ample boot provides an excellent dispensary for the picnic before making room to transport all the kids' clutter back home again.

That's not to say there is no fun to be had with a Volvo. I went to a public school in Scotland that was not terribly posh, and hence could not pick and choose its pupils. As I reached the sixth form, the school had been reduced to accepting all manner of waifs and strays and even those who had been expelled from other schools. One such incoming pupil had a bad name since he had been expelled from Eton. Whenever he was quizzed on what he had actually done to merit expulsion, he would cryptically reply 'cumulative misdemeanours'. Eventually he revealed the final straw – during the annual Eton–Harrow cricket match, he had been a little bored and had livened up the day by opening all the Volvo estate cars in the car park and swapping the black Labradors around. The owners drove home with the wrong dogs and took some time to discover the prank. Expelled? The guy should have been given a medal for 'Originality in Practical Joking'.

With Richard well and truly converted, we hit the motorway at Junction XYZ, wondering whether our left turn gamble had paid off. There were no other Gumballers to be seen after ten miles or so, but feasibly that could have meant that we had come out behind them. Fuel consumption is not any car's strong point when travelling at insane speeds, and 12 mpg was the best that we could muster so it was not long before the trip computer was warning us of impending shortages.

'Fuel in 22 kilometres; we'll pull off there, Richard.'

'Right you are. I'm knackered. We should think about swapping over.'

He had only been driving for about an hour, and I thought this was a bit odd. Richard confessed that his strenuous night on the Parisian tiles had caught up with him and he was a bit too shagged to drive any further. It was not a problem as I was feeling fine, but it was not really in the spirit of pulling your weight. I remembered something else about the Arctic trip I read in Marcus Armytage's *Telegraph* 'Diary'.

While Richard lost 10 lb on the trip – something he used to do in two hours in a sauna in the old days – Tony lost a stone and a half, so it's fairly evident who did all the pulling.

It was quite a surreal night. We had travelled about 300 miles and seen no Gumballers at all. This was not right. Although we were travelling at a considerable speed, relative to some of the people we had seen earlier, it was pretty average. Surely the likes of Fat Boy Kim or some of the crazy Lamborghinis would have caught us?

As the evening wore on, we got more and more puzzled, until eventually delirium fatigue had set in and we were convinced that the whole shebang had been cancelled for some reason or other, and everyone was locked up in some grotty jail in the middle of nowhere. Contingency plans were drawn up: proceed to Marbella, chill out, enjoy a week in the sun and see what mischief we could find down in that neck of the woods. Richard, who had clearly spent some time in the environs, was confident that two men of insufficient means and morals, such as ourselves, could be royally entertained in a place like Marbella. Richard reminisced eagerly about holidays with the lads from the weighing room, which left me in no doubt that not only was there mischief to be had in that neck of the woods but also that I had pursued a really rather tame tourist plan on my previous holidays. Up until that point, I certainly had not considered that to be the case.

When Richard speaks of racing, apart from the thrill of competition, what is obvious is how much he misses the camaraderie of the weighing room. It is clear that they all give each other a merciless slagging, but it is by all accounts largely good natured. Even when there are times that it is not, jockeys would seem to have a thick enough skin to be able to laugh it off. The anecdotes from the weighing room were a glorious antidote to the tedium of a long night's drive, though sadly most of them are unprintable.

This made me wonder why no jockey has ever won the Sports Personality of the Year Award. What is the award for? It's clearly not for 'personality' or else jockeys would be in the running year after year, and Nigel Mansell would never have got a sniff of it, let alone won it twice. David Beckham has won it, and, although he's undoubtedly a talented sportsman, you would not award him points for personality, not least because no one apart from his hairdresser has ever heard him talk. Allegedly, he is a legendary swordsman, but if Richard's weighing room tales are anything to go by he is nothing compared to jockeys. Indeed, if you stand Beckham next to your average jockey, you would have to attribute any success on their respective techniques to Beckham's looks and a jockey's personality.

One could understand if it was only footballers who won it. There would be a certain logic in accepting that, with football being the most popular sport, it would inevitably garner the most votes of the Great British public. Bafflingly, this is not the case. Tony McCoy made the shortlist the year he broke Richard's record of riding 1699 winners to become the most successful jockey of all time. How did he do? He came third behind Paula Radcliffe. Paula Radcliffe broke a world record but it was for glorified jogging. And the year before Ellen MacArthur polled massively more votes than he did. Sorry, who is she? She is the lady who sailed around the world single-handedly – perhaps if she had more personality she would have had a few mates to go with her.

I asked Richard if he ever involved himself in the media side of racing, as I imagined that he would be pretty good at it. He has quite a lively wit and, in many cases, the truly fun side of a sports star's character only comes out in the media after they have given up the serious business of competition. It is an understandably widely held belief that top sportsmen/women and athletes have difficulty adapting to life on the other side of the fence, since it's a reminder that, while they have achieved great highs, they are now over the hill and the only way is down the other side. That said, the retired greats of a sport generally make the best media pundits and commentators since they have the confidence to say what they think, and it is difficult to question their views in light of their experience.

James Hunt, former F1 World Champion, and now sadly dead, was one who made a successful, if initially difficult, transition from the track to the commentary box. When he started he said he 'felt like a spare prick at a wedding' and took the analogy further by regularly getting pissed up at lunch before the speeches. While I suspect Richard misses the banter in the weighing room, Hunt refused to visit the pit garages for different reasons.

'The only reason I ever walked up and down the pit lane when I was a driver was to look at the crumpet. But now, with the modern pass system, there aren't any women around and you have to go outside. Pity, that.'

Boris Becker displays similar characteristics to Hunt. As a seventeen-year-old winner of Wimbledon and three-time champion, he knows what he's talking about when it comes to commentating on grass-court tennis. His other great talent is for womanising and occasionally he manages to combine his experience of the two. When asked how he would cope with Roger Federer, generally regarded as the finest grass-court player of today, he said, 'Federer, eh? I'd just get him drunk and try and sleep with his girlfriend.'

Having played an earlier blinder, notwithstanding my musings, Richard was not exactly oozing personality himself at that moment. He had not spoken for some time, though I knew he was not asleep. He was properly spent from the previous night's exertions and, although he was clearly incapable of stringing a sentence together, it was approaching 3 a.m. and I needed some intelligent conversation to concentrate on staying awake. Sadly, I was unlikely to find any so I decided I'd have to make do with Richard's.

'Shut up, Richard, your chat stinks.'

'Eh? What?'

'Be quiet. I can't hear myself think.'

'What are you on about?'

'I am being sarcastic. You've gone into some sort of coma, saying nothing, but clearly awake as you are flinching from time to time at my driving.'

'Yep, that's right, I am knackered after last night, but too scared to go to sleep.'

'What exactly did you get up to last night?'

Richard grinned his Dunwoody grin. 'Well, you know Jess?'

'You didn't, did you? You jammy bastard!'

Thankfully, it turned out that nothing had happened at all. Jess was the cute Gumball press officer we had both taken quite a shine to. After stringing me along for a minute, Richard admitted that he had simply got pissed up with her and the Irish lads and they all had a fine old time, but sadly there was no room for hi-jinks. There was some talk of a Swedish lady, although he could not quite remember why she had gone home in a huff, but he decided that it was probably because he had turned his attentions to Jess. He had returned to the hotel at sometime after 5 a.m., though he couldn't be sure. It was no bloody wonder he was zombified having done a full marathon the day before as well.

In the absence of intelligent conversation, I was more than happy to discuss Jess's considerable charms, though obviously in a most gentlemanly manner as only two chaps like myself and Richard would. This line in banter developed agreeably and after some time Richard suddenly shouted the now familiar cry of 'Fuck me, I'm famous!'

'Settle down there, mate, you've got no chance,' I said, sniggering.

'No, you fool, that was a Gumballer we just passed. I saw the sponsors' logos.'

I slowed down, consulted the mirrors and sure enough there was the friendly Gumball logo. Strangely, it was plastered all over some four-wheel-drive vehicle, which didn't seem right. Damn, maybe we were last after all and it had taken us this long to catch the slowest car. Richard pointed out that there was a toll for the Spanish border in just a few miles, so we could collar them then and see if they knew what was going on.

At the toll the 4 × 4 slowed down and pulled alongside us, windows wound down. Speak of the devil.

'Helloooooooooo, Richarrrrrd,' purred Jess, rolling her Rs like a pro. 'What are you up to? We're the crew vehicle; we're supposed to be hours ahead of you. Did you go to the racetrack?'

'Indeed,' I answered quickly before Richard could get a word in, 'we left there ages ago but we haven't seen a car since. Have you?'

'No, you're the first.'

'Splendid, well, we'll see you in Marbella.'

I tore off from the toll with renewed enthusiasm for our driving adventure.

'I know it's not a race, it's a rally, Richard, but we're in first place.'

'Did you hear that?'

'Yeah, we're the first car, in the Volvo!'

'No, I meant did you hear "Helloooooooooooo, Richarrrrr-rrrrd"? There was not much "Hello, Clement", was there?'

'Yes, Richard, of course I heard it. Shag off and go to sleep, I need to concentrate on driving.'

We entered Spain and upped the pace, and I convinced myself that speed, adrenaline and the goal of reaching Marbella before all the sniggering supercars was more than enough of an incentive to keep me awake.

Before long, a car loomed large in the mirrors, and the speed in which it was approaching indicated it had to be a Gumballer. Within seconds, it passed us and I instantly recognised the outline of the Mercedes 600CL. Kim Schmitz, Kimble or Fat Boy Kim as we had christened him by this stage. If any confirmation that we were at the sharp end of proceedings was needed, Kim's road presence was it.

Minutes later a Ferrari 550M passed and then the JUMP Porsche, christened such because of its number plate J1 UMP. The increased speed had the typical adverse effect on the mpg, and, as we pulled in for fuel, we heard the unmistakeable exhaust note of the 'Spirit of the Gumball'. We might have enjoyed a good run down so far, but the quick chaps were catching and passing us rapidly.

After another 25 miles or so, the heavens opened and we were driving in appalling conditions of torrential rain and hideous visibility. My immediate thought, again not charitably, was that I was sure the chaps in the Caterham weren't laughing so heartily now.

The Volvo, with its excellent acceleration, 300 bhp and top speed of 155 mph, up until now had been more than capable of making good time across France and Spain and keeping up with the more exotic machinery. Sure, it could not keep pace with some of the very fastest Porsches that were capable of running for distances at speeds in excess of 170 mph, but it was by no means a slouch. It was at this stage that the car truly came in to its own. The lashing rain was terrible, creating vast lakes of standing water on the motorways. It was not long before we caught the hitherto mentioned Porsches and Ferraris nervously twitching their way through the puddles, frightened that the immense horsepower channelled through their rear wheels would spin their cars.

The Volvo on the other hand is fitted with an all-wheel drive, as well as a fancy traction control system, and shot through the water at speed with ease. One by one, we left the technically faster cars literally trailing in our wake. Richard woke up briefly, and clearly decided that whatever nightmares he was having were infinitely preferable to watching me sail a Volvo to Madrid.

The rain passed and the morning dawned. By that stage, we were well ahead of all the cars that we had overtaken in the floods. Richard woke again, with a comment that the seats were terribly comfortable.

'How are you feeling?' he asked.

I was slowing down. 'I'm shattered. We're not far from Madrid. We'll stop for petrol soon and then you can take over.'

'Sure, no problem.'

At that moment, the 3-Series Diesel BMW shot past us. These guys had a similar stealth vehicle to us and, combined with their less frequent petrol stops, were making excellent time. An indication of how tired I was showed itself in my willingness to simply accept they would make it to Madrid before us. We had to stop for petrol, and I had to stop driving.

Richard came out of the fuel station like a man possessed, with the bit between his teeth and, after sensing an upset in the running order, he was well and truly off. We were fifteen miles or so outside Madrid, and he was determined to get us there as quickly as possible. And quite right too. I had not done all that hard work during the night for nothing.

All I had to do was work the maps. We were heading to the Bernabeu, Real Madrid's football ground, supposedly for breakfast with David Beckham and his team-mates, though it was highly unlikely that they were going to be there at all, never mind at 7 a.m. Beckham had allegedly been embroiled in some scandal with a personal assistant named Rebecca Loos, and I was fairly confident that the last thing he needed was to entertain a pile of messers, cracking jokes and repeatedly asking to use the 'loos'.

I had pinpointed the Real Madrid stadium on the map, and directed Richard straight to it. There was a huge Real Madrid crest, the colours and the whole shooting match. We drove in but something was not right. The place was like a building site, with a few beaten-up old Portakabins and a shabby stretch of grass.

'I can't see David Beckham doing his pre-match eyebrow plucking in there,' I ventured, nodding towards the Portakabin.

Richard scoffed. 'You're damn right, he doesn't; this is the training ground.'

Oops.

Back out on to the main road and Richard was flying in the face of the 'make haste, not speed' maxim. Stop, start. Left, right.

'Where is it?' he said, mid-three-point turn.

'I don't know. Why don't we ask someone who does know?'

'Look at the route card.'

I read from the route card, as instructed, '*Upon entering Madrid, simply ask anyone for directions to the most famous football club in history.*'

We opened the window to speak to a local. I knew Richard was learning Spanish so I thought I'd let him do the talking this time, but sadly he insisted on chatting in European again. Not only that but he was in such a rush to get the words out, get the answer and follow the directions that he tried to do all three before the poor Spanish chap had worked out what we wanted. I looked out of the back window as we tore off and saw the Spaniard pointing to the left. On our immediate left across the road, was the biggest, most unmissable football stadium imaginable, with the words 'Real Madrid Bernabeu' in giant twelve-foot script across the top.

'Left!' I shouted as Richard raced straight on. He slammed on the brakes, and, after committing what would usually be a suicidal manoeuvre, but was just about survivable at that time of morning, we pulled into the car park. Three cars had arrived before us. Jump Porsche, Fat Boy Kim and the diesel Beemer. Evidently, we would have been first if we had not taken a tour of the training ground.

Breakfast at Real Madrid sounds glamorous, but in reality, after a gruelling drive, it is a little exhausting. We only really had the energy to quaff a coffee, pose for a few photographs and decide that it was best to proceed direct to Marbella rather than hanging around. Thankfully, Richard had developed a new lease of life and was full of beans, right up for a stint of spirited driving.

As we were preparing for our departure, a camera crew spotted us. They approached Richard, who was getting into the driver's side with some excitement.

'Goodness me, Richard Dunwoody, you're here in good time. Will you say a few words for camera?'

'By all means,' Richard said, beaming in full media mode.

'So, Richard, it's 7 a.m., and you and the Volvo have arrived in very good time; the fourth car in by our calculations. You must have had a very good drive down.'

'Well, yes, the car was magnificent, sure-footed all the way, comfortable and relaxing to drive at speed.'

That's the stuff, Richard. I knew he'd come round to the merits of the Volvo.

'But I have to say a big thanks to Clement,' he said, gesticulating towards me, as I was thinking, What a decent fellow, all that driving did not go unappreciated. 'Clement was excellent on the maps; he has some experience in this department and I could not have made the pace without him.'

'Cut,' said the interviewer, who wandered off, satisfied with the sound bites.

Momentarily speechless, I finally spluttered, 'You're some tosser, Richard. You've driven practically sod all apart from the last twenty minutes.'

'Yeah I know, but I wasn't going to tell them that, was I,' he said, laughing.

'You can make up for it now. When we get out of here, I'm having a doze.'

Madrid to Marbella

Leaving Madrid, I first became properly aware of something a little peculiar about Richard's driving, and a habit that was destined to become increasingly infuriating. His behaviour had hitherto hinted that there might be some issues, but I was left in no doubt after our tour of the streets of Madrid.

I mentioned earlier that, on leaving Les Puids, Richard had a quick glance at the maps. That was to be expected from a meticulous and thorough professional such that he is, but it did not prepare me for his habits that were to become known as 'multitasking'. This was not an affectionate piece of terminology.

Richard is literally unable to drive a car and allow someone to map read beside him. He has to do both and preferably at the same time. As Richard tried to keep one eye on the road and one eye on the map, I raised both mine to heaven. In the end I had to resort to the tactics of a school kid protecting my answers to a spelling test by contorting my body around ninety degrees and using all available forearm, bicep and shoulder as a protective shield. Luckily for the kid in the classroom, he might be separated from prying eyes by a couple of feet and have the added protection of the scary schoolmaster. I had neither protection and, cooped up with Richard in a car, his beady eyes were only a matter of inches away. It was too much for him to resist holding the wheel with one hand and trying to disrupt my map-censorship position with the other. Needless to say, his driving deteriorated even further.

'Let me see, let me see,' he said, as he grappled with the wheel and my arm.

'Piss off, you're driving and I am map reading. This is a team effort, not an exercise for you to demonstrate your multitasking abilities, which are pretty poor, I might add. Take the next left.'

'I am going straight on.'

'Why the hell are you going straight on? We need to turn left.'

'I want to go straight. Why do you think we should turn left?'

'Because I am looking at the bloody map and that's the way out of Madrid.'

'I am going straight.'

We went straight on.

This crazy talk continued for some time until eventually I left him to it, and after some time, by some convoluted route, we got out of Madrid and on to the road south for Marbella. Exhausted I fell asleep.

A little later, I awoke, still clinging to the maps and relieved to find Richard had not tried to relieve me of them. Looking around for signposts, I had no real idea where we were or how long I had been asleep.

'How are we doing, Richard?'

'Good, steady progress, making time; we've not been going quickly.'

I looked at the speedo. We were doing 110 mph. 'Richard, 110 mph is quickly!'

'Well, yeah, but you know what I mean.'

I knew exactly what he meant. In the past twelve hours, our whole concept of speed had been somewhat recalibrated. Speeds of 110 mph appeared to be perfectly appropriate for the road and the conditions, notwithstanding the speed limit. The car was certainly within its limits, although it would be debatable whether we as drivers were within ours. To really have a sensation of travelling quickly was to be at 130 mph plus. As a responsible passenger, I wholeheartedly agreed with Richard's cruising speed, more concerned with getting to Marbella sooner rather than later.

It wasn't until we passed the police at such speeds that I really considered we were doing anything wrong. We passed a lorry in the blink of an eye, but I had time to make out 'Guardia Civil Horses' on the side. There were sirens on the roof but they were surely an optimistic fitting.

'Richard, that was the police.'

'What, where? Rubbish, I didn't see them.'

'The truck we just passed was Guardia Civil, full of horses, I think.'

'Mounted police, they don't count. Anyway they will never catch us.'

It was a reasonable statement that they couldn't catch us, and perhaps if I had spent more time riding into Grand National and Cheltenham Gold Cup Winner's Enclosures I could have been more confident of their ersatz policing role, but my experience of mounted police was that they were particularly vicious buggers used to quell rioters and football hooliganism. Whatever their duties, I was slightly concerned that they would have friends who not only counted but were perfectly able to catch us. I need not have concerned myself since there was no police action at all.

We were on our way to Marbella, having seen nothing of Madrid and we had covered the whole of France under darkness. It was just as well that we were not overly interested in taking in the sights. I looked out of the window to admire the view but the Spanish countryside just seemed to be a bit brown and dry. If you are travelling through Spain at speed, the only thing of note you will see are the giant bulls on the hills by the side of road. They are massive steel silhouettes originally built as advertising hoardings for the Osborne y Cia brandy distillery. The first one was erected in 1956 and by 1960 there were more than 500 all over the country. They have since become something of a national icon.

In 1988, the Spanish Government implemented a 'clean-up-the-environment' campaign, and ruled that there should be no advertising billboards visible from a national motorway. Undeterred, the company simply painted over the slogans to leave the plain black bull silhouette you see today. In response, the government targeted the 'Osbornes' directly with new regulations, and for a period it looked like the animals' days of watching over the motorways were numbered.

But the government suffered an unexpected backlash. The Spanish, more usually associated with massacring bulls, rose up in the Osbornes' defence. It turned out that most Spaniards regarded the Osborne bulls as a symbol of their country, like the Eiffel Tower in France or America's Statue of Liberty. Writers, artists, broadcasters, TV personalities, political parties all joined the 'Save Our Bulls' cause.

The government's objective had been to eliminate advertising. In appealing one of the many decisions against it in lower courts, the Osborne company came up with the argument that its bulls shouldn't be classified as advertising at all. They were actually art, expressed in a peculiarly Spanish way. A Madrid University professor who gave evidence said, 'The Osborne bull has become a symbol, a historic monument, a piece of popular culture that transcends advertising.' The court agreed, thereby setting a precedent that Spanish culture is a load of old bull.

Nowadays, drivers use them for directions in a 'take the first exit after the bull' fashion, and children alleviate long journeys by counting the number of bulls between towns, like Eddie Stobart lorries in England. Under the circumstances it did not seem like such a bad idea.

'Look, Richard, there's a bull ... and another one ... and another one ... and ...' I muttered repetitively.

'Do you think that might get irritating after a while?' said Richard, with some justification.

Richard had done a monster drive and taken us to within a couple of hours of Marbella when we decided to swap. All that was left was a clean run to the hotel where bed awaited.

The road into Marbella is awesome, all bends and curves. The sweeping nature of the drive is similar to the road into Aix-les-Bains in France, where I had enjoyed a great drive racing with a Jaguar XK140 on a Monte Carlo rally. I was excitedly describing this to Richard and lamenting the lack of dicing with Gumballers when all of a sudden Jose, the local hombre, in his Renault Megane, was all over my mirrors. For a couple of miles we were having a mighty scrap. Now we're Gumballing, I thought, but it was a long way to go for a dice with a Renault Megane.

Richard was on the maps, and I was content to leave him to it. I had further confidence as he had told me that he knew exactly where we were going, and finding the hotel would be no problem as he knew Marbella 'like the back of my hand', as you do if you're a playboy jockey type. Great, I thought, the last we thing we need after a gruelling drive is to bugger about the Marbellan suburbs.

Half an hour later and we were buggering about the Marbellan suburbs. It had become clear that Richard had no idea at all where we were going.

8. MARBELLA

We arrived at the hotel considerably flustered having spent 45 minutes getting thoroughly lost. It turned out that Richard had no sense of where we were going, and stubbornly refused to obey any 'Marbella-Centre' signs, having convinced himself that we were staying in some shanty town outskirts. Although 45 minutes were wasted, we discovered that we were actually the third car to arrive, ahead of all the Ferraris and Lamborghinis and even in front of arch nutter and speed freak Fat Boy Kim. Obviously, being gluttons for punishment, we did a bit of mental arithmetic to ascertain where we would have been if we had gone straight to the hotel. Second place. Oh, well. 'It's not a race, it's a rally.'

'I'd much rather be third than second,' Richard declared.

'That's just ridiculous. Don't talk such rubbish. I'd much rather not add forty-five minutes on to an 18-hour drive so you can revel in third place. What the hell are you talking about?'

'When I was racing I always found second distinctly unsatisfactory, as if I had not tried hard enough for first. With third place, at least you know you were soundly beaten.'

Really, Richard? Interesting logic, but complete and utter bollocks. If you had tried hard enough to read the maps instead of relying on your legendary local knowledge of Marbella, we would have had 45 minutes extra in bed.

The Hotel Puente Romano was a predictably five-star affair with a copious amount of helpful attendants and valet parkers. While valet parking might seem an enjoyable luxury on the back of such a long drive, in reality it was a bit of a pain. The hotel was a mini resort, and all the rooms were scattered around in whitewashed 'casitas', sort of little cottages. The idea was that Mr Valet Parker would take our car off to some far-flung car park and transport us in a golf cart to our lodgings. The problems occurred when we remembered that I did not know where my luggage was, having last seen it in the back of the Hummer in Paris, and Richard wanted to bring all his luggage to the hotel, requiring a trailer or at least something with a more substantial load space than a golf cart.

I was slightly concerned by my lack of luggage. In Paris, it had struck me as a reasonable idea to offload it. After all we would be meeting up with them the next day, at the first hotel stop. Now, at the first hotel stop, Paris felt a long way away, and feeling like I had not seen my bags for a week I wondered whether I would see them at all. I would not have liked to undertake such a long drive in a Hummer and was worried that the lads might have had a complete sense of humour failure, and have decided to stop somewhere and enjoy a regular Spanish holiday like normal people.

After leaving detailed instructions with the check-in staff warning of my bags' impending if not imminent arrival, we were finally successful in shunning the advances of the golf-cart driver. We had decided to take advantage of our early exit, and parked the car near our quarters, in preparation for a quick getaway in the morning. This had the advantage of making sure that all arriving Gumballers would see it, and realise that the Volvo had the measure of them.

There was a great temptation to enjoy the sun and soak up the atmosphere, watching the cars as they arrived. But, in reality, the drive had just been far too tiring and we decided to have a light lunch and get some much needed sleep. We lunched with Ant and Pete in the diesel BMW, who had arrived in just before us, and some friends of theirs in a Ferrari 360, who arrived shortly afterwards.

We were all giddy with tiredness and there was much laughter concerning the lunacy of such a long drive. At the same time, we were undoubtedly feeling rather pleased with our-selves. There were bravado rights to arriving before anybody else, but there was a great feeling of *schadenfreude* knowing we were about to hit the sack whereas there were some poor bastards who still had not even reached Madrid.

The Ferrari driver was laden with police memorabilia, and was wearing what looked like an official UK police force badge around his neck. Surely he could not be a cop?

'Are you a policeman?' I asked him.

'What? Are you kidding? How many cops do you know with a Ferrari 360?' he said, laughing.

'I just saw the badges and thought . . .'

'Oh, yeah, they're from a mate; he's in the police and he told me that the Spanish cops like to collect badges from police forces around the world. I thought they might come in useful, but we did not see a single cop in Spain.'

Neither had we, and nor had Ant and Pete. We raised our glasses to the Spanish cops and toasted them for their Gumball-friendliness factor.

We had a certain respect for Ant and Pete in the BMW and I think it was reciprocated. They had also gone for the less glamorous approach to Gumballing and were as pleased as us that it had paid off. Out of more than one hundred and fifty cars, there was a diesel and a Volvo estate in the top three arrivals after the endurance stage. Not so strictly rock 'n' roll. They had the added bonus of knowing their car would need nothing more than a good wash on its return, something that had not occurred to us since ours would be going straight back to Volvo but we could understand the logic. Those in more temperamental machinery would be facing some pretty hefty maintenance bills on their return. Pete pressed the point home by suggesting that his mate's Ferrari would need a serious service after the Gumball.

'Service?' he scoffed. 'I'll be damned if I'll give it a service. I am going to sell it! One careful owner – 4000 miles only!'

Although at the very limits of physical exhaustion, I found that I was unable to simply fall into a deep sleep. Rather than counting sheep I reached for the local literature provided by the hotel. In the Marbellan magazine, there was a lengthy feature on Prince Alfonso de Hohenlohe-Langenburg, or Alfonso Maximiliano Victorio Eugenio Alexandro Maria Pablo de la Santisima Trinidad y todo los Santos to give him his full name. He had died recently of prostate cancer, and, according to the article, as well as being the founder of Marbella, he was quite a character. I felt that he would have approved of the Gumball, and not only because of his fondness for rally driving.

With a name as long as that, Alfonso was clearly from something of a smart family, more Eurotoff than Eurotrash, although the magazine claimed he grew up with most of his family's vast fortune depleted. His father's side were princes of Württemberg in Germany until Napoleon's invasion and traced their history back to the sixth century. His mother was a bit new money, granddaughter of a Basque adventurer who had made a fortune in Mexico, but such wealth had led her to rise to the dizzy heights of 'marquise'. Reading this sort of stuff makes one wonder where the rest of us came from. Did our families just miraculously appear in about 1956, in a sort of 'and on Day 176,897,645,909,836,588,302,847,475,769 the Lord created the plebs' fashion? Do I have sixth-century ancestors? Do you? They might well have been plumbers with less of a fetish for archiving their existence but presumably they existed nonetheless.

His mother, possibly from spending too much time 'basquing' in the glory of her traceable family history without worrying about its future, lost estates in the Mexican Revolution; and, after the fall of the Third Reich, property in Germany and Czechoslovakia disappeared behind the Iron Curtain. The article added that Alfonso grew up with private tutors in Bohemia and Spain, learning fluent German, Spanish, French and English, suggesting that money was not too tight.

In 1946, as an adult he toured Spain with his uncle, the Marques de Soriano, and economised by undertaking the journey in a charcoal-powered Rolls-Royce. They were travelling from Gibraltar to Malaga when they stopped by the old fishing village of Marbella for a picnic and, seeing the potential of the place, sheltered by the dramatic Sierra Blanca, they decided to buy the crumbling farmhouse adjacent to where they had stopped, with 24 acres of land. Alfonso persuaded his father to sell off his wine cellars in Malaga and build the first of Marbella's new houses.

Alfonso must have realised that, for chaps of his ilk, the days of the 'Grand Tour' were long gone, to be replaced by more hedonism and less culture. His aristocratic ancestors of the seventeenth and eighteenth centuries would surely have spent the obligatory two to four years travelling around Europe in an effort to broaden their horizons and generally prepare themselves for the tricky aristocratic life ahead. The Grand Tourists in a loose sense could be likened to the legions of Ruperts and Camillas of the modern-day gap year, but the young and the feckless had infinitely more panache and flair in those days.

Instead of the Grand Tour, Alfonso was planning tourism on a grand scale. Not grand in the sense of the sheer volume of commoners in nearby Torremolinos, but with a little more emphasis on the grandeur. Prince Alfonso began persuading his aristocratic friends that Marbella would be a little more stylish in the summer than clichéd San Sebastian or Biarritz.

The magazine went on to describe how after a successful start it all got a bit tacky. Guests were culled from the Alamanach de Gotha, the royal houses of the Middle East and Hollywood's emerging 'jet set', a period when the title still meant something. When the Prince ran out of spare rooms, he sold his house to the Rothschilds, and in 1954 converted the farmhouse into a luxury hotel – the Marbella Club. The club boasted a piano player by the name of Don Jaime de Mora y Aragon, the Prince's Spanish nobleman friend who was directly descended from 56 kings, and also happened to be the brother of the Queen of the Belgians.

Soon there was a disco, with raves on Tuesday and Friday; the Horcher family, the great restaurateurs of the Third Reich, came out of exile to open La Fonda. Photographs from the time showed everyone from Sophia Loren to the Duke and Duchess of Windsor enjoying themselves. There was James Hunt in his bell-bottomed trousers playing golf, and Patrick Lichfield cradling his camera. Alfonso took a close interest in every aspect of his creation, from the architecture to the menu, from the layout of gardens to the decor of the bedrooms. Marbella's hillsides became studded with new pueblos, hotels, restaurants and sports clubs. Jose Banus built the marina of Puerto Banus nearby, a magnet for Adnan Khashoggi and other multimillionaires with their yachts.

King Fahd of Saudi Arabia built a gleaming white palace (modelled on the White House) and a mosque for his entourage. As head of the Costa del Sol Promoters' Co-operative, Hohenlohe lobbied successfully for improvements in roads, airports and water supply. His conference and exhibition centre spurred the growth of Torremolinos as a mass-market holiday destination. But by 1978 his vision had been eclipsed; Marbella was out of control and he decided to sell up to a consortium of Arabs.

Marbella has cleaned up its act a bit since 1978 and once again attracts the nobs if not quite so much nobility – its clientele being the moneyed types that Alfonso was keen to cultivate. It is not, however, his passion for the 'jet set' or the parties that suggested he would approve of the Gumball; it was his passion for cars and motoring.

As well as tourism Alfonso made his money in cars. Firstly, he married Princess Ira Furstenberg, a Fiat heiress and the niece of Gianni Agnelli. She was only fifteen at the time and as such the marriage raised a few eyebrows and required special dispensation from the Pope. And then he turned his business prowess to selling cars.

As I read, I was developing quite an admiration for Alfonso, so you can imagine my delight when I discovered that a man of such charm, good taste and vision chose to make his fortune selling Volvos. He obtained the franchise and brought Volvo to Spain. If a Volvo was good enough for a hard-partying, international playboy, ladies' man, and jet-set founder of Marbella, it was good enough for the Gumball. A common catchphrase doing the rounds was 'If Batman took a vacation, he'd do the Gumball.' Balls to Batman, I thought, if Prince Alfonso did the Gumball he'd do it in a Volvo.

Later, after a good sleep we headed for the party at about 9 p.m. On the way we spotted the black cab arriving, prompting a discussion about its occupants. This was a regular happening; we would pass a car, point and make some remark like, 'Look that's the guy who plays porn all day long on his in-car DVD', or whatever their defining characteristics might be. We had met two of the taxi's drivers, Chris and Graham, at the parties and had both agreed that they were good lads. They had hired a working London taxi and drove the whole way with the meter running. Chris was a tailor and Graham worked in financial PR, evidence, if it were needed, that Gumballers are not exclusively muppets with more money than sense. This is a common misconception, and one I must admit to thinking might be true before I actually went on the Gumball.

While inevitably most are very wealthy indeed, there are many like Chris and Graham who have regular jobs and regular incomes. The common factor uniting Gumballers is not money but a sense of fun. There were many like ourselves and Chris and Graham, who felt that the money involved was a worth-while investment in having fun. The only difference between 'us' and 'them', as it were, was that we were all justifying it on the grounds of work. Chris swore blind that it was well worth the money, as he would get the opportunity to network with some new clients and sell a few suits. Nonsense, of course, but endearing nonetheless.

One of the reasons it was such nonsense was that the Gumball is a peculiar environment where no one asks the staple small-talk question 'What do you do?', which made it difficult for Chris to open the sales pitch. In this sort of company, nobody really cares how you make your money, or indeed how much of it you make. Generally, there are only two reasons anyone asks that sort of question: firstly, to place you on a social ladder and, secondly, to ascertain if you're worth talking to. If, for instance, you met somebody at a drinks' party who told you that they were an actuary, you might think, Fine, now I know you are well paid but boring, so I'll talk to somebody else.

On the Gumball nobody is interested because the assumption is that either you've made (or inherited or stolen) a great wad of cash, or else you're simply well up for a laugh at any cost. Or probably both. A Gumballer could even be an actuary but you would know he was not boring. Or course, there are exceptions, and in any group that large, particularly with so many bankers, you are bound to come across some dullards and those with arrogant egos, but by and large they were as fun a group of characters as you would be lucky enough to meet in one place.

The other interesting observation about a gathering of Gumballers is that you notice in many ways that, at this level, money is irrelevant. People of great wealth tend to stand out under normal circumstances. In day-to-day life most of the participants would be the big fish in their local pond, with all manners of underlings at work to bow down to them, people who envy the size of their house and where they holiday, and they would be confident that their sports car makes them look good. On the Gumball all that goes out the window. There is not much point in shouting about your Ferrari if there are 65 other Ferrari owners in the room. Even if you drive the £250,000 Enzo, so what? There is another one here, and did you hear that someone wrote one off on the way? Perhaps you are a big cheese in Norwich? Wow, big deal, that's a Saudi prince over there. This sort of one-upmanship just does not happen. Everyone takes each other at face value, which makes a very refreshing change.

One thing they do ask, as has been noted, is 'What are you driving?' Under normal circumstances the marque of car would usually be a sufficient response. If, at a dinner party, somebody said to you, 'What do you drive?', while thinking, What a git, you might reply with a Volkswagen, Audi, Ford, BMW, Porsche or whatever it might happen to be. On the Gumball the question is perfectly appropriate, but the interesting thing is everyone refers to their cars by their model names or numbers. No one drives a Porsche – they drive a Carrera 4 or a GT2, or a Turbo something or other, and a Lamborghini would be a Murcielago or a Gallardo. It sounds confusing but most petrol heads are aware of the differences, or at least when it comes to exotic machinery.

Up until now, we had been answering the question with 'the Volvo' since it stood out and everybody had spotted it. We decided to take a leaf out of the other Gumballers' books and see if we could have a bit of fun the next time somebody asked what we drove.

'So what are you in then?' came the usual opening gambit.

'A V70R,' I said, imbuing the title with a certain mystique.

The Gumballer looked puzzled. 'That's quick, yeah?' he ventured.

'Oh yes, 300 bhp, 0 to 60 in about 5.6, limited to a top whack of 155 mph. It will sit at 150 all day.'

'Just what you need for this sort of thing then.'

'Indeed, and you?'

'I'm in a Boxster,' he replied, without needing to say it was a Porsche. 'It's fast, but not quite as quick as your car.'

At this stage only about two-thirds of the field had made it to Marbella. The good news was that my luggage had arrived safe and sound and gradually the Hummer lads drifted into the party. Far from having suffered a sense of humour failure, it was impossible not to notice that they were in high spirits. Closer inspection revealed that, having jettisoned the Belgians somewhere, they were expecting to be joined by a hen party from Dublin they knew to be living it large in nearby Puerto Banus. Much excitement evidently ensued, as with wives, girlfriends and assorted groupies left behind in Paris, the Gumball female contingent was noticeably thinner on the ground in Marbella. It never really occurred to us to ask how they had so conveniently located a hen party.

We spotted Jodie Kidd, and Richard suggested it was time he introduced me properly. A couple of years earlier I had met her once before when she was participating in a polo match in Dublin. We wandered over, and Richard said, 'Hi, Jodie, how's things? Let me introduce my co-driver Clement Wilson.'

She held out her hand, as I said, 'Actually we've met before.'

Quick as a flash Jodie was in with: 'Indeed, I remember it well. I may be a model but I'm not stupid.'

Feeling rather pleased with myself, as you do, when you discover that you have made an indelible impression on international supermodels who are fresh off the polo field, I continued. 'Indeed, that polo game in Phoenix Park a couple of years ago.'

'Oh, really? I was thinking of a couple of days ago when you stopped me in traffic for a lighter.'

As the evening progressed it was happily clear that our Volvo's early arrival had not gone unnoticed. Less happily, we discovered that its 'podium position' had aroused feelings of resentment which gave rise to some conspiracy theorists who suggested that we were cheats. Just as Richard had been less than amused at being told that his flash Jag was slower than a Volvo estate, those in high-powered, high-maintenance supercars were reluctant to concede that the Volvo had made it to Marbella ahead of them. A popular rumour was that we had flown the car from Paris to Marbella, and even more ludicrously we heard a story that we had two identical cars, and had simply swapped the plates around. We were too tired to argue, and anyhow it was gratifying to discover that the Volvo was rapidly becoming the most talked-about car. Whenever somebody questioned its position or whether it was a standard Volvo, and not some Ferrari in drag, we simply smiled, confirming it was completely standard and stressing that the only preparation required was to remove the roof box.

At 1 a.m. there were still cars wearily checking in, and those who had arrived later were unaware of the running order at the top. The talk had shifted slightly from 'What are you driving?' to 'What time did you get to the hotel?'

'What time did you get to the hotel?' asked a gentleman I knew to be in a heavily souped-up Japanese contraption, and he likewise knew of our Volvo. As he had arrived quite late, I suspected that he had singled us out in the hope of finding someone who had arrived after him.

'A little after twelve,' I replied, and followed up with the bait, 'It was a very long and tiring drive. What time did you get in?'

He looked at his watch: 1.00 a.m., and he smugly said, 'We were here at nine o'clock, just in time for dinner thankfully. That's tough on you guys, straight to the party with no time to sleep. But, hey, that's Gumball.'

I smiled and turned to Richard. 'Tough? Gumball? How many hours' sleep did you get, Richard?'

'Oh, a good eight hours, my recommended daily dose.'

The guy chuckled. 'Ha, I suppose that's one advantage of a Volvo; you can stretch out and get some proper sleep,' he said rather patronisingly. 'But I feel sorry for you, you must have done all the driving.'

'No, I got my eight hours as well. One of the advantages of the Volvo is that we arrived here a little after twelve midday, just in time for lunch and a lengthy siesta. I'm pleased you made it for dinner though.'

The party proceeded to the hotel nightclub, at which stage the hen party arrived. Sure enough, there were a dozen or so lively Irish lasses who had clearly come out for a good time. Inevitably though, only one was pretty and, while Richard was chatting to Jess, I thought it was sensible to make hay while the sun shone, or at least while the rest of the competition were necking Sambucas at a powerful rate. A great failing of mine – and it is a characteristic I discovered Richard shared – is that, if I am chatting to a girl I consider attractive, I tend to be far from subtle. This is possibly a subconscious thing, but for whatever reason I always manage to be completely unambiguous. Perhaps it's because I believe that way you don't find yourself having some awkward chat along the 'I thought we were good friends' lines. My modus operandi is as clear as day to both the object of my affections and to anyone who might be casually spectating. In addition, I have always found it useful to let all her pals know as well so there is no confusion. For instance, Steve, who had miraculously produced this hen party, deserved a hearty congratulations for laying on such entertainment. He wasted no time in letting me know that he agreed one stood head and shoulders above the rest, and that she was his wife-to-be, hence the convenience of the hen party.

Some indeterminate time later I turned for bed. I last saw Richard heading for the dance floor.

Marbella to Tangiers

We had cunningly positioned the car for a quick getaway the previous day. Satisfied with our third place to Marbella, we were keen to remain at the sharp end and had both agreed on the vital importance of departing for the ferry at no later than 7.30 a.m.

So it was with some surprise that I awoke to find Richard throwing his clothes into the bag and screaming, 'We're late, look out the window!'

Where the previous day there had been over a hundred and fifty cars crammed in, there was now only one Volvo, albeit one in pole position. Mayhem ensued as we packed our stuff,

Right Autographing the flag in the George V.
© Gumball 3000 Films Limited 2004/James McNaught

Below Torquenstein arrives in an ambulance; it wasn't the last time his fondness for vehicular lunacy landed him in an ambulance.
© Gumball 3000 Films Limited 2004/Fiona McLeod

Above left The Irish on the Gumball.
Left to Right; Steve, Clement, Richard, John, Mark, Bob and Shane.
© Gumball 3000 Films Limited 2004/Mark Kershaw

Above right Richard and Clement with Chris and Karron Eubank in Paris.
© Gumball 3000 Films Limited 2004

Left Jess and a friend in Paris; we live in hope.
© Gumball 3000 Films Limited 2004/Fiona McLeod

Right One of three Ferrari Enzos on the rally.
© Gumball 3000 Films Limited 2004/James McNaught

Left Clement with Mandy in Marrakech, before the first Moroccan crash.
(© Author's collection)

Right Moroccan children were delighted to receive Gumball stickers and top trumps.
© Gumball 3000 Films Limited 2004 /James McNaught

Below The London taxi with £7,253 on the meter: Chris has just woken up and is admiring the view. Graham is on the back seat.
© Gumball 3000 Films Limited 2004/FLY

Above A Mitsubishi Evo follows us into the 'Gumball Lane'.
© Gumball 3000 Films Limited 2004/James McNaught

Above 'Assessing the damage revealed that the most immediate problems were the front wheel and wing' – Chapter 11.
© Gumball 3000 Films Limited 2004/James McNaught

Left A closer look at the front valance indicated without a doubt the unfortunate victim – Torquenstein. The shrapnel discarded from his car was advertising his website…
© Gumball 3000 Films Limited 2004

Left Not Clement's best side, but clearly Jodie Kidd has done this before.
(© Author's collection)

Above Sunday driving, Tony Hawk style.
© Gumball 3000 Films Limited 2004/FLY

Left 'The Spanish police took a dim view of our hijinks' – Chapter 12.
© Gumball 3000 Films Limited 2004/Maurizio Fabris

Left 'We found Richard kicking off his quiet night on the roof of the Hummer' – Chapter 15.
© Gumball 3000 Films Limited 2004/James McNaught

Left In Cannes, looking presentable for the first time in a week, thanks to Cordings of Piccadilly, who were our not-quite-so-bling outfitters of choice.
© Gumball 3000 Films Limited 2004/James McNaught

Below left Adrien Brody collecting his Burt Reynolds bust with more pride than his Oscar.
© Gumball 3000 Films Limited 2004/Mike

Below right Richard with his Burt trophy, for which the Gold Cup will have to make way.
© Gumball 3000 Films ltd 2004/Fiona McLeod

checked out of the hotel and loaded the car. For once Richard's multitasking was much appreciated.

We got on to the road, and Richard agreed that it was probably a safer bet to follow the signs for the port rather than rely on his unrivalled local knowledge. After a short while we caught up with some stragglers, and were able to relax a bit. We needn't have worried – a staple of the Gumball is the immense hanging around at every stop. This is somewhat inevitable with the volume of cars and associated administration and logistics required to baby-sit so many messers.

We arrived at the ferry port, admittedly one of the last half-a-dozen cars, and joined the back of a queue to get on the boat that did not display any signs of moving particularly quickly. Entertainment was on hand in the form of Chris Eubank, the boxer, or former boxer, now star of *The Eubanks*. While he comes across as a bit eccentric on television, it cannot prepare you for meeting him in the flesh. He appeared to scoot everywhere on his little scooter while his apparently long-suffering wife would manoeuvre his colossal Bentley a little further up the queue. He would scoot for a bit and then spy a likely target, flip up his scooter in one deft movement and then proceed to hold forth about God only knows what with an authority and understanding sometimes not always comprehensible to everyone else.

The ferry journey was characterised by yet more queuing chaos, yet all Gumballers were in a state of heady excitement. The African adventure was about to begin and there was a feeling that the real fun was ahead of us. After we eventually confirmed that our vital documents for our persons and our car were in order, I left Richard to have some lunch and went out on deck to enjoy some rare peace and quiet, fresh air, a spot of sunbathing with some ambitious notions of sightseeing.

We were sailing through the Straits of Gibraltar and I was particularly keen to take a close look since at one stage we had considered undertaking this particular route by car. After returning from Geneva I had had some discussion with the managing director of the company who manufactures the Gibbs Aquada, which is an amphibious sports car guaranteed to excite all small boys, grown men and James Bond aficionados alike. After a brief test drive in the London docks we had discussed the rather hare-brained plan of crossing the Straits. A little research had suggested that it might be a bit hairy since the Straits were rather congested. Now, looking at the sea-faring traffic from the safety of our large ferry, I was thankful that the company had not shared my mindless enthusiasm. All manner of ships, large and small, were cutting across each other with a blatant disregard for their fellow seamen. The aggressive nature with which a trawler would take on a rowing boat made the Arc de Triomphe with Gumballers look positively novice, and the size of the waves was far scarier than anything road rage could produce.

As we passed Gibraltar I remembered I had read that the residents were gearing up to celebrate the three hundred years since the Anglo-Dutch occupation and subsequent Union Jack waving. The Spanish Government, on the other hand, were gearing up to give the British a piece of their mind to remind them that they were occupying a piece of their land. I laughed thinking that they could do with a few lessons from the Irish. The humour value was inspired not from any patriotic pride of courageous Irish freedom fighters rebelling against an occupying force, but from a recollection of how John Magnier and JP McManus dealt with Sir Alex Ferguson.

They had all been involved in a recent debate over the ownership of a horse called, ironically enough, Rock of Gibraltar. Sir Alex, allegedly, claimed that John Magnier had given him a half-share in a horse. John Magnier, allegedly, claimed he had not, since, while a generous man by nature, he was not a fool of a businessman. To cut a long story short, Sir Alex, although famous for being fairly ruthless in the cutthroat world of football, discovered that he had bitten off a little more than he could chew when he tried to tackle a couple of heavy hitters in the horseracing and breeding industry.

Sir Alex Ferguson operates in a sporting world where he manages players who get paid sums of up to £100,000 a week for their ball-dribbling skills, although footballers seem to spend a lot of time dribbling in nightclubs, flashing their wages and trying to get laid. Magnier operates in a sporting world where he gets paid hundreds of thousands of pounds for his charges to get laid. With such testosterone and all that talk of sex flying around, it was inevitable that it would come down to whoever had the biggest balls when disputing how to divvy up the proceeds every time the Rock of Gibraltar got his rocks off.

There was a Gumballer beside me and I made the mistake of trying to engage his interest in my ruminations. Predictably enough he was a Manchester United supporter and did not share my enthusiasm for the cheap jokes at Ferguson's expense. Bizarrely, he went off on a rant about the ownership of Manchester United. This was a further complication, since, in a series of transactions that could not be disputed, Magnier and McManus had bought thirty per cent of Manchester United. The fan did not share my view that Ferguson was pretty stupid to pick a fight with major shareholders of a company he worked for, and suggested that as it was a club they did not really own it anyway. Apparently, the fans had not completely given up on the idea that the pair should give them the shares back. I decided not to continue the conversation, as there were still clearly some pretty stupid people in and around Manchester United, notwithstanding Beckham's departure. As he was a staunch Ferguson supporter, I also decided not to point out the irony of Ferguson's views that while at Manchester United Beckham should have concentrated on what he was good at, without dragging undue attention to the club from his extracurricular activities and fancy friends. Apart from anything else I realised that I was being rather boring with my pontificating.

I found Richard downstairs lunching with the Irish lads and speculating as to what Morocco had in store for us. We were nearly there.

9. MOROCCAN MADNESS (PART 1)

> We bring you Morocco – Welcome to Africa. Prepare to
> enter another continent and a different world.

So said the Gumball route card that I studied on the ferry. All
the Gumballers had been scrutinising the route card on the ferry
with some speculation, and we were no exception. It made for
interesting reading.

> Upon entering Morocco the government and the King's
> security are specially looking after all us Gumballers. So, if
> the police stop for you for any reason, please respect their
> requests.

> TIPS: If you get 'stopped' by the police or need to ask for
> directions, it's really useful to have a quantity of Gumball
> stickers and Top Trumps to give away. People will be very
> appreciative.

Goodness me, this all sounded pretty intriguing stuff to us. We
had driven well over twelve hundred miles at speed and,
although we had heard countless Gumballing tales of woe
concerning the cops, we had hardly seen the police let alone
had a tricky time about speeding. Now we were entering a
country where the police 'stopped' you, whatever stopping in
inverted commas might mean, and they could be bought off
with stickers and games.

We got off the ferry into gridlock and were marshalled like
cattle by all sorts of police and security types. At this stage their

assistance was not in doubt, but after hanging around the port for about half an hour it seemed that they were a little too keen in their assistance to keep us waiting. Predictably, cars started jockeying for position, sneaking up inside lanes, moving bollards and cones to try and get closer to the front. We managed some fairly professional queue-barging and ended up about the tenth car.

For some time we appeared to be going nowhere fast. This in itself was not a great problem, as again it was a lot of fun to be sitting in a supercar traffic jam. Understandably, the local Moroccans were fascinated at the spectacle, and every one of them was genuinely pleased to welcome us. We wondered how long that would last. The real frustration of sitting in the port was that we all started to worry that our entire Moroccan drive would be held up by bureaucracy, and overeager security staff who were just too happy to help.

How wrong we were.

The police activity had involved organising an escort for us through the town of Tangier. This was not your standard 'take care with a wide load' sort of escort, but a full-on high-speed job with motorcycle outriders. The sort you often see in London, when visiting dignitaries have their swift progress ensured by a team of police working in unison to control the inconveniences of public road users and traffic lights. Except this wasn't London; it was a dusty town in Morocco, and the visiting dignitaries in question were not confined to the back seat of an upmarket luxury saloon, but consisted of 150 supercars. We tore through the town; it was awesome to experience and must have been phenomenal to witness, and only two miles into Morocco it set the scene for a succession of events that were simply mind-boggling to Gumballers and Moroccans alike.

As we approached the outskirts of the town, we were about the fifth car in the procession. Cars were three abreast on a single-track road and the police at the front were gamely trying to stay in front, an activity that was always destined to be futile.

At the earliest available opportunity, as soon as the road straightened out of the town, one by one Gumball cars put their foot down and flew past the police. It did not take long for them to simply peel off and give up. As we passed them they were waving, but in that split second it was unclear if they were waving for us to slow down or simply waving us on. As nobody took any notice of them, we waved back and pressed ahead.

As I have mentioned, the Volvo had been a serious contender on the rally up until now, and we felt that Morocco was going to be where it really came into its own. In a rather naïve, and admittedly slightly ignorant, frame of mind, we had assumed the Moroccan roads would not be of any great standard, and some of the spicier cars would need to take it easy. The road out of the town was fairly dusty and had the odd pothole, but it was by no means Third World. We decided that was probably because it was a major road to the port and needed to be better than most. The lads in the low-slung machinery had better make the most of it.

Once again we had underestimated the Moroccans. We paid our dirham at a toll-booth and rounded a bend to see a road that was surely built with supercars in mind. It was impeccably surfaced, wide and straight for as far as the eye could see. Well done, Morocco! This was not a road; it was a runway that Heathrow would have been proud of.

I was driving; I turned to Richard to see that the significance of this had not been wasted on him. No chance. He was as wide-eyed as I was.

'OK, Richard, look at this road. Would you agree that the Moroccan cops seem fairly friendly?'

'What are you suggesting?'

'I want to go absolute full tilt on this thing. Worst-case scenario we get a fine, which I'll gladly pay, just for the experience.'

A 911 was at the booth beside us; they paid and took off. If Richard was having any doubts about giving me the green light, the desire to remain ahead of the rest put paid to those.

'Absolutely, go for it; just watch your mirrors.'

Allegedly, I once drove a Ferrari at 150 mph on a long straight road in the UK. It was early in the morning and the road was empty, but it was still quite a nervy experience. I swore then that I would never again drive at such insane speeds on a public road. Less than two months later, and only about fifteen seconds after leaving the tollbooth, I was nearing 160 mph in a Volvo.

At that speed the car felt surprisingly sure-footed, and no doubt the all-wheel-drive system, combined with the quality of the road, was partly to explain why these speeds in a Volvo in Morocco felt safer than a Ferrari in Wales. The real reason I suspect was to do with the traffic. Ironically enough, in Wales, where there was no traffic, it was scary because you knew that if you met another car it might only be travelling at a third of your speed. Here in Morocco the road was busy; we were travelling in heavy traffic at 160 mph but were being overtaken. Watching the mirrors became more important than the road ahead.

Looking in the mirror I saw the distinctive shape of a Ferrari Enzo going head to head with a Porsche. The Porsche was staying with the Enzo, which indicated that it could have only been the finely tuned GT2. Within seconds they passed us, travelling at the sharp end of 200 mph. Not only did we find it mesmerising to see this on a public road, but also the police looked fairly awestruck as well.

We had passed a large number of Moroccan police armed with speed cameras. Initially we lifted off and went by at perhaps 130 mph. When that did not seem to trouble them, and after seeing others not bothering to slow down at all, it began to dawn on us that perhaps we had immunity from the speed limits. But why then were they standing at the side of the road with speed cameras?

It turned out they were clocking the Moroccan traffic coming the other way. In the most incredibly blatant affirmation of the theory that there is one rule for the rich and another for everybody else, the Moroccan police were pulling over their countrymen for breaking the speed limit to the tune of 5 km/h. As they were getting booked or fined, they had to stand back and watch us pass at speeds in excess of three times the speed limit.

I insisted we stop.

'Why on earth do you want to stop? We're losing time,' Richard asked slightly impatiently.

'I don't care, Richard, let's just watch this. It is not every day that you get to witness cars of this calibre going absolutely flat out on public roads. Under normal circumstances, you would never see one and today we have the opportunity to see 150 of them.'

'We'll stop for a minute or two but not for the whole 150.'

On the bridge watching these cars, and catching the brief glimpses of the grins on their drivers' faces, I decided that the Gumball was worth every penny. We had debated among ourselves and heard a few others venture the theory that, although it was all good fun, £8000 was a little steep for what was essentially a long, and pretty tiring, drive. A £160,000 Lamborghini drove under the bridge, and if the engine roar had not been so deafening I guarantee we would have heard its occupants hooting with delight. That is a lot of money to spend on a car, particularly as ordinarily three-quarters of its ability is effectively redundant. Under those circumstances, £8000 for this one short drive alone had to be considered a bargain.

As we watched, we were approached by some French tourists. Sensibly they had decided to pull off the road as well, since their rent-a-car road-trip plans had not included near-death experiences. They realised that we were part of the madness unfolding as our car was proudly bearing its Gumball badges. An odd conversation ensued. They could not quite get their heads around what we were all up to. Clearly, it was not an official race or else they would not have been allowed to stray into its path. That said, equally clearly, these cars were in a hurry. I tried to explain that 'it's not a race, it's a rally'. The bridge shook as yet another 200-mph car went under, drowning out my explanations. What's a rally then? Well, sort of a motoring holiday, rather like yours but with other like-minded car enthusiasts. Other like-minded idiots was their definite impression after our brief conversation. Richard's babbling attempts to explain in his now all too familiar, but resolutely incomprehensible, language simply confirmed to them that we must be from some other planet, which had suffered a literal brain drain.

It was time to go. If they had followed, a mere two minutes later they would have needed no further proof that we all needed locking up. A couple of miles down the road we passed a police lorry. I looked in my mirrors and saw a Lamborghini Gallardo and BMW M3 approaching fast. I pulled in front of the police to allow them past.

Just ahead of our car there was a Moroccan truck travelling at about 50 mph, and another local car behind him in the slow lane. The car pulled out to overtake.

'Oh, shit, Benny Maroc, look behind you!' cried Richard.

At that moment the Lambo and Beemer were barrelling past us and the police. In fairness to the local driver, he probably did check his mirrors and could be forgiven for thinking that all was well. Under normal driving conditions, rear-view mirrors do not lie. He would have seen a Volvo estate car and a police van, in the slow lane, and naturally assumed it was perfectly clear to overtake.

Except it was far from all clear, and these were not normal driving conditions. If he had checked his mirrors again when he was alongside the truck, he would have discovered that, while all clear a mere moment ago, they were now stuffed to the brim with a yellow Lamborghini. In reality he probably did not have time and literally didn't know what hit him.

To picture this, anybody unfamiliar with the shape of a Gallardo should realise that it is aerodynamically designed, with a low sleek nose. It is deliberately designed this way so that it can cut through the air with the greatest efficiency, reducing drag and increasing speed and stability. However, an unhappy side effect of such a wedge-shaped design is that, if the car comes into contact with a Renault 4 with knackered rear suspension and the aerodynamics of a brick, it attempts to drive underneath it.

The hypothetical scenario, which surely never occurred to the designers, was unfolding in real time before our very eyes, and those of the police I might add. The only person who did not enjoy such a smashing view was the Renault 4 driver. Before he knew it he was airborne, and spent a few split seconds soiling his kaftan before he came to land facing the other way on the far side of the hard shoulder.

Happily for him, the far side of the hard shoulder was a big pile of sand, and the car landed on all four wheels like a cat, though without the composure. The Lamborghini slammed on whatever was left of its brakes, and pulled in to be joined by the police. We rubbernecked our way past, speechless in astonishment, and delighted to see the Moroccan emerge, understandably shaken, but in good health nonetheless.

'At a guess, I'd say the fun's over now,' I said to Richard when we had regained our composure.

'No doubt about it. The police had as good a view of that as we did. They won't be quite as cordial when word spreads that a Moroccan citizen was punted off the road.'

'Punted off the road' summed it up perfectly. It was as if his car was a piece of tumbleweed that had strayed in the way and bounced off the Gumballer. We speculated as to what lay in store for the Lamborghini driver and reckoned that he would be trying to buy his way out of trouble by at least replacing the car.

Although it was in serious circumstances, it conjured up an amusing image. Mohammed Moroccan might turn up at his local that night, for a strongly deserved stiff drink, and tell his friends about his new car.

'All right, chaps, good evening.'

'Ah, Mohammed, what are you having?'

'Make mine a double, Achmed. I've had a bitch of a day. I was driving along minding my own business and a big yellow Lamborghini came out of nowhere and drove underneath me. My car flipped off the road and spun right round. He hit me at about 180 mph. I'm very lucky to be alive, lads. Anyway, the gentleman in the Lamborghini apologised profusely for the inconvenience and bought me a car. An S-Class Mercedes, come outside and have a look.'

'Listen, Mohammed, there will be no doubles for you. You need to stay off the drink, mate.'

As mad as it sounded, we'd witnessed it and we proceeded towards Casablanca at a reduced pace showing a lot more respect for the Moroccan people, their police and their speed limits.

Casablanca was bedlam, as we arrived in the thick of lunchtime traffic. The map we had was worse than useless since it appeared to have been made redundant by somebody's decision to rename every street 'King Mohammed Whatnot Boulevard'. Presumably that decision had been King Mohammed Whatnot's. We got hopelessly lost and were most thankful to take advantage of the welcoming nature of the Casablancans. A young couple, with no regard for their own schedule, took it upon themselves to show us the way. They had spotted us leading a number of Gumball cars around in circles, clearly planning on going somewhere specific but with no idea where. Without prompting they gesticulated for us to follow them.

'What do you reckon? Will we follow them?' I said to Richard, as it seemed a positive move.

'Why? Where are they going?'

'I don't know, but clearly they do, which is a lot more than can be said for us.'

'But they could be going anywhere. How the hell do they know where we're going? We haven't even asked for directions?'

'Look, they're not leading us off to kidnap us and sell our kidneys. We are in a group of ten Gumball cars, stickered up and obviously these people know that we are going to Rick's Café to meet the rest of the cars.'

'If you say so.'

I was wrong. Not about the kidney thing, thankfully, but about Rick's Café. It turned out that the Casablancan Motor Show was on that very day, and the helpful people had assumed this cortège of glamorous cars were exhibits. A fair assumption perhaps, until you consider that Geneva, Tokyo and Detroit are the big three in the motor show league table, and about the only venues imaginable that could gather a collection of cars to rival the Gumball entrants. Even the British Motor Show struggles to get the most exotic cars, so, notwithstanding our guides' touching patriotic faith in the Casablancan Automobile Club, it was an unlikely scenario.

As soon as we arrived at our destination, we realised the mistake. The organisers were more than happy for us to gatecrash their party, because their exhibits did indeed consist of a couple of last year's BMW models, and an admittedly fine display of Renaults. Unhappily for them we filed out of a gate just as soon as we had entered. The local enthusiasts had time to clock the arrival of a range of cars and quickly realised something special was afoot.

Thus we arrived at Rick's Café with a bit of a fan club, stolen from the motor show. When we got there, they were in for another treat. Like Sam, the GT2 driver was playing it again, performing inch-perfect doughnuts on the congested street outside the café. Congestion was not present in the form of cars, merely people and police spectators. Once again the Moroccan authorities had displayed their helpfulness by making sure that no traffic could get in the way of the Gumballing fun.

Predictably, as we had swapped driving, Richard was once again under starter's orders and keen to get back on the road after a light lunch. Once again we had another fine display of high-adrenaline town driving, map reading and multitasking. We were on route to Marrakech and, as Richard read the maps, I read the route card for want of something useful to do.

> Head south out of Casablanca, getting directions may be easier than map-reading.

I thought I'd keep that bit of advice to myself. Richard had his hands full as it was without trying to converse in a combination of languages. We were looking for the motorway towards Settat, and unexpectedly found it after a little trial, error and frenetic three-point turning. The first glimpse of the motorway confirmed that there was to be more of the same speeds and it was Richard's turn for some fun.

'Make the most of it,' I said, then read the route card aloud again.

> TIPS: After Settat the road narrows into two-way traffic, and the 'real' Moroccan experience begins. Keep your speed down and watch out for donkeys, shepherds with sheep, camels and stray dogs.

I must admit that I was nervous. Prior to the rally itself my only slight concern was that I might have to listen to Richard banging on about horses; now I was more worried about him banging into donkeys. At this stage, I was experienced enough to judge Richard's driving style and it did not seem compatible with animal traffic. It is not that I thought he was a bad driver, he just never seemed to be terribly relaxed. Any sign of traffic, two-way or otherwise, and he started frenetically bobbing up and down in the driver's seat, and swinging from side to side in a bid to manufacture an overtaking opportunity.

At the end of the motorway we met some more of the King's security, who rather inexplicably took our number plates and time of arrival at their checkpoint. They had witnessed so many shenanigans that morning in good humour that we felt it was unlikely that they were trying to keep us in check, monitoring who was speeding. We joked that perhaps they were betting on the finishing order in Marrakech. This hold-up had the unfortunate effect of backing up the Gumballers and then unleashing them into quite heavy traffic. We were particularly unfortunate to re-enter the road stuck behind a wheezing lorry that was struggling to make it up a steep hill.

Inevitably Richard started bobbing and swinging. The Moroccans drive on the right, and we were in a right-hand drive; hence I was in the passenger seat with full view of a suicidal blind brow of a hill when Richard swung the nose of the Volvo out for a peek.

'What the fuck are you doing?!' I screamed at him.

'The lorry won't make it up the hill; it's rolling back. It's going to roll into us,' he replied at 3000 words per minute as the revs struggled to keep up.

'Far better it "rolls" into us than some fucker comes over that hill and smashes into us.'

A terrifying two or three minutes followed. The agitation in the driver's seat continued and, just when I thought we were safe, Richard would make another lunge.

'Calm down, Richard, you mad bastard! It's crazy to go over that hill blind. And stop jumping around in your seat; you'll shag the suspension if you keep that up.'

'I can't see; I'm trying to get where I can.'

'That's the point: you can't see, but I can. Trust me, it's suicidal.'

Thankfully the lorry eventually crept over the brow and we went after it. At the crest, before Richard could make a bid for freedom, I had a good look at the road. 'OK, clear!' We overtook the lorry safely and were on our way. We agreed at this point that, on single-track roads, whoever was driving had to put their faith in the passenger's judgement of whether or not it was safe to overtake.

From that point to Marrakech the drive was exhilarating. On the motorways the Gumballers had been spaced out over fairly lengthy distances, whereas here we were in close quarters engaged in car-to-car combat with the ever-present threat of camels. It was exciting stuff, particularly when we were three abreast with a Lamborghini Gallardo and an AMG Mercedes. Richard resolutely held the inside line as we undertook them approaching a bend. It would have been a ballsy move on the pit straight at Silverstone, but on the N246 something or other to Marrakech it was outrageous. There was a photographer hanging out of the window of the Merc, but it was his face that was the real picture.

In addition to the chaos of the Gumballers' cars, the Moroccans were out for a drive as well, going about their business as usual. Generally, the bemused people simply gave us a wide berth and looked on in astonishment. As most Moroccans were driving fairly beaten-up old and slow cars, on the straight roads for most of the time, the Gumballers passed them with ease.

The very quickest Porsches, capable of phenomenal bursts of acceleration, passed us with ease on this stretch of road as well. It was made easier as I implored Richard not to try and dice with them, as four abreast was just taking the piss. Three overtook in one go and lined up directly ahead of us and behind two trucks, as we rounded into a bend. Approaching the bend they uncharacteristically decided that discretion was the better part of valour and they would dispatch the truck after the turn.

Porsche number one did not count on truck number two having the same idea. Coming out of the bend the second truck pulled out to overtake the slower lorry ahead of him. Slower is all relative, as he tried to overtake at 50 km/h. This slowed us all down and set us up for a ringside seat of yet another breathtaking display of vehicular lunacy.

The three 911s were weaving behind the two trucks three abreast. We were behind them, weaving a little as well, though I was unclear if that was because Richard was looking for a point to penetrate or he simply couldn't sit still. Suddenly the middle Porsche floored it, having spotted a gap open up between the two trucks, and flew right through the middle of them accelerating out into the open road ahead of them. It happened so quickly that I daresay the truck drivers didn't see him until he was ahead and spent some seconds wondering where he came from. Seconds later he was gone, out of sight.

These sorts of antics were becoming commonplace, and while difficult to condone they were undeniably fabulous to witness. As it dawned on some of the Gumballers that they were enjoying immunity from the police and the authorities, they were driving ever faster, with decreasing concern for their own safety. In defence of the driver who had driven between the lorries, it must be stressed that it was only his own well-being, and that of his passenger, that he risked. If the trucks had hit him, undoubtedly he was going to come off worse.

It must also be stressed that the Gumball rally management and staff in no way condoned or encouraged such madness. Of course, no matter what the official line was, they turned a blind eye to speeding, but we had been expressly told that we were 'important guests in Morocco, don't take the piss'. It was quite an achievement by Max to have the King on side, but at this stage I felt that he might have some uncomfortable explaining to do.

I was worried that I might have some uncomfortable explaining to do of my own. We were a hundred-odd miles from Marrakech and Richard was enjoying himself. It was getting dark and I was concerned about the fact that it was apparently legal to drive in Morocco at less than 20 mph with no lights.

'Just take it easy, Richard. There's a lot of madness going on. It would not be a great career move for me to return this car in anything less than one piece,' I said.

'Relax, mate, you're too uptight.'

Perhaps he was right. I was particularly uptight, and manically gripping the seat. And how ironic. He was supposed to be the uptight one.

While we had been warned about stray camels and donkeys there had been no mention of the random fashion in which the Moroccan people crossed the road. Like the famous chicken, they seemed to be doing it purely to get to the other side, as between the towns there were no discernible activities or attractions on either side yet the crossings continued unabated. In fact, maybe it was a game of chicken, since they must have noticed a steady stream of ridiculously fast cars.

After debating this, we realised that they must be hitchhikers, crossing to get to a purple patch in the direction intended. We had seen quite a few hitchhikers in situ, notwithstanding the fact that all Moroccan cars we had passed were stuffed to the gills with about a dozen passengers. A hitchhiker would have a long wait.

Suddenly I had a plan. Despite appearances, surely Richard was an inherently responsible individual and would not take any mad risks with the car, and indirectly my career, if we had a passenger on board? I did not really count since a) I had gone into this madness with my eyes open and b) I had driven everywhere with scant regard for Richard's nerves.

'Let's pick up a hitchhiker, Richard,' I suggested.

'Sorry, excuse me? I know it's not a "race" but nor are we on some Sunday drive. We can't just give Benny Maroc a lift; he'd be scared shitless.'

'Nonsense, these lads believe death is preordained. It's all fate, they'd be fine. And by the way, just while we're on the subject, who on earth is Benny?'

Richard had repeatedly been talking about Benny this and Benny that. When Benny became Benny Maroc, I realised that this was his version of my Moroccan Joe. So far we had encountered Joe French, Jose in Spain and Moroccan Joe. As far as I was concerned these generic nicknames were fairly self-explanatory but I could see no logic in Benny.

'You Benny! You ride like a right, proper Benny,' Richard said and laughed at the recollection. 'It's a tribute to the comedian

Benny Hill; hence Benny was a nickname used by a jockey called Tom Morgan, for somebody who is possibly not the sharpest tool in the box. He was an established jockey who recommended me to a trainer for one of my first professional rides. He'd said to the trainer, "I know this lad, Richard Dunwoody; he's a good young jockey, give him the ride." I rode the race and made a complete dog's dinner of it, getting beaten by Tony Mullins. Tom Morgan got some serious stick from the trainer for recommending me and it wasn't until I'd won a Gold Cup and a couple of Nationals that he conceded I no longer rode like a "Benny". Ever since then I call people "Benny", like your man, or whatever.'

Fair enough, it made as much sense as my Jose. I spotted Benny Maroc with his luggage ahead. 'Come on, let's pick him up, Richard. It will be a laugh, certainly more fun that that idiot you offered a lift to in Paris.'

We pulled over, and I got out and gestured to the fellow to join us. 'Pour Marrakech, Monsieur.'

He already looked terrified, but glancing around there were no other in cars in sight other than sports cars already carrying two, and saloons carrying ten. Reluctantly, he approached the car. The stickers obviously had already given us away as potential killers, but as he surveyed the unmistakeable lines of the Volvo estate and the welcoming leather, he seemed less nervous. The integrated child seats, seatbelts and clearly marked airbag in the roof lining might have convinced him that we were a safe bet. He climbed in, bowing and thanking us.

We set off again, and I rummaged around in my Gumball goody bag for some Top Trumps and stickers to give him and for a few moments he must have thought that it was his lucky day.

His luck changed when a hairdresser's Porsche Boxster overtook us. We had seen them a couple of times and I had to agree with Richard that they drove like a Benny. They had also made the mistake of cracking ill-informed jokes on the ferry about the Volvo's performance. Richard needed no encouragement.

The thing I fell in love with most about the Volvo was its ability to surprise. We had been having great fun surprising all sorts with its turn of speed both at top whack and accelerating through the gears. Now it was our passenger's turn to be surprised. Pinned back into his integrated child seat, he did not share our enthusiasm for putting manners on those who had underestimated our car's capabilities.

In fact, he did not seem enthusiastic about anything other than getting out there and then. He did not speak much English or French and he was having difficulty making himself verbally understood at Mach 3. His body language, however, can only have meant one thing.

Unbelievably, I had misunderstood his gesticulations. I was less concerned about the traffic now, as the road had straightened and widened. Richard had everything under control and without a constant stream of traffic had stopped hopping about in his seat. Or perhaps he realised that it was unwise to continue such energetic movements as the Moroccan's jumping around far surpassed anything Richard had achieved. At high speed, the two of them moving in conjunction would definitely have threatened the car's stability. No, stupidly I thought the Moroccan was waving madly for us to slow down because he saw the police ahead.

As we passed the police, waving happily at four times the speed limit, our passenger stared despairingly looking for help. I helpfully explained that we were important guests of the King, so he could count himself lucky and we'd be in Marrakech in no time.

Our new friend was not counting himself lucky at all. In fact, unluckily for him, since we so comprehensively saw off the Boxster, we had caught a BMW M5 and a TVR and were now involved in a spirited three-way dice. My anxieties earlier had been caused by a concern that Richard might try and involve himself with three 911 GT2s. This I knew to be futile, but I certainly was not going to object when he wisely decided to show up the BMW and TVR upstarts.

There was a shock in store when I turned around to see how our passenger was enjoying the fun. Benny was now looking for a way out. He was contemplating his own style of vehicular lunacy, eyeing up the door handles and assessing the risk/ reward ratio of making a jump for it. It would have been no use, since even if he had calculated the odds to be in his favour he would have discovered our child-friendly Volvo central-locking system was just as effective at keeping our passengers in, as it had been in Paris at keeping them out.

I suggested to Richard that we ought to stop and let him go.

'What? I thought he wanted to go to Marrakech?'

'Not any more he doesn't.'

10. MACBETH

10. MARRAKECH

Marrakech

'OK, Richard, we're coming into Marrakech,' I said, waving the ample supply of maps, town plans and route cards at him. 'Trust me on this one. I know exactly where we're going. Stay on this road until we hit a T-junction; take a left on to Avenue de France and then we will see the Kempinski Hotel on our right.'

Simple, you would think, but at the sight of a town, traffic lights and a few junctions, Richard could not help himself. He made a grab for the town plan, but as an old hand, at this stage, I deftly swept it out of reach. Undeterred in his attempts at getting us lost, he stopped a local. 'Monsieur, Señor, Sir, Hotel Kempinksi,' he enunciated, carefully but not clearly.

I gave up, deciding there and then that, as frustrating as it was, he was beyond help. From now on, in towns I would let him fart about in his frenetic fashion and try and remain calm. It would not have been so infuriating except for the fact that, invariably when we arrived at towns, we were exhausted, and our senses of humour and patience were wearing thin. What made the whole fiasco even stranger was that Richard, on account of his superior party staying power, was invariably more exhausted than I was as we finished a stage. One would have expected him to be delighted to complete the last few miles on autopilot.

'I am absolutely knackered,' declared Richard after completing yet another draining dialogue with a confused Moroccan. 'I am going to have a quiet one tonight.'

'A quiet one?' This sounded unlikely. I needed clarification.

'Yeah, a quick bite to eat, stay off the drink, and straight to bed after dinner.'

He was serious. It was comforting to know he did not have unlimited reserves of stamina after all. I have never been known personally for shying from a party but so far that week I had been amazed at Richard's ability to stay out all night, on the back of so little sleep and prodigious quantities of driving. Not forgetting the Belfast marathon he had run the day before we left. I had had to cut short both of the Gumball parties since I had simply ceased to function.

We arrived at the hotel in about fifteenth place, and parked the car. Richard was becoming increasingly incoherent and announced he was going straight to bed, asking me to wake him in time for dinner.

While I accept that from the organisers' point of view this fatigue is part of the 'pushing yourself to the limits' experience, it is the only thing I would change. I was also exhausted but was reluctant to go to bed as I had just arrived in Marrakech, hardly an everyday experience, and was keen to savour it. It was a privilege to watch the Moroccans soak up the atmosphere. There were chaps arriving with camels festooned in Gumball stickers, and we were constantly harassed for postcards and other such memorabilia.

I have read many times that travelling in Morocco can be something of a hassle as the people are so eager to make your acquaintance and earn your money by making a nuisance of themselves and their 'tour-guiding' abilities. It could not have been more different for us, notwithstanding the fact that it was unlikely they had ever seen so many moneyed folk in one place. Adults and children alike were not interested in money, but they had a voracious appetite for Gumball souvenirs. They had a genuine respect for the machinery on show, and one could sense their delight in having the opportunity to see it all up close. This welcome and hospitality was all the more remarkable when you consider the disrespect we had shown the speed limits and traffic laws. After the events of the day, and especially remembering that many Moroccans got pulled over for speeding while we sped past them, a collective jealousy, resentment and outbreak of national road rage would have been entirely understandable.

After a couple of hours enjoying the Moroccan welcome and the camaraderie of the arriving Gumballers, it was time to wake Richard. As I walked through the hotel lobby, I noticed an uncommonly large amount of beautiful girls, loitering. This was another marked difference from our arrivals in France and Spain. Rich guys with flash cars are ten a penny in Paris and Marbella, but as the town's best-looking daughters were filling our hotel they were clearly pretty scarce in Marrakech.

Richard was not asleep, but collapsed on his bed, zombie-like, and wittering with delirium. As I have discussed at length, I had heard Richard babble incomprehensibly on a number of occasions. This was different from his usual daytime witterings, which were generally created by a lack of local language knowledge; as he lay on the bed, eyes rooted to the television, this breed of nonsense was more of a stream of consciousness.

'Have you had any sleep?' I interrupted, somewhat apprehensively.

'Watching television.'

'Anything good on?'

'Don't know.'

'Well, what are you watching then?'

'This girl.'

I looked at the television, and a rather large girl was being interviewed about something of no great consequence. She was lying on a bed in much the same manner as Richard, though taking up considerably more of it. Richard was fixated.

'Look at her, she is enormous,' he drooled.

'Sorry, what's your point?'

'That's the point: she's enormous. I mean huge. Normally, I like big girls but she is enormous,' he said wearily, and sighed heavily, still transfixed by the television.

'Richard, you're not making any sense.'

'Imagine sleeping with her,' he continued.

'I'd rather not, thanks.'

'Wow, just imagine the effort involved. I couldn't handle it. I mean I know I like them large but that's just ridiculous.'

He gave an involuntary shudder, as he pictured the extent of the exertions, while he did not even have the energy to get off the bed. I was beginning to worry about him. Not about his tastes and preferences, that was his own business, but, to my medically untrained eye, he appeared to be in an advanced state of exhaustion, and was making matters worse by imagining strenuous physical activities.

'Richard, you need to get some sleep. It's time for dinner now but I think you're right to have a quiet one,' I suggested.

Suddenly he swung his legs off the bed, sat up and snapped out of whatever trance or fantasy he had been inhabiting.

'I'll be all right,' he said. 'Anything interesting happening when you were downstairs?'

'Oh yes, there's a lot going on. And the hotel is jammed full of young, beautiful Moroccan girls, but they might be a bit slim and conventionally good looking for your tastes.'

At dinner, we took a table with the Irish lads from the Hummer, who were equally tired and also looking a little shaken. Richard grabbed a beer and announced his intention to have a quiet night. There were sniggers all round. Richard looked blank, as they all heartily agreed that it was hardly surprising he was in the market for a quiet night after his performance in Marbella.

'Was I up late then?' he enquired nervously. 'I don't really remember going to bed.'

'Richard, we had to encourage you out of the place in the interests of health and safety,' said Bob.

'Do you remember dancing?' asked John with a knowing grin.

Richard did not respond. It was obvious that he was sufficiently aware of his capabilities and talents not to enter into a discussion about his dancing style.

'At the last count there were six injuries, one serious.' Mark had joined in.

Richard clearly was suffering the embarrassment of someone who routinely enjoys a dance after a few drinks, only to swear 'never again' on each occasion. John seemed to sense this and appeared to be changing the subject. 'There was a lot they could have done in the way of entertainment in Marbella. There was a huge stage in that club, and it was a waste of space. Having paid a whack to be here, the parties could be made to really rock,' he said with the confidence, experience and authority of one who knows a thing or two about cheesy nightclubs.

Richard nodded in agreement, glad that the talk had moved on.

John was not finished. 'What I really mean is, last night in Marbella was a lot of fun, but eight thousand quid seems a hell of a lot of money to watch Richard Dunwoody make a fool of himself on the dance floor.'

For the rest of the meal there was little respite for Richard. In the way that blokes do, we latched on to the theme and flogged it like a dead horse. As if someone had been listening to both John's gripes and his jokes, further ammunition was at hand when a troupe of belly dancers, snake charmers and assorted performers appeared on stage for our enjoyment.

The audience were captivated, and I looked around the room and noticed that some people had moved from the back to get a better look. One couple in particular were standing out at the side of the room, locked in an affectionate if not loving embrace. I nudged Richard and nodded towards them. He raised an eyebrow.

It was Jodie Kidd and her apparent boyfriend of some years, Tarquin. I say apparent because, although I understood them to be an item, on the rally one did not often see them together. Richard had introduced me to Tarquin, as he had met him through some polo connection and from conversation I had just assumed he was Jodie's other half. Some weeks before the Gumball, Richard had assisted in arranging their participation in a charity horse race. He had told me that Tarquin had fallen off in the race and there was speculation that Jodie had run over the top of him. I got the distinct impression that there was rather less sympathy from Jodie than might have been expected. I had heard that they had a famously tempestuous relationship but surely this was a bit much? I had some experience of my own from being on the receiving end of a model's high-maintenance tantrums and, although unpredictable and unpleasant, she at least drew the line at running over me on a horse.

It was watching the reactions of the audience that made the belly-dancing troupe such a spectacle. The dancers left the stage and proceeded to circulate themselves around the tables. As one gyrated her stuff in front of a chap at the next table, it was fascinating to watch him focus. Tears came to my eyes watching a man who has had no sleep for 48 hours trying to rotate his eyes to keep up with the high-speed action less than two feet from his face. Eventually he fainted.

The two guys in the Caterham were also on our table. In Paris, we had registered for the event at the same time as them and had overheard their names in the queue. When I had recognised one of the names, I had made the mistake of informing Richard of the significance. One of them, Oli, was the boyfriend of Georgie Thompson, the unfortunate and unsuspecting girl I had accosted in London, issuing invitations on the Gumball. Predictably, Richard had thought that this was hilarious when I told him what happened, and as soon as he realised who the Caterham driver was he wasted no time in introducing us. Richard had done this out of pure badness, as he reckoned there was a reasonable chance that Oli would have heard of my invitation from his former beloved. To my immense relief and Richard's disappointment, Oli showed no sign of whether he was aware of the fact or not. In fairness to Richard, I do not think that I would have resisted the opportunity for mischief either had the tables been turned.

Oli and his co-driver seemed a lot more concerned about the wine situation. We had arrived at the table and promptly devoured the contents of whatever wine was in whatever bottles that had the misfortune to be in range. We did not give it a lot of thought, and as soon as it was pointed out that these bottles had been ordered by our new Caterham friends, we happily ordered replacements but sadly the waiters did not share our sense of urgency. After some time, the wine had still not arrived and they disappeared muttering about thieving Volvo boys rather more vociferously than either the quality or quantity of the wine merited. Richard, who is a hospitable and generous character, was slightly taken aback at the suggestion that he did not get his round in; we did however see the funny side and wondered aloud that, on that evidence, the potential reaction had Miss Thompson accepted the invitation might have been quite something.

At this dinner, the food was a little disturbing. There was great debate about whether it was chicken or fish. Ordinarily, this would have been an obvious distinction, but since the question had been raised we thought it best to decide by the results of a quick poll. Unfortunately, this failed to come up with a definitive decision since the vote was split exactly 50–50, resulting in the table collectively rejecting the dish whatever it was. Thankfully, the drink had arrived by this stage and spirits rose again.

It became clear that the Irish boys were looking a little shaken since Bob, at the wheel of the Hummer, had not been holding back. As they spent the day being continually overtaken by cars going flat out, Bob had not been able to resist racing the other yellow Hummer when they came across it coming into Marrakech. A Hummer is built for bulk not speed, and apparently it came into its own on a head-to-head. Outright top speed mattered less when the roads simply emptied on being confronted with two raging trucks. John winced with particular feeling when he recalled that Bob had 'lost the back end' going the wrong way around a roundabout.

It is a great truism that nobody likes to think they are a bad driver. People will begrudgingly admit at a push that their choice of music might not be to everyone's liking or their taste in fashion might strike some as less appealing than others, but no one likes to be slagged about their driving. Bob's response was to open a can of worms of driving horrors from the Hummer. Mark seemed to have been fairly exempt from the criticism, presumably as a) he owned the Hummer and b) he had acquitted himself with some respectability in single-seat racing. John and Steve were not so lucky and, if the stories were to be believed, driving with Richard sounded positively relaxing in comparison. It would be impolite to name names, but apparently one of them had taken out a barrier at a French tollbooth much to the horror of the rest of the Hummer's occupants. There was some, unsubstantiated, suggestion that, as the toll was close to the Spanish border, it was just as simple to keep going, screaming something about brake failure to the bewildered *péage* employee.

It was difficult to tell if any of this had actually happened or was the result of grossly exaggerated teasing, as the four of them engaged in an incessant line of banter that had Richard and me repeatedly in fits of laughter, while their conversational routines would continue unabated in a deadpan fashion. After they had finished shredding each other's driving ability, they began to berate the Hummer for its lack of speed.

'I tell you it got quite tedious today, sitting in the Hummer at 100 mph, while every Tom, Dick and Harry flies past you,' John stated in quite serious tones. 'If it wasn't for us making our own fun to amuse ourselves, the days would be very long indeed,' he continued.

'Oh yes, four blokes in a car, we know how to make our own fun,' added Mark. I looked at Richard and realised that, yes, he too, was beginning to wonder where this was going. 'Making that porn movie, for instance . . . that was a laugh, wasn't it, lads?' Now I was really concerned.

'Porn movie?' I ventured.

'Well, you know, boys will be boys; we had the camera so it seemed like a fun idea,' Steve said, laughing.

No, actually I did not know. I was fully aware that light entertainment was required to keep the jovial ambience in the car alive, but the thought of making a 'boys will be boys' porn movie had not entered our minds and I was sure it was not just because we did not have a camera. We had got as far as working out our porn-star names, by taking your first pet's name and combining it with your mother's maiden name. It was definitely entertaining as we speculated whether my 'Fudge McMeekin' would be a bigger box-office hit than Richard's 'Nipper Thrale' but we had stopped short of giving the characters a screen debut.

'We cracked the hundred-positions' target; four ways offers a lot of combinations. After that, it just got silly when they all joined in,' John continued, now grinning as it became clear that there was more to the story.

All that is required to make a hard-core porn movie on the move was apparently for sale in any good continental motorway service in the form of Gummi Bears, those miniature little jelly sweets. Most of us will admit to a puerile moment of setting up copulating Gummi Bears or Jelly Babies, but these guys had taken the idea to new heights, and staged a full-blown orgy on the dashboard. It was fifteen minutes long with full sound effects and assorted voice-overs, and they had high hopes of finding a backer when they got to Cannes for the Gumball party at the Film Festival. A lot of thought had gone into it and, as they explained the plot, it was clear that this was more than your average 'boy comes to clean pool' script.

'They were all at it like rabbits, those Gummi Bears. Even the ugly little pasty see-through guy that nobody likes got laid,' explained Steve, practising his pitch for the producers.

After the meal and the show, Richard disappeared. I assumed that he had gone for his quiet night. Good for him, I thought, but I am off to the club for the party. As I left the hotel, a fellow Gumballer introduced himself. His name was Aidan, and he explained that he recognised me from driving with Richard; he was a big fan and asked if I would introduce him? Aidan was a third-generation bookie, hence his familiarity with Richard and his achievements. Of course, I could introduce him, but he would have to wait until tomorrow, as I explained, 'Richard's not as young as he was when he was riding his winners, you see, and he's having a night in.'

At that point Richard appeared, bobbing up and down in much the same way as he did in the car. I looked at him and noticed that he had indeed been to the room, but not for a lie down. He had gone to engage in some of his mixing and matching and emerged in Cordings finest. This unusually high level of bobbing, even by his own lofty standards, indicated he was in a rush.

'Right, come on, where's the party?' he said hurriedly.

'Whoa, Richard, settle down for a second. Meet Aidan, he's a bookie.'

'Hi, Aidan, good to meet you. Do you know where the party is?'

'Hello, Richard, nice to meet you too. The party is in the town somewhere, a taxi drive away,' Aidan replied, a little taken aback.

'Right, come on, let's get a taxi.' Richard bobbed off towards the rank.

'Don't mind him, Aidan, he's not usually like that. Well, actually he is, but normally that's because he wants to get somewhere quickly in the car. I think he's decided that a "quiet night" means cramming his usual length of session into a highlights package. I can't think of any other reason he's in such a rush.'

'No worries, mate. I've got to wait for my pals, but I'll catch up with you guys later,' he replied affably.

I sauntered over to the taxi rank where Richard was agitatedly trying to flag taxis off the main road in a high-speed version of three languages. He was with Chris, who was driving the London taxi on the rally, a fabulously laidback individual, who hadn't seen this side of Richard before either. We exchanged looks that said 'Ignore him until he finds the taxi.'

The taxi was a Fiat Uno, curiously bedecked with beads and buttons, and blaring Moroccan music. After three days of bombing around at breakneck speed, it was a thoroughly weird sensation to be travelling at 10 mph. The taxi driver, for whatever reason, saw absolutely no reason to go any faster. He saw no reason either for Richard to wear his seat belt, possibly because he felt a crash at 10 mph was unlikely. I think Richard wisely thought that, no matter what speed, a crash was infinitely possible as a direct result of whatever our driver had been smoking. He eventually won the seat-belt argument and the driver really should have been thankful as it restricted the range of his movements. Richard was still in a mad rush and consequently jumping around. Up until now my in-car experiences of this had been in a sturdy Volvo, and they had been unsettling purely because one wondered about his ability to drive at the same time. In a lightweight Fiat Uno, he physically unsettled the car, as it jumped up and down to his rhythm. I felt a dancing joke coming on, but decided it was not the time. Chris and I merely convulsed in laughter in the back.

The nightclub in Marrakech would not have been out of place in Soho, with lashings of chrome fixtures and fittings, populated by bright young things. Before long, it became clear that it was just too hard-core for some of the more fatigued Gumballing crowd. In a not very rock 'n' roll vibe, Gumballers began heading back to the hotel. Rumours were circulating that there was quite a posse gathering in there, and the ambience was less techno. Richard had been doing a bit of circulating himself and, deciding that he was getting too old for the likes of Marrakech's trendiest spots, announced he was off to the hotel club. I told him that I'd hang around for a while and see him later.

My motivation for hanging around was Mandy. For some reason, and it was certainly no good reason, I had got it into my head that she was flirting with me a little. After Richard departed I found her again with Sonia and Sonia's love interest, Conor. A nice little gang, we could have been double-dating.

'Hi, guys, I'm a bit too wrecked for this carry-on. I'm thinking of heading back to the hotel,' I said.

'Yeah, we were thinking the same; we can all share a taxi then,' Mandy replied.

That's all the encouragement that I needed to convince myself I was on to a racing certainty. It is most unclear what evidence I had apart from the potent Moroccan wine, but I was in no doubt at all. Back at the hotel, as I interpreted it, there was the inevitable playing for time, while Conor and Sonia went about the business of sloping off. Meanwhile, I was trying to steer Mandy in the direction of the residents' bar. Mandy set off in the opposite direction with purpose. Oh yes, here's a development then, I thought.

'Not in the market for a late-night drink, then, Mandy?'

'No, I'm going straight to bed,' she replied in a distinctive tone: a tone that said 'And you can clear off!' Unfortunately, it was a tone only perceptible to a sober man. To someone who had indulged in local beverages it said: 'Go on, my son, you're in there!'

'Wahey, straight to bed, eh? Is that a bit of an invitation, Mandy?'

'I think not, Clement,' she replied in a tone that very definitely clarified matters. Just in case I had not quite got the message, she wisely followed up with a raised eyebrow in a look of annoyance and incredulity. As she wandered into the lift, she finished off with a mirthful chuckle that plainly said, 'You are as stupid as you look if you think I would invite you to my room.'

Looking and feeling that stupid, I felt I needed another drink, and headed for the hotel nightclub. In a darkened basement with an abundance of mirrors, it was as seedy as the other place was trendy. Nearly every guy in the place seemed to be a Gumballer and there seemed to be scores of girls around, huddled in their own groups. Richard was settling in at the bar. In my absence, he seemed to have caught up with Aidan and introduced himself properly. He had also stopped hopping around madly, which was a welcome relief to all. It must have been the effects of a soothing drink, and I made a mental note never to offer him a Vodka and Red Bull.

'Hello, chaps. Richard, I thought you were having a quiet night!'

'I am just having a quiet drink, getting to know Aidan here. His dad was a well-known bookie. Aidan now bets full-time on the exchanges. An "internet entrepreneur", as it were.'

Here we go. Horse chat. I looked for my escape, and saw a Moroccan guy, chatting animatedly nearby. I still felt I needed to meet some Moroccans after our surreal day. I began to move away from Aidan and Richard.

'Wait, Clement, where are you off to?' Aidan asked hurriedly.

'To talk to that Moroccan guy; we have to make some effort.'

'Oh, I wouldn't do that; he's been pestering us. He's a pimp and he is trying to hoist a load of prostitutes on us and the rest of the Gumballers; he won't take no for an answer.'

Richard confirmed matters. 'Honestly, he harassed us for ages. When he heard I was a jockey and Aidan was a bookie, he tried to sell us the idea of staging a Gumball race through the hotel. His idea was that Aidan would open a book on it.'

'What do you mean a Gumball race?'

'Ten Gumballers and ten girls through the hotel foyer. Bareback. For some reason he thinks I should be favourite,' Richard continued.

'Leave it out, lads, you're taking the piss.'

'Honestly, it's true; he's looking for runners and riders at the minute. It'll never happen though; the hotel surely wouldn't allow it.'

Bedtime, I decided. I had seen and heard enough Moroccan madness for one day. As I emerged from the nightclub into the car park, a Porsche Cayenne was undergoing a highly elaborate pit-stop outside the hotel. Closer inspection revealed that the gearbox was receiving emergency attention in the form of a replacement. There was quite a crowd gathered, and I turned to one chap who was armed to the teeth with spanners.

'Where on earth did they find a Cayenne gearbox in Marrakech?'

'Simple, they flew it in by private jet,' he replied matter-of-factly.

11. MOROCCAN MADNESS (PART 2)

At 8 a.m. be in your vehicles ready to follow the Wali of
Marrakech (The Mayor) on a short 'parade drive' from the
hotel to the Medina, where the flag will drop and you'll be
on the road towards the ancient city of Fez.

Eight a.m.? Not a chance. By 9.30 a.m., we had dragged
ourselves out of bed and checked out of the hotel. The car park
was still chock-a-block with everyone jostling for position to get
out first. Sadly, the arrangement of cars at the hotel meant first
in last night was last out this morning, so we had some extra
loitering to do.

Richard appeared with a photographer called James, who
needed a lift for the day. Despite Richard's form in offering all
manner of idiots a lift, James was a good lad. I had met him
before and, apart from anything else, it would be very useful to
have some photos. Since our camera had run out of batteries in
Paris, it had idled in the back seat.

One thing James was not useful for was directions. After
screeching around the Medina in our high-speed parade lap, we
shot straight past the sign for 'Fez' as James indicated straight on.
I was driving, with two conflicting navigators. Two minds were
certainly not better than one in this case. In fairness to Richard,
he was shouting to go the correct way, but it seemed more fun to
give him a taste of his own medicine and simply ignore him.

That is how we ended up in it what is best described as a
shanty town. Having realised our mistake, we tried to be clever
and, instead of turning around, took a short cut through
Shitsville. Kids, camels, donkeys, stray dogs and gnarled men with

no teeth were everywhere, a perfect photo opportunity. We stopped outside what looked like a shop, but smelled like a morgue, and were mobbed by the kids. It was difficult to tell who was more excited – James or the kids. James was snapping away deliriously having finally had an opportunity to get some human-interest shots that did not involve suicidal overtaking manoeuvres.

Back on the road, James explained that the life of a Gumball photographer was fraught with danger. In order to get the best shots, he needed to lean out of the rear windows, while cars weaved in and out of traffic. We realised that he was the nutter in – or rather hanging out of – the AMG Merc we had been chasing at high speeds yesterday. I had been terrified simply watching him, hanging on with one hand as the car lunged from side to side, and adjusting his shutter speed with the other. He explained all this in a rather matter-of-fact manner, as if it was all in a day's work. Later, he admitted his ultimate ambition was to be a war photographer, which explained a thing or two.

An hour out of Marrakech we swung on to a long straight road and saw quite a commotion in the distance. A long line of cars was parked on the side of the road, and there was quite a gathering in the field off it. It was unlike Gumballers to stop for anything other than a party so something was clearly up.

We pulled in at roughly the point where a monster set of skid marks left the road, and saw that an Escort Cosworth had finally come to a halt some 300 yards beyond that, and was now lying on its roof, having scattered its contents over some distance. The driver was up and about, apparently without serious injury but obviously in a state of extreme shock. His co-driver had been filming at the time, and not strapped in, and he was thrown from the car with the rest of the contents. By the time we arrived, he had already left in an ambulance and the extent of his injuries was unknown.

It was a sobering sight for one and all. Except James. Now he had some human-interest shots combined with the evidence of a suicidal overtaking manoeuvre.

'Sorry, guys, I know it's morbid, but I have to get some shots.'
He would make a fine war photographer some day.

Morbid wasn't the word. From surveying the wreckage, it was
difficult to see how anyone not wearing a seat belt could have
survived such a tumble. The car had clearly barrel-rolled a
number of times and both front and rear ends were to all intents
and purposes missing. It had a full roll cage, which had held
up well under the circumstances, but it was impossible not to
imagine the very worst, picturing a passenger being thrown
around bouncing off the cage.

Tish, the press officer, was going about her job telling us to
move on; there was nothing to see here. She confirmed the
passenger was alive. Max was parked on the side of the road
with a look that was praying for best and fearing the worst.

In a more serious frame of mind, we pressed on and eased
off, agreeing to maintain a sensible pace for the day and make
the most of the Moroccan scenery. Though not literally.

Some thirty minutes later, we came across another congregation of Gumball cars, and immediately feared the worst
particularly as they were parked on the side of a steep cliff.
Thankfully, the gathering was simply feeling like us, having
experienced the same reaction as we had to the crash, and was
taking time out to enjoy a fine view of the Atlas Mountains. We
stopped to join them.

The highly modified Cayenne, with the private jet support
crew, had blown its gearbox again, and all the others were
simply chilling out. We chatted to Aidan for a while, admiring
his Lamborghini Murcielago and soaked in the sober atmosphere.

I was mesmerised by the Atlas Mountains. Having driven
extensively on the mountain roads of the French Alps and the
Pyrenees, enjoying hairpin after hairpin, I was finding all the
straight motorways and roads of the Gumball somewhat
monotonous. I had mentioned this to Richard on a number of
occasions and now I was pointing excitedly into the distance.

'Wow, Richard, look at that; we're going up there this afternoon.'

I got the impression that he did not share my enthusiasm.

No matter where, or in what conditions, you are driving, if you witness the scene of an accident, it will have two guaranteed effects. Firstly, you will slow down to get a good look at the carnage, praying that all involved are safe, while simultaneously rubber-necking to see as much gory detail as possible. And, secondly, as you drive on, your speed will be tempered by what you have just seen. Sadly, though, an equally guaranteed fact is that you will have forgotten all this half an hour later and will revert to your old ways.

The first indicator that things were back to Gumball normal-ity was my overtaking an ambulance. In my defence, I must stress that it was holding us up. I had often thought that one of the quickest ways to travel by road would be to follow an ambulance that was speeding to an emergency with sirens blaring, but from first-hand experience on the road to Fez I can assure you that theory does not always stack up.

We then came across a couple of Gumballers, a Ferrari 360 and Aidan in his Lambo. We all pulled out to overtake a Moroccan car and, when the other two pulled back, I kept my foot down and passed them. Richard was shaking his head.

'Christ, I just told them we were taking it easy,' he scolded.

'We are taking it easy; I just couldn't resist those two.'

Meanwhile, James, in full action-man mode, complete with multi-purpose combat waistcoat for film and stuff, was dis-gusted to think that we might be taking it easy, and his disappointment led to despair as we came across a long line of local traffic. He looked behind us and saw that we were leading a pack of about six Gumball cars.

'Lads, go up the Gumball Lane,' he suggested. The 'Gumball Lane', as I have mentioned, is a euphemistic term for the hard shoulder. It looked a bit treacherous and dusty. 'Please,' implored James, 'I can hang out the back, and it will make for some great shots with the dust and the following cars.'

I had to concede it was another good photo opportunity. 'What do you reckon, Richard?'

'Sure, what harm can it do? Be careful of those puddles, though, they could be deceptively deep.'

'OK, James, we're going for it; get yourself out of the window and in position and give a good bang on the roof when you're ready. And, if you hear Richard banging on the side, get back in instantly.'

James manoeuvred himself and his cameras into position, as I noticed that a Mitsubishi EVO behind was having much the same idea. Behind the EVO was the usual collection of Lamborghinis and Ferraris and I felt fairly confident that their ground clearance would not be up to following us. It was all happening in the Gumball Lane and the last thing that we needed was a traffic jam.

With far more confidence than his actions merited, James hammered the roof. I hammered the throttle, on to the hard shoulder, and pulled alongside the Moroccan cars. The Mitsubishi followed and James snapped happily.

I was aware of what was going on behind and in front, but not alongside, apart from the fact that we were rather ignorantly undertaking, as opposed to overtaking, the traffic. I looked intently ahead, partly because it required all my concentration to dodge the puddles, but also because, out of the corner of my eye, I was dimly aware of Richard's discomfort. He had the unfortunate position in the passenger seat of getting a close-up view of the Moroccan attitude to this style of driving and, as he grimaced, I sensed that they were understandably not best pleased.

Looking ahead, I saw some added complications, in the form of a few of the infamous stray camels and donkeys and an almighty and unavoidable puddle. Also ahead was a service station. Looking behind I noticed that the Mitsubishi was having trouble getting off the Gumball Lane as the following pack had closed in tightly. At this point, there were a few decisions to be made to say the least.

The sensible thing would have been to simply plough on straight ahead, avoiding the strays and pull into the service station as if that had been our intended destination all along. That was the sensible thing at the time and, unfortunately, that old chestnut about hindsight confirms it beyond doubt.

I was toying with this idea when, to add insult to injury, I ploughed through the puddle creating a bit of splash. If we were looking for a silver lining, at least this wave brought James back into the car fairly smartly, but had the unfortunate side effect of drenching the adjacent traffic. Another negative consequence was that the splash had woken, and visibly angered, a few camels and donkeys, who looked dangerously ready to lunge.

The EVO had got back on to the road, and now there was a gap for us to slot back in. Splendid. Back where we started, but things were only just beginning to hot up. It was all getting a bit crowded and I was keen to make a bid for freedom away from stray animals, Gumballers and angry natives. A camel stood up with intent and I pulled into the middle of the road to give it a wide berth, and simultaneously to explore any potential overtaking opportunities.

'OK, go, clear for two,' Richard shouted with authority and confidence.

We had been operating this 'clear for one, two, three, four or whatever' overtaking system throughout Morocco. With the better view, it was the passenger's responsibility to judge whether it was safe to overtake. This had worked with no problems at all, and, of course, the vastly superior power and acceleration of our car compared to the average Moroccan runabout made the whole operation straightforward.

In this instance, it was not quite so straightforward as we encountered traffic that deliberately bunched up to make absolutely sure that we not would not be able to get back in after the two. Undoubtedly, this bunching was as a direct result of our previous antics and I had to admit that I could not really blame them.

Your average Moroccan runabout is a twenty-year-old Mercedes and it was one of these that was heading straight for us now. A quick check of the mirrors confirmed that two Gumballers had decided to follow our overtaking lead rendering any sudden braking a little tricky.

Hitherto, I had revelled in the Volvo V70R's power, pace and comfort. I had not given a lot of thought to its other great strength – namely, its great strength. Numerous detractors had disparagingly likened it to a tank, but with a certain crash on the way, it was a tank I was happy to be in. I felt utterly confident that, with the abundance of airbags – there was even one in the roof – and the solid frame, we were going to escape the rapidly impending road-traffic incident relatively unharmed. I was delighted with our car.

Indeed, at that split second in time, if there had not been so much going on to distract my attention, I would have turned to Richard with a told-you-so tone, and said, 'Hah, I bet you're pleased we're in a Volvo now, eh? And while we're here, I'm sure you'll agree that travel insurance I recommended is looking like a pretty good buy.' There is a time and place for such smugness, and this was categorically not it, but I made a quick mental note to crack the joke later.

So, the Volvo was going to look after our interests, but it's a great truism that one man's gain is another man's loss. As we were getting increasingly closer to Benny Maroc, I am sure that he was not so pleased we were in a sturdy Volvo. In his rusty Merc, I knew that if we crashed into him he was as good as dead; the plan must be to avoid hitting him at all costs, even if it meant a nastier accident for ourselves.

Of course, he could not know what on earth was going on in my head, and could have been forgiven for thinking that it was not a great deal. As I went for the hard shoulder, so did he. Thinking he was making a bid for safety, I turned back into the road and so did he. He was like a magnet, whichever way we went, he followed. There was only one thing for it – I was going to have to launch our car right off the road. But we were going to have to leave the road at pace.

With the vast acceleration differential between the two cars, I was confident that if I floored the throttle we would miss the Mercedes even if he decided to head in the same direction, in other words, our paths would cross in a diagonal but without impact. If I braked, a collision was unavoidable. Thankfully, as I unleashed a vast surge of acceleration, although he headed for the same escape route, he braked and, like ships that pass in the night, we shot straight past his nose. After some furious braking, he came to a safe halt on the hard shoulder, as we became airborne.

Phew, we missed him, but now our problems were only just beginning. From the relative safety of the road, the field off it looked to be fairly innocuous. A big, dusty, open space. The ideal place to land a flying Volvo. I hadn't counted on the blind spot concealing a bloody great trench followed by an enormous, wide drainage ditch. The trench was dealt with in flight, but that time in the air cost us some precious braking ability, and consequently we hit the ditch at a considerable speed, nose first and heading for the apex. If we hit that apex head first, the car was going to roll.

What happened next remains a considerable point of debate between Richard and me. He maintains that our exit from the ditch in one piece was a sheer fluke, while my side of the story insists that it was only fortunate in as far as my evasive driving worked as intended. Whatever the case, it's largely irrelevant since Richard always wins the moral high ground by reminding me that we should not really have been in the ditch in the first place.

Suffice it to say that the rear end of car, whether by accident or design, suddenly flicked around and hit the apex at such an angle that the momentum sent us back up the way we came: out of the ditch and towards the road. I managed to straighten up(ish) the car and fishtail along the side of the road in the dust.

Hard braking was still not an option, as that would have caused a spin, and controlling the twitchy, fishtailing rear end was a more pressing concern. The car was still not completely under control but things were definitely looking up.

At this stage, the car was still undamaged. It would be unrealistic to suggest that 'there wasn't a scratch on her', since the vast quantities of sand, stones and dust pluming from its backside would undoubtedly have had a detrimental effect on the paintwork, but given its unorthodox route to get to this point it was holding up fairly well. Perhaps I would not have to make that awkward phone call to Volvo after all.

No such luck. Straight ahead was a fairly substantial concrete bollard supporting a road-safety warning, the wording of which escaped me. Sadly, the car did not escape the bollard. It started its campaign of terror on the front headlight, tore off the front wing and made steady progress ripping its way down one side of the car: Richard's side incidentally, something that later sparked another 'accident or design' debate.

Anyway, at least it slowed us down. We came to a halt shortly after that, but a considerable distance from where we originally left the road. Some distance behind us our following troupe of Gumballers had pulled in and were looking through the dust to see where we'd got to. There were some mighty relieved faces, when they eventually realised we'd popped up in front of them. By their description of proceedings, it seems it looked scarier to watch than it was to experience.

Assessing the damage revealed that the most immediate problems were the front wheel and wing. The bollard cum tin-opener had done such a comprehensive job on the wing that removing it was simply a matter of giving it a light tug.

A large group of Moroccan men were congregating, chewing tobacco and spitting great wads into the dust. They had the look of a lynch mob, which would have been fair enough, but amazingly they were on hand to help and immediately set about removing the wheel. All that was left for us to do was to locate the spare. Easier said than done. It was buried in the cavernous boot of the car, not only under our entire luggage supply but also under the 'woofer', and when after some twenty minutes we managed to locate it we discovered it was a damn 'spacesaver'. A 'spacesaver' is one of those spindly, skinny little tyres that you see on Fiat Puntos, so the spare wheel does not take up the entire boot. What the hell was one doing in a Volvo estate with an enormous boot? The shagging woofer that had taken us a good half-hour to extract could have done with some economies of space itself. A dispirited glance at the wheel confirmed it was for emergency use only – 'DO NOT EXCEED 50 MPH'. Fifty mph? We had a ferry to catch, a grand prix to see and a 1,200-mile drive at 50 mph was not possible.

Our Moroccan mechanic deftly changed the wheel and then refused payment. Once again, it occurred to me that we were experiencing a very different sort of Moroccan to the stereotypical harassment-for-money tactics. If any one deserved harassment for money, it was us, as well as owing a liberal helping for recklessly endangering other road users.

Eventually, after a good three-quarters of an hour, and some profuse thanks and apologies, we were back on the road and it was time for a post-mortem. None of us had spoken much, except to curse at the woofer, and generally concentrate on the task in hand. First, I had to commend Richard and James for their composure.

'Lads, I have to say a big thanks that you guys remained so calm. Nothing would have been worse than if you two had been whooping and screaming and making unhelpful suggestions.'

Richard raised an eyebrow. 'I just thought it best to sit that one out and see what happened,' he said.

James, on the other hand, couldn't contain his excitement. Richard was displaying a steely calm; I was coming out of shock but James was high on adrenaline. 'Wow, Clement, great driving,' he roared enthusiastically. Richard looked at him as if he was mad. James carried on excitedly, 'My very own Gumball experience, what fun. You hear all these stories, but I have been sitting in all these different cars for the last few days, and nothing happens. Then I hop in with you guys and we have a great crash. Good work, fellas!'

I looked at him for a moment. 'James, have you had a bash to the head?' I asked.

'Oh, yes, I wasn't wearing a seat belt and I got thrown about a bit, but I'm all right.'

Richard started to laugh. There was a definite childish humour developing in the car, with a reluctance to acknowledge how serious the incident was.

'What's so funny, Richard?'

'Well, I think it's the best thing that could have happened to us. I'm delighted that you narrowly avoided killing us this morning, before you had an opportunity to do a really great job of it this afternoon up in those mountains.'

Well, all was fine then; everyone was in super form whereas I had been expecting a particularly frosty reception. For future reference, if you are going to subject passengers to a frightening car crash, you'd do a lot worse than to make sure that they are a wannabe war photographer and a retired jockey.

Once again, Richard was off, chuckling to himself.

'Now what's so funny?'

'Do you know why all those cars bunched up and wouldn't let you back in?' he asked.

'Presumably because they didn't appreciate being undertaken on the hard shoulder. I'd say the splash didn't help either.'

'It was a funeral procession.'

I looked at him in horror. 'Tell me you're not serious?'

'I'm deadly serious. I saw them when we were alongside, the coffin, the mourners, the whole shebang.'

'Hmm, Richard, you might have mentioned that. Do you not think that might have been a useful piece of information to know?' I said haughtily, and looked at him seriously.

With the merest hint of a grin, but in a completely deadpan tone he simply replied, 'Mentioned it? I was speechless. I could not believe you were undertaking the undertakers.'

I am ashamed to say that we all roared with laughter.

Moving on to more serious matters we were concerned how the car had held up. While it had clearly taken quite a knock, potentially it was only cosmetic damage. It was impossible to tell from driving it since it was all over the road, as you would expect with one wheel a fifth of the size of the rest. More disturbingly, there was a big notice on the dashboard announcing in a cheery manner: 'You have 4 New Messages.' Four new messages? We're in luck. We had been staring at this '0 New Messages' chat for two thousand miles and it had caused much speculation as to what a message might be. Was it connected to the in-car phone? Was it going to wish me Happy Birthday? It is safe to say that speculating as to what they might be was a lot more fun than actually reading the delivered missives.

Select 1st New Message – Brake Settings Service Required.

Select 2nd New Message – Engine Settings Service Required.

Select 3rd New Message – Chassis Settings Service Required.

Select 4th New Message – Skid Control Settings Service Required.

Hmm. Well there's a bit of news. It's amazing what these onboard computers can do nowadays. I think the above was a polite way of pointing out that we had just had a crash. I'm sure that if the Volvo hadn't been so family orientated it might have been tempted to deliver a simpler message along the lines of 'You idiot, the car's rightly fucked.'

We proceeded as quickly as we dared on the spacesaver – about 80–90 mph. We had to make the ferry at Nador, or else we would be spending the night in the ferry terminal and would miss the Grand Prix in Barcelona.

At the next town, there was yet another commotion. Towns were always busy, and normally upon entry the spectators would be attempting to crowd the car, while the police batoned them out of the way, waving us through at speed. We knew something was up in this town since, as soon as we entered the main drag, the spectators saw us and made a run for it, giving us as wide a berth as possible.

Coming out of the far side of a roundabout, we realised why. A Ferrari 360 had pulled in with a shattered wheel rim, broken in four places.

'Jesus, you must have given that some smack. What happened?'

'We lost the back end coming around that roundabout, applied it a little too much opposite lock and spun. We twatted the wheel off that kerb.'

'What speed were you doing?'

'About 90 mph.'

The in-town speed limit was 20 mph. It sounds reckless behaviour, but you have to remember that this sort of thing unfolded right under the police's nose. Indeed, they were positively encouraging it. Every town we passed through was manned with police and security, clearing our passage for us to drive through as quickly as possible.

Even so, losing it at a roundabout at 90 mph in a packed town was pretty stupid by any circumstances. I was tempted to laugh until the 360 driver pointed at our car, now proudly missing its wing.

'What happened to you then?' he asked.

'I had to take some evasive action on the hard shoulder, came off the road and hit a bollard.'

'Right.' He nodded, thinking that seemed a reasonable explanation but something was not quite right. Then he twigged. 'How come it's the passenger side wing missing then?'

'It wasn't our hard shoulder; it was on the far side.'

I forgot about laughing.

His problems were significantly greater than ours were though. For all my cursing of the spacesaver, at least we had something that would keep us moving. The Ferrari had nothing, and now he was facing the unattractive prospect of leaving it at a local garage in the depths of Morocco until he could find a tow truck or replacement wheel. A long wait, I would think.

Having left him, it was only another fifteen minutes before we came across the next casualty. We had come off the straight bits by now, and the roads, although excellently surfaced, were undulating, twisting and turning. We came round one bend to be greeted with the now familiar site of shocked-looking Gumballers speculating as to how the latest disaster might have occurred – in this case a Ferrari 360 Spider had spun off the road at 180 degrees, and gone backwards into a tree. Deflated airbags were hanging out of the side of the car and, despite having gone in backwards, the front was as mangled as the rear. Apparently, he had hit a tractor. Miraculously, there were no injuries, apart from the odd scratch.

Emma, the ersatz porn star, had been in this car at the time as opposed to her normal transport of a Bentley Continental GT. Rumour had it that she had been chatting to the Ferrari driver at the petrol station, and, with a flutter of the eyelashes and an 'ooh, what a nice car, I have never been in a Ferrari before', had arranged to go for a short spin, though not quite as literally as things had turned out.

This particular Ferrari driver had been one of the noticeably more sensible Gumballers and, when we first realised who it was, we were somewhat surprised. After hearing that he had a passenger, his momentary brain fade explained itself. With all six foot two inches of Emma in the car, excited by his big red Ferrari, the smart money was on this particular driver momentarily thinking through his trousers. The foolish money now was going to have to be spent sorting out this wreckage, which looked suspiciously like a write-off. The look on his face suggested that he was facing the realities of a third-party insurance policy on a leased Ferrari.

However, his loss was another man's gain. Now the chaps in the 360 who'd lost it on the roundabout had themselves a spare wheel.

Back on the round, we decided to skip Fez. Our off-roading excursion had cost us a lot of time and the direct consequences were now seriously affecting our average speed. A look at the maps indicated that there was a right turn at a major crossroads and that would cut out a major chunk for us. All very simple apart from the inevitable squabbles involving the maps. Richard was driving at this stage, but predictably had not released full control of the navigational responsibilities.

What we had not counted on was the heavy police presence at the crossroads. Of course, they had been positioned there to stop any troublesome traffic and allow us to speed through unhindered. They were somewhat confused when we approached cautiously to ensure that this was the right turn that we wanted. Recognising the stickers, the police whooped themselves into a frenzy, waving madly, gesticulating towards the road to Fez.

I was quite glad that I was not driving, since I am not great at ignoring instructions from authority. I always tend to follow the road-traffic police's instructions. Richard, however, is excellent at doing his own thing, and showing a characteristic disregard for all that was going on around him, and concentrating only on what was going on in his head, swung right. Behind us, the police did not know what to do. They had been instructed by the King to send Gumballers speeding to Fez and now we had blatantly disregarded their orders. Two cops hopped on their bikes, lights on and came after us.

At long last, we had some Gumball police action, being chased by motorcycle cops, sirens blaring. The Gumball, particularly from its time in America, is famous for the role that the police play. Numerous annual Gumballers maintain the whole thing would be no fun without some heavy-handed cops, and the cat and mouse element of avoiding the speed traps and road blocks. We had yet to experience any of this, and I was secretly disappointed.

Thanks to the good old King of Morocco, our bad-ass, high-speed police chase was a bit of a farce. Firstly, on our puny spacesaver, we could not get away from them and, secondly, when they pulled us over, it was not to show us the error of our ways concerning bad-boy driving, but to show us our error in turning right. We gave them a couple of Gumball stickers to thank them for their helpfulness and explained that, since our accident, we had decided to skip Fez and make up time. Surveying the damage to the car, they seemed satisfied that we were hard core Gumballers after all, and this lapse in speed and behaviour was uncharacteristic. They let us off with a caution.

'OK, gentlemen, we understand why you're going slowly and respecting the speed limits. We'll let you go this time, but just get that wheel fixed as soon as possible and don't let it happen again.'

While obviously that's not exactly what they said, it's not far off it. And it was miles away from the reception two Gumballers in a Ferrari F50 received in Texas the previous year.

Gumballer: 'Sorry, officer, how fast was I going?'

State Trooper: '200 mph plus and now yo goin' to jail. You boys ain't from round here, are yo?'

Gumballer: 'No, sir, we're from London.'

State Trooper: 'Well, when yo get out of jail, I suggest yo get yourselves back to London. Cos yo'all not welcome round these parts.'

The Moroccans could definitely teach redneck Texans a few things about hospitality and manners.

Back on the rally route, we emerged in some Gumball traffic. Our car had definitely upped its Gumball factor as now every passing photographer and cameraman strained to get a picture or some footage of the wingless Volvo. In fact, such was the excitement it seemed odd that it was all purely on account of the missing wing. At the next fuel stop we had a closer look around the car and discovered that, while we had lost one wing, we had gained two more.

Roadkill! A rather exotic-looking, multicoloured bird had got itself wedged in the front radiator. The grill had scooped up much of the body bar the head and wings, leaving the beak facing straight ahead and the wings spanned across the grill. It looked like a rather upmarket mascot, similar to the flying wings of the Bentley badge. You could not have positioned it better if you tried and, while it looked great, the position sadly indicated that the poor bugger must have been flapping his wee heart out to try and fly away from us.

At this fuel stop we had the bonus of picking up a route card from Fez:

Head north from Fez following signs for Taza, Guercif and Taourit to Nador. Follow the towns listed – do NOT take another route, despite some road signs suggesting an alternate route to Nador. The other routes have very poor road surfaces.

Vindicated. A furious debate along these lines had developed in the car. From looking at the maps there appeared to be two alternative routes to Nador. I was adamant that we needed to establish which one we were supposed to take, and such information was easily available by simply flagging down another Gumball driver. Richard, for some unfathomable reason, simply refused. He insisted that we take what appeared to be the shorter route, but was clearly a monumental drive through a mountain range. I refused to agree with him, at which stage the debate was over, since he simply switched off.

By his own admission, he has this infuriating ability to shut his brain down. It is a sort of autistic mode, whereby he is locked into his own little world and does not hear reason from anyone. It is a particularly advanced form of stubbornness. Its not that he refuses to listen; when he gets into this mode he literally just does not hear you. I had been getting used to such levels of obtuseness, but James looked on aghast, only slightly amused by the professional standards of bickering.

I knew our only hope was to keep my fingers crossed that there might be another Gumballer refuelling when we stopped. With immense relief, I handed Richard the route card. He read it carefully.

'Well, we'll see what the road looks like when we get there.'

'Aargh!' I screamed out loud and perhaps even stamped my feet. 'Richard, you damn eejit, you've been telling me all day how important it is to catch that ferry and now you're going to fuck up all our good work by your intense stubbornness.'

'Good work? You crashed the car. I don't think you're in any position –'

'Just shut it.'

I just had to hope that he would see sense when we got there. Either that or I would have to enlist James and stage a mutiny, and leave him tied up in the boot with the maps stuffed in his mouth. In the meantime, we needed to eat.

Eating at service stations is the ultimate in fast food. Beloved by sales reps, truckers and any motorist in a hurry, it is most convenient simply to grab a sandwich as you pay for the fuel. We were pressed for time and Richard announced that he would go in and order us a cheese sandwich each. I sat down with James outside.

'Richard seems like a good bloke then,' said James.

'Most of the time, yes, but he can be infuriating,' I replied.

'Yeah, but you seem to get on together. How well do you know him?'

'A lot better now than I did this time last week.'

I was about to enlist James for the mutiny when Richard returned, having ordered the sandwiches. In high spirits, he began to tell us an indiscreet story. How we laughed. It was really most amusing, told against himself and involving a bit of splash and tickle in his hot tub. Instantly, I realised there was no need for a mutiny.

'Richard, we should write a book about our Gumballing adventures,' I suggested, not for the first time.

'Absolutely, do you think it would sell well?'

'Undoubtedly it would if we include all your anecdotes like that one,' I said, grinning.

There was nothing autistic about Richard's level of understanding now, as he said, 'We'll follow the rally route to Nador.'

After a good twenty minutes, it was clear that the Moroccans did not fully grasp the idea of eat 'n' dash service station food. When it finally arrived, it was also clear that they had not fully understood the request for sandwiches. They produced a veritable feast of kebabs, a glorious tomato salad and an assortment of breads. Richard swore he ordered sandwiches, and for once I believed that it was not his language skills that were at fault. There were five or six enormous carcasses of indeterminate origins hanging nearby, and I suspect the staff had seen us as an opportunity to make an impression on them. Whatever it was, it was delicious, if a little cannibalistic.

A chap in a Porsche pulled into the garage for fuel and wandered over to exchange pleasantries. He was looking a little flustered having created a bit of confusion in the last town. He explained how, for most of the afternoon, he had been enjoying a long dice with a TVR. The last town we passed through had a long straight road running through the middle and, as he approached, he noticed that there was the usual gaggle of kids waiting to wave the Gumballers through.

'And I suddenly realised that, if I threw all my stickers out of the window, they would scatter like confetti. The kids would scrabble around for ages to pick them up, and the TVR would be well held up.'

'Good thinking,' I said. 'But was it safe to do that?'

'Oh yes, no problem, the TVR was about a mile behind me, and as the road was so straight he would have seen all the kids in plenty of time. That was the idea anyway.'

'So what happened?'

'Well, I had a big stack of about two hundred sitting in the console above the gearbox tunnel. So I grabbed them and just flung them out the window.' He shook his head. 'It seems so obvious now though.'

'What seems so obvious?'

'Well, I hadn't thought of the heat. The stickers had been sitting there for three days and had all congealed together. It was a solid disc. Far from scattering like confetti, as soon as I threw them, they frisbeed out of the car, like a weapon of mass destruction. They hit some poor kid in the eye, and took him clean off his feet. And then all the kids piled on him to find the stickers. The sad thing is, I had deliberately thrown them in his direction to cheer him up. He looked miserable.'

We agreed that he was probably still fairly miserable. Once again, there was a surreal comic value in what had happened. One can imagine him going to school on Monday explaining away his shiner, saying, 'Honest, sir, I was not fighting again, I was hit in the eye with a stack of stickers thrown from a moving Porsche.' An unlikely story by any standards, and you could imagine his teacher adding to his woes with an extra stint of detention for not only fighting, but also lying about it.

We made steady and uneventful progress towards Nador and, thankfully, we went the right way. I think Richard still intended to do his own thing, but, at his favoured turn, we were greeted by the police who pointed out the traffic jam heading into the hills, and a large sign to indicate the road was more of a dirt track.

It was dusk at this stage, and in the distance we could pick up Gumballers' brake lights in a sequence, snaking around the route in procession. Suddenly they all jammed on and pulled in, with such immediacy that even from a mile or so away we knew something major had happened. Another crash, but unbelievably this crash eclipsed anything we had seen throughout the day. As we approached the gathering, there was debris everywhere. The front valance of whatever car had crashed was lying off the side road, isolated. The first impact from leaving the road would appear to have been a vertical smack on the nose, which had been ripped clean off. We pulled in, shocked and speechless. Whereas the previous crashes we had witnessed looked pretty senior, first impressions gave hope that the occupants sustained serious injuries rather than death. In this case, as we struggled to ascertain even what sort of car had been crashed, the first impressions were significantly worse.

A closer look at the front valance indicated without doubt the unfortunate victim – Torquenstein. The shrapnel discarded from his car was advertising his website www.torquenstein.net. Beyond that, it was difficult for anyone bar the dullest petrol-head anorak to recognise the car. What was easier to ascertain was what had happened. The ferocity of the damage to the front and the rear suggested that, as opposed to rolling in a conventional manner, the car had violently cartwheeled from end to end.

Once again, the Moroccan authorities were on hand to sort things out, with no hint of judgement. The early news was that Torquenstein and passenger were both alive, but seriously injured and had been taken away in an ambulance. The irony of his arrival by ambulance in Paris had not been wasted on anyone present.

Inspecting the wreckage I was struck for the third time that day (fourth if you include our crash) of just how well modern cars are constructed. While the car was to all intents and purposes unrecognisable, the central section where the occupants were seated was bashed and bruised a bit, but had held up surprisingly well. The airbags had been activated, and there was a gruesome smattering of blood, but encouragingly it was possible to imagine some survivors.

The Ferrari that had gone into the tree had been the same. It had hit a tractor at high speed, which had ripped the front off and then sent it spinning backwards into a tree. The wreckage was terribly dramatic to look at and obviously the car was banjaxed, but the cockpit was basically unharmed as were the occupants. The Cosworth had a roll cage, which had done its job admirably, and any serious injuries had to be apportioned to the stupidity of not wearing seat belts.

I mention this because, in a curious way, it's actually terribly heartening to see outrageous accidents that have taken place at such monumental speeds. You don't often get the chance. We are all familiar with the crash-test procedures of modern manufacturers. They belt those odd-looking dummies with black and yellow ears into the car, and send them off to meet a wall at 30 mph. Well that's all very well but it does not translate into the real world where a car might cartwheel off the road at 140 mph, or where a red-blooded male will stuff his Ferrari into a tractor. These things do happen, as we had witnessed that day, and, although I doubt the testing procedures involve unrestrained speeds on African roads, it's encouraging that modern vehicles are well prepared for it.

That said, despite the fact that we could have confidence in our cars, all Gumballers departed the scene of Torquenstein's epic accident in a slightly more subdued frame of mind. There were only seventy-odd miles left of Moroccan madness to the ferry, and they were completed by one and all at no more than 60 mph.

As we departed, James was the first to speak, capturing the mood with a long sigh, and a simple 'Wow, that was quite something. It really makes you think.' We simply nodded our agreement. He moved forwards and stuck his head through the front seats. 'I'm really glad I wasn't in a car with some mad bastard today.'

I looked at Richard in surprise. He looked at me, then at James and, jerking his thumb in my direction, incredulous, he exclaimed, 'What, you mean like this mad bastard?!'

12. NADOR TO BARCELONA

Nador ferry

The subdued mood spread through the ferry. After all the worry about not making the 11.00 p.m. departure time, the ferry was going nowhere fast. Max had still not arrived, and it made sense to assume he had been delayed somewhere, tending to the carnage.

On my first attempt to find our accommodation, I headed for Cabin 416 and, sure I was in the right spot, just wandered in. The lights were off and Richard was in the bunk as I crashed around dumping my luggage and generally making a nuisance of myself.

'What the hell are you doing?' Richard asked.

'I'm looking for my bed, the bathroom or at least the damn light switch.'

The lights shot on, and the Norwegian racing driver shot up and shot me a glare. 'You won't find your bed in here, now piss off.'

We had met this guy in the queue on the ferry going to Morocco. He had told us that, as well as being a racing driver, he worked as a commentator and, as such, it was a matter of life and death that he made it to Barcelona where he was covering the Grand Prix. Presumably, he had hit the sack as soon as he got on the boat to get a good night's sleep in preparation. As I slunk out of the room, I thought better of telling him not to be so narky as the boat still had not left yet, and he was highly unlikely to be clocking in for work tomorrow.

Somehow or other Richard had secured the Captain's cabin for us, with an en suite bathroom and all the trimmings. He was making full use of the facilities while I wandered aimlessly around the vast ship. Unfortunately, his habit of not listening had rubbed off on me, and I didn't really take any notice when he told me the cabin number. The only thing to do was to wait for him in the bar, as he'd be sure to turn up there sooner or later.

In the meantime, there were some administrative issues to attend to. Having got the car safely out of Morocco, it was time to call Volvo Assistance for a bit of assistance. Volvo had provided us with a telephone number of the 24/7 variety and the inference was that anywhere and any time an army of ruthlessly efficient types would rally round and sort any problems out instantly. The reality was a little different, since when I called I had the misfortune to be put through to the biggest Benny on night duty.

'Hello, Volvo Assistance, how can I help you?' he started ambitiously, but as I explained the situation it was apparent he was a little unhelpful. The problem was he thought that I was winding him up. Another Volvo driver had crashed in Morocco and was looking for assistance, and he decided that this was just too much of a coincidence, and he was not going to be tricked into sending cars and parts all over the country on a wild goose chase. He must have been the repeated victim of practical jokes and wind-ups from his friends and colleagues as he was clearly pleased with himself for having spotted this one. Rather than investigate my troubles, he simply kept patting himself on the back, and saying in curiously nasal tones, 'Well, I'm not going to fall for that one.'

I was too tired and amazed to get angry, as I realised that losing my rag would simply make the game all the more fun to him. At this stage, we were only looking for a replacement wheel to be delivered to the port of Almeria, where the ferry docked. We had decided that we would drive on a new wheel to Barcelona and assess whether it was safe to continue. Apart from anything else, the next day was a Sunday, so we could not get in touch with the Volvo press office and I did not fancy abandoning the car until I had spoken to them. I was getting increasingly concerned about the impending arrival of that conversation, and the least I could do was still be in possession of the car.

With the car in such a sorry state, I was kicking myself for tempting fate by cracking jokes with the driver who had delivered the car to me a couple of days before we left London. Receiving a press car is much like a hire car in that you sign for it confirming there is no damage. As the driver parked, he kerbed one of the rims, inflicting a little light damage and was most apologetic insisting he marked the exact spot down on the forms. As he made his apologies I told him to relax and not worry about it, since as we were bringing the car to Morocco on the Gumball, I thought a light scratch on the rim was the least of its worries. The quip did not seem so funny now, and with that very wheel rim buckled beyond repair and the passenger side front wing ripped clean off, I thought it unlikely that I would be able to point to his X marking the spot on the damage forms.

A Gumballer who had been listening to my increasingly exasperated requests for a spare wheel offered his advice, which, while lacking in legality, more than made up for it by its ingenuity.

'Hey, you in the Volvo?' he asked.

'That's us,' I replied, thinking now was not the time to tell him how fabulously quick it was. Safety was the new black.

'I couldn't help overhearing your conversation; you did not sound like you had much luck getting a wheel. But, if you think about it, it's dead easy, there's only one place you'll find an alloy for a Volvo on a Sunday in Spain.'

'Where's that then?' I asked, neglecting to add 'Smart arse'.

'A multi-storey car park.'

Thanking him profusely for his excellent advice, and promising to consider it, I moved to join the Irish boys in the bar who, although subdued like the rest of us, still found the time to wind up John. They had been enjoying tormenting John, who was keen to get some sleep, for the last thirty minutes by doctoring the room number on the key. Originally, the joke had been intended merely to put him in the embarrassing situation of wandering into someone's room but they had unwittingly come up with a number that did not exist at all, and the joke became infinitely more amusing and with a longer shelf life. When John reappeared for the fourth time swearing blind that the room did not exist, they simply swore he was blind.

Eventually Richard joined us; we had a couple of beers and then he announced he was off to bed. I wanted to stay up and find out what was going on, as it was now past midnight and the boat had gone nowhere. It turned out that what was going on was the predictable post-mortem of the day's events with everyone gobsmacked and swapping ever-more gruesome reports of what they had seen and heard. It soon became clear that there had been a few other incidents that we had not witnessed.

Rather splendidly, our crash was big news. Or I should say Richard's crash was big news. One of the advantages of driving with Richard was that most people recognised him and knew who he was. This came in useful if he had wandered off somewhere he shouldn't have, or fallen asleep under a plant for instance. It was always easy to find him if I was looking for him as I just had to ask. As his co-driver, I was fairly anonymous among the wider group of Gumballers and as I sat eavesdropping on the rumours of the day I realised that this was a positive bonus.

'Did you hear about the Volvo?' people were asking each other.

'Yeah, that mad jockey Dunwoody nearly totalled it apparently.'

'What a nutcase; he has that look about him, don't you think?'

'Story is he went right off the far side of the road.'

I felt I had to clarify matters for them, so I leaned over and said, 'Yeah, I saw it first-hand; he had just undertaken a funeral on the hard shoulder. What a lunatic, eh?'

Awaking early on the ferry, we discovered the ferry itself was very late. It was 8 a.m. and we should have got in at 5 a.m. The Grand Prix was looking unlikely, particularly with the space-saver. We had five hundred miles to do and at suicidal pace we might have made it in a little over five hours. Even then, we would arrive at about 1 p.m. and it would have been tricky to get in at that time. I was really disappointed by this, as the Grand Prix was a major highlight of the whole trip for me. Richard wasn't too bothered as he had been to a few before, but I had never seen one live.

To get over the disappointment I procured a passenger. The previous day, we found it fun to have a third person in the car, and today we spotted Lucy, who was a sort of token model who seemed to be hopping from car to car. She was delighted by the invitation and needed no encouragement jumping in.

First impressions of Lucy were that she talked a lot. An awful lot, and generally about 'boys, tee hee, my flirty friends', as she called them. It looked like it might be a long journey. Quickly, we realised that not only did she talk a lot, but also perhaps she was all talk and no action. All fart and no poo, or all big hat but no cattle, as George Bush would say. She was a sweet girl in essence but clearly had been corrupted by travelling with assorted Gumballers, and I think that she felt she needed to play the role of 'pretty girl, on tour, amuse the boys' sort of thing.

'Who were you with yesterday, Lucy?'

'The Irish lads in the Hummer.'

That explained a thing or two. Richard's phone beeped and one of his interminable text messages arrived. He laughed and handed me the phone, and not for the first time I was shocked at the graphic nature and imagination involved. What was doubly shocking was the fact that it was 8 a.m. on a Sunday morning, 7 a.m. GMT where the text message had come from. Thinking we might see a bit more of a genuine Lucy if she realised that her flirty chat could never compete with the sordid texts Richard received, I passed her the phone.

'Goodness me, that's revolting,' she shrilled. It worked – from then on, she was perfectly charming.

A short distance out of Almeria, Jodie Kidd pulled alongside us, and started laughing and pointing at the damaged wing. She wound down the window, and over the engine noise shouted, 'What on earth happened there?' Richard was driving, hence I was alongside her. Confident that she would not be able to hear his protests above the traffic, I saw the opportunity to exact a little revenge for Richard's sound bites in Madrid.

'Well, Jodie,' I shouted, 'you know what Richard's like. Mad jockey type, he was taking it a bit too quickly and ran out of talent.' I shrugged my shoulders as if to say 'What can you expect?'

Jodie laughed, rolled her eyes in sympathy and understanding, and then tore off. I grinned at Richard, who definitely was not amused and about to get a little shirty, when Lucy, who had been watching all this intently, interrupted.

'How do you guys know Jodie Kidd?' Presumably as an aspiring model type, Jodie was something of a role model to her.

'I don't. I only met her this week. Richard knows her; he introduced me,' I replied.

'I know her through polo mainly,' explained Richard.

'Really?' Lucy sounded surprised. 'I didn't take you for a horsey type.'

It wasn't long before we were reminded that the Moroccan boys in blue were exceptionally friendly. As one Gumballer put it, they were as sophisticated as any police force in the world, only they had a better sense of humour. Back in Spain, we got pulled over at the very first toll, along with about twenty other

Gumballers. The Spanish Police were on to the Gumball early, after they received dozens of complaints from the Sunday drivers, who had been blown off the road by eager would-be Grand Prix fans. The strategy of the police seemed to be to hold us up as long as possible, meticulously checking the cars' documents and insurance. They were manning the tolls, and without any evidence of speeding pulled over any car bearing Gumball stickers. Our strategy of pretending that we had lost the tollbooth ticket was looking to be a smart one.

We were somewhere in the middle of the pack, and as things got lippy the police warned us that we would end up in jail. They had already escorted forty cars to jail and five people were being held overnight. Whether it's Gumball fact or fiction, rumour had it that one car had sped past the mayor at 150 mph and given him the finger. I was kicking myself now for the crash. I am sure we would have been overlooked completely had we stripped the stickers from the car. It is doubtful that they would have pulled a Volvo estate in and, even if they had, we could have done a good impression of being two fairly dim blokes on a motoring holiday. As they were not actually policing the roads between the tolls, we could have maintained a sufficient speed to reach the Grand Prix. Damn. What might have been.

As it was, we were trying to keep them away from the crash damage of our car, since given the mood that they were in we were convinced they simply would not let us drive any further. Lucy came into her own here, posing flirtatiously on the bonnet, and cutting off any cop who threatened to inspect the passenger side of the car. Meanwhile, we produced the documents and, thankfully, Richard stuck to English. This scenario was repeated at virtually every toll, and the police strategy worked. For us, and most of the rest of the field, the Grand Prix was abandoned, and we regretfully decided to head straight for the hotel in Barcelona.

Mid-morning, I received a call from Marco, a friend of mine from Ireland, who was in Barcelona.

'Hello, sir, I am at the Grand Prix. I see a big Gumball car park, but no cars. I was hoping that you might be able to find me a cheap ticket; the touts are looking for €450.00. Where are you?'

'Well, Marco, you're in luck, because we're not at the Grand Prix, nor are we likely to be. And neither is anybody else. You can have our ticket.'

I told him to find Jess who I knew had gone to Barcelona straight from Marbella, and was fairly confident she would be armed with hundreds of Grand Prix tickets that were going to be binned.

In Spain, they have these monster petrol stations, similar to the Motorway Services in the UK, with all the trimmings. Whenever I am in Europe, I enjoy poking around these establishments as it gives an excellent insight into the national psyche and culture, what stock they consider vital to their customers who are making a roadside stop. For instance in England, it's all jazz mags, pies and in-car air fresheners. As truckers' staples, these items are understandable and indeed complementary. The English one I don't understand is that ubiquitous stand selling money belts and travel plugs. Why on earth would you need a global travel adaptor on your way to Birmingham? A money belt perhaps, but a travel plug? It is hardly for the tourists, as they would be unlikely to be visiting Birmingham, and, if for some reason they were, having been cruelly conned into believing England's second city was worth seeing, surely they would have sorted their electrical appliances on arrival?

On the other hand, in France it's all baguettes and foie gras and, splendidly, you can smoke in these places as well. Poking around the Spanish service station, I was alarmed to discover they were selling a mean-looking line in truncheons. There was a sort of man-sized truncheon cum baseball bat thing, and then some mini weaponry for junior. The really disturbing thing was that they were all available in your favoured football team's colours. While I know the English have a well-deserved reputation for football hooliganism, I could not help thinking that Spain were taking the preparations for meeting them in Euro 2004 a little too far. I was sorely tempted to buy one, both for its surreal souvenir value, but also to have it on hand for the next time Richard tried to steal the maps.

With no pressure to get to the Grand Prix, and the spacesaver's speed restrictions, for the first time the Gumball was quite relaxing. It was quite literally so for Richard who was receiving an in-car massage from Lucy. He was enjoying himself immensely, and providing a running commentary on her progress, the innuendo of which appeared to go straight over her head. She was vigorously massaging his right shoulder and she could not fail to notice his repeated wincing and grimacing.

'What's wrong, Richard, am I hurting you?' she asked innocently.

'Its just a bit sore there, whiplash, you know?'

'Is that from the accident in Morocco?'

'Oh yes, it's been sore since then.'

'That's bollocks,' I interrupted, 'don't listen to him, Lucy. Whiplash, my arse, he's pulling your leg.'

'Are you sure?'

'Yes I am sure,' I said, at the same time that Richard was muttering about solicitors, damages and compensation. 'He's had it for years; I really don't think it will stand up in court. He fell off a horse.'

'I didn't "fall off a horse",' said Richard, mimicking my tone. 'It was a racing accident.'

'Ooh, were you a racing driver?' she asked, wide-eyed in admiration.

'No, I fell off a horse,' said Richard, and then gave up, deciding not to bore her with the nitty-gritty of the 2.45 at Fontwell.

As one of the few unattached girls on the Gumball, it was clear that Lucy had enjoyed a certain amount of attention and admiration, though was adamant that she had been 'terribly well behaved'. When the Gumball started, Max the organiser had been a single young man in his twenties and rumour had it that there was a lot more emphasis on the female contingent. One Gumballer who had been on the first two had told us that everybody was busy getting off with each other after a hard day's fast driving. With fast cars and fast women, he joked, the original Gumball experience was an extreme form of Speed Dating.

I had been trying to persuade Richard to try Speed Dating on our return to London. It struck me as perfect for someone so rushed and keen to get a job done quickly and, having done it once before, was convinced that Richard's efforts would be hilarious.

I had gone Speed Dating just after I moved to London thinking it would be a laugh, and perhaps a good way of meeting people in north London, since I lived there whereas all my friends lived in south London. As I turned up to the venue in Camden, it was clear that the exclusivity of the venue referred to the lack of walk-in punters as opposed to the desirability of the establishment. It seemed to make sense to arrive early for a spot of window-shopping, and my first impression was how delightfully pretty the hostess for the evening was. Inevitably this led to all sorts of amateur flirting as she pinned on my name badge and recorded my vital statistics, and I must commend the company on the professionalism of its staff, although presumably the unwanted attentions of single men is something of an occupational hazard in her line of work.

Armed with my scorecard I settled at the bar to familiarise myself with the dos and don'ts, appreciating that an event of this nature would require a certain amount of rules, regulations and etiquette. The format is very simple – each participant has a number; you start at the table with your number, engage your opposite number in conversation for a total of three minutes, at which stage a bell is rung and the male participants move round one place, eventually arriving back where you started, having ticked those people you would like to meet again. If they ticked you as well, you are provided with their email address the next day. In order to get the most possible value from the allotted time, the organisers provide suggestions to make conversation more interesting and productive.

First things first. Get any deal-breakers out of the way immediately. Hate smokers? Ask now if he'll be looking for an ashtray on the break. Horribly allergic to cats? Find out quick if she's a magnet for four-legged strays. You'll save yourself some trouble later if you get the deal-breakers out on the table.

Fighting talk indeed!

Speed Daters are also encouraged to avoid asking the typical, unimaginative starters for ten, for example, 'What do you do?' and 'Where do you come from?' This was something of a mixed blessing for me personally; while I was obviously keen to avoid raising the subject of my unemployed status, it meant that I would miss out on the 'simple Irish lad, lost in London' line.

Apart from the above wisdom, the scorecard also provides the means of recording the essential information required to keep track of meeting thirty potential partners. Apart from the yes/no tick boxes, there is copious space for taking notes and those milling around were already keeping their scorecards close to their chest, though the mind boggled at what information they could have collected at this early stage.

I must admit to being a little intimidated by the scorecard. Before studying the document closely, I was enjoying a rather carefree attitude to the whole idea of Speed Dating, satisfied that I was neither sad nor desperate, simply someone looking to meet new faces in a new town. The talk about 'deal-breakers' and the spreadsheet marking layout reminded me that Speed Dating is potentially quite a clinical way of having one's character analysed and assassinated. Not for the fainthearted then.

As the bell went to signal the off, I tried to stride confidently to Table 9. With the evening's accessories of freshly sharpened pencil, scoresheet and clipboard, I felt as if I was off to attend a lecture or even an interview, and, on seeing Denise, my first date, I sensed I was quite possibly in for both.

Denise, a formidable-looking character, unleashed the deal-breakers straight away. 'Are you a dog or a cat man?'

'I love dogs.'

She nodded with approval. 'Arts or sciences?'

'Strictly arts.' Positive vibes once more, I thought.

'What is your favourite sport?'

'Skiing and cricket.'

More smiles, I am saying the right things. I am out of my depth here and determined to do something about it.

'I hate smoking. Do you smoke?'

'Oddly enough, Denise, I smoke sixty a day. I would smoke more if I could, but it is terribly difficult to physically find the time. I know it sounds a lot but if a job is worth doing it is worth doing properly, don't you think?'

Believe me, while it doesn't sound much, three minutes is an awfully long time to endure if you do not get off to a good start. I was tempted to use the remaining two and a half minutes for a sneaky cigarette but decided that might have been pushing my luck.

After this baptism of fire, I thoroughly enjoyed the whole experience. My performance on Table 9 simply confirmed that I really was so shallow that I could decide in the first thirty seconds of meeting someone whether I would like to see them again, and, since that is the whole point of the concept, that Speed Dating is intended to be a ruthlessly efficient way of separating the wheat from the chaff, I decided to wholeheartedly embrace it.

This theory lasted until Table 21, where I met Charlotte. I had spotted her some way down the line and had ticked her yes box prematurely while I was supposedly listening to Table 15 tell me about IT recruitment. Admittedly, this tick was based on looks alone, but the true motivation was not wishing to be fumbling with scorecards and clipboards with only three minutes to make an impression. Although I had not actually tested the theory, I was confident that the time limit would pass very quickly indeed if you were trying to score positively.

This proved to be the case, all the more so since the first minute was spent furiously back-pedalling about the views I had expressed on Table 20. One of the flaws in Speed Dating is that the tables are placed very close together and, if one is inclined to take more of an interest in a conversation on an adjoining table, it is a very simple matter to do so. It might not be instantly obvious why one would bother to waste one's own three minutes on the chat next door, but at this stage I had not consciously spotted that, since most female Speed Daters hunt in pairs, and arrive together, they are issued with consecutive numbers and are thus seated at adjoining tables. No doubt this adds much enjoyment and hilarity for the female Speed Dater since they can exchange knowing glances and winks, but to the uninitiated and unsuspecting male it is a serious banana skin. Charlotte's best friend Rebecca was seated at Table 20, and for no better reason than to amuse myself I had subjected her to a gratuitously controversial rant concerning the merits of fox hunting, and had described actors as 'work-shy'. Rebecca understandably found this offensive, not least because she was a vegetarian actress, and, from the shocked look on Charlotte's face, I thought she might be too.

I managed to explain, in all honesty, that the views expressed were not necessarily my own, and had been aired to spice up the three-minute conversation. This obviously opened the hornet's nest of suggesting that her best friend was something less than scintillating company, a subject which inconveniently occupied the second minute of my three-minute window of opportunity. When the bell went, I ruefully reflected that the third minute did not allow enough time cogently to develop the argument that most people were probably lying to make themselves sound more interesting or appear more pleasant, and I was simply bucking the trend. Body language gave nothing away as to whether there was to be any further ticking than the ticking off, so I was resigned to wait and see if we had matched.

An added inconvenience of the table positions is that the dates have the opportunity to eye up your competition, the guy bringing up your rear as it were. It was my misfortune that the heart-throb of the Camden Speed Dating scene was the participant directly beside me, as so many of my dates spent the three minutes ogling him. It was, of course, particularly galling to see him take my place at Table 21 after my departure.

Suitably chastised, I was a little more circumspect for the remainder of the round, and continued to enjoy the banter and the jokes. As the evening proceeds, inevitably more drink is consumed with nerves and shyness retreating. This makes the final five dates infinitely, but understandably, more fun than the first five.

There was only one further girl I ticked: Sarah, a charming sales assistant from west London. From the start, conversation flowed freely with a good combination of factual exchange and idle banter. Just as I was thinking that we were on to a good thing, and Speed Dating was quite effective after all, she told me that she had been to 'two or three' events previously and would probably go again. I'm no mathematician, but there was certainly enough time remaining to calculate that potentially, if she went twice a week, she could meet 240 men a month. I ticked 'yes please Sarah, serial Speed Dater' nonetheless, but with those odds reckoned there was more chance of getting Charlotte's email, perhaps even Rebecca's.

From my experiences, there was much amusement to be had imagining Richard bobbing up and down at his table, impatiently trying to break the Speed Dater's record, thinking that, if three minutes was the norm, he would get the job done in two. It is a naturally competitive environment and Richard would take to it like a duck to water.

On the outskirts of the city we approached the final toll before Barcelona. Beyond the tollbooths, there was a vast congregation of angry-looking Spanish Police and even angrier-looking Gumballers. There was a more menacing aura to proceedings and some instinct suggested that this was about a little more than insurance and registration documents. Rather stupidly, but luckily for us, the police had chosen to carry out their business in such a position that left two lanes available to go behind them. As a precaution, they had a spotter, keeping a beady eye on these lanes, and under normal circumstances that would have been sufficient. But what if somebody crept through under the cover of an articulated truck?

I veered right, in an alarming fashion, across about ten toll lanes, amid much wailing, gnashing of teeth and honking of horns. 'Bear with me here, guys,' I explained to Richard and Lucy, 'we have nothing to add to whatever conversation is going on over there.'

In the lane at the extreme right, I crept towards the tollbooth, waiting for a truck to pull alongside us. There was one behind, but he was maintaining an irritatingly slow pace towards the booth, though possibly not anything like as irritating as us in the eyes of the increasing traffic jam behind us. Eventually, we reached the booth, and I reckoned that Richard's tomfoolery would give us a few vital seconds. Sadly, he simply handed over his credit card without any attempt of conversation. On the other hand, the Jose in the truck was engaged in some pretty professional flirting with the toll attendant, and ironically all those behind us were honking their horns madly while we waited for his horn to calm down. I think he was Italian.

Luckily, I have quite a high embarrassment threshold. Firstly, I enjoyed a childhood with embarrassing parents who thought nothing of creating the most almighty scenes in the most public of places. No foreign holiday was complete without my father summoning waiters with the title '*garçon*' or '*fraulein*' at the top of his voice, while clicking his fingers, and proceeding to tell them exactly what he thought of their third-world standards of service. After becoming accustomed to such outbursts we affectionately christened them 'strops' and looked forward to them intently, even manufacturing one or two of our own so we could sit back and enjoy the show. Shyer children would have cringed with embarrassment but for us it was an infinitely more enjoyable pastime than sightseeing. Secondly, I have endured a relationship with a girlfriend whose tantrums were on the mental side of monumental, and the more public the better. While not as much fun as my father's antics, they undoubtedly steeled me to the stares of other diners and passers-by.

Richard has a fairly thick skin as well, as you might expect from someone who has been in the tabloids for lapping up a lap dancer, but poor Lucy was mortified as we stubbornly sat at the booth, deliberately delaying some pretty angry hombres. Thankfully, the police could not see what all the commotion and horn blowing was about, because we were now enjoying the full cover of the lorry, which we maintained when he eventually moved on and we sailed right past them undetected.

Arriving in Barcelona, we were delighted to see the Hotel Rey Juan Carlos towering above the skyline, which negated the need for the usual urban navigational nonsense. The hotel itself was quite something, a strictly Star Trek affair of a tall glass structure. There were seventy-odd floors, but with only one ceiling, as each floor clung to the outer walls and overlooked the vast lobby. Richard, who was displaying a similar deliriousness to the one last experienced in Marrakech, headed straight for bed as soon as we had located our room. I watched the Gumballers arrive in the lobby for as long as my resistance to vertigo would allow.

13. BARCELONA

Check into the hotel, freshen up and then follow the red carpet to dinner in the Garden Marquee. After dinner, dance the night away at the hotel nightclub – The Tati!

Looking forward to a night in The Tati, I investigated the possibilities of lounging in the vast bath for the afternoon, but with water cannons for taps it was obvious that even filling it would wake up Richard. And then I'd probably start to sing. He needed his sleep, so I went to the bar instead. There was a fine old party brewing up as everyone had resolved to get rightly pissed on the back of missing the Grand Prix and a fairly testing day at the hands of the Spanish Police. I discovered that hiding behind the truck had saved us a hefty fine for participating in an 'illegal road race'. No evidence of speeding was required, just a Gumball sticker on your car. Some who had removed the stickers had got done anyway on account of driving something like a Ferrari on foreign plates, and were then easily identified by the Gumball ID around their neck. A holidaymaker from Munich was honeymooning in his Porsche with his wife, minding his own business, when he got pulled in and fined for little more than being German and having a fast car. There were a few Gumball wives, who presumably were recalling their own honeymoons, who seemed to think the unimaginative Hun deserved everything he got.

There was a great camaraderie among the Gumballers, who had clearly enjoyed the police activity. Underneath all the indignity, it was evidently a fun day out, a cracking Sunday drive, as it were. Most had realised that since the boat was delayed the Formula 1 was a non-starter anyway and the police had provided alternative entertainment. All those present could easily afford the fines, with some admitting that it was well worth the cost simply to have the opportunity of attaching a Gumball sticker to a cop's arse while he was writing a ticket. There were five or six drivers still in jail, awaiting a court appearance in the morning and, although their views remained to be heard, the overall spirit was high.

I noticed that the Belgian girls that the Irish lads had picked up in Paris had reappeared, and presumably not by coincidence. It turned out that they had been to the Grand Prix and enjoyed a fine lunch and a great view of the race in the empty Gumball grandstand. They had met Marco at the race and shared a lift back to Barcelona with him, along with the American divorcees, and, as we got chatting, it dawned on them that I was his friend.

'Where's Marco now then?' I asked.

'He's in the hotel somewhere.'

'And the divorcees?'

'They're here too.'

Not together, I hoped. The American divorcees were two ladies of a certain age, both flush after a recent lucrative divorce, and were following the Gumball, hell bent on spending some of their ex-husbands' money and perhaps some of a future husband's as well. They had caused quite a stir in Paris and, having found no man to latch on to, they proceeded to latch on to each other, and staged a show for some onlookers. This story had done the rounds of the Gumballers, although the girls hadn't.

The American girls then appeared in the bar, thankfully without Marco, and came to sit with their new Belgian friends. The Belgians had been recounting the tales of their crazy night in Paris and, fortuitously, without their realising the company they were keeping, began to tell the story of the two lesbian hookers and their exhibitionism.

'And then these hookers began to perform oral sex, would you believe it.'

'My dear girl, those weren't hookers, that was us,' one of the Americans replied.

The Belgian was taken aback for a minute, and then gave them a look as if to ask 'what's the difference?' Composing herself, she simply said, 'Oh I am sorry, I didn't recognise you with your clothes on.' Turning to the brunette she said, 'You had your eyes shut,' and delivered her damning verdict to the blonde by saying, 'And, as for you, I didn't get a good view of your face.'

As the assembled crowd were suppressing our sniggers, Marco arrived in the bar, and I got up to greet him, expecting some gushing thanks for the free ticket and amazing experience.

'Hi, Marco, how was the Grand Prix?'

'It was shit. Loud. Noisy. And boring. First lap was OK but the rest was crap; lunch was good though. Thanks for the ticket, though I'd have paid the full price not to have had to endure it.'

'Oh well, poor you, sorry you had such a shitty day.'

'Oh no, on the contrary, the rest of the day was a real laugh. I've got quite into the whole Gumball vibe.'

Marco explained that, after meeting Jess and getting tickets, he had hooked up with an American fellow in a big yellow Chevrolet. He had missed all the fun in Morocco because he had suffered some car trouble in Marbella. In the meantime, he had been to Madrid and bought two new Chevrolets for spare parts.

'After meeting him I then clumsily asked an American girl about "hooters", the aerosol things that make even more noise than the cars at a Grand Prix. I stuttered and stumbled, and choked as the American shoved her plastic breasts in my face and said, "Oh I brought my own." I regained some of my composure and realised I was on the Gumball and could turn off some of my inhibitions,' Marco carried on animatedly. 'On the way back to town we picked up those Belgians hitchhiking and I was very proud of you guys when I discovered they had come to Barcelona for the mad Irishmen. Then I was a bit disappointed to find out they were talking about completely different people.'

Speaking of mad Irishmen, I suggested that it was time to wake up Richard.

'Oh, he's awake,' said Marco. 'I met him in the lift; he's just been for a run and to the gym.'

'Mad as a brush, that fellow; I've been sitting in this bar all afternoon, so he can get some sleep.'

Marco surveyed the empty bottles. 'It doesn't look like you have suffered too much.'

We sneaked Marco into dinner, and took a table with the Irish lads, Jodie, Tarquin and one of Jodie's co-drivers, a sports-car dealer called Joe Macari. Joe had sat Morocco out, and stayed in Marbella to get a badly needed suntan. Although every second Gumball car seemed to be festooned in Team Macari colours, when I had met Joe in Paris he had no colour himself. To look like 'death warmed up' would be one thing, but Joe was literally whiter than white, and as a former car dealer myself I knew that this appearance was definitely deceiving.

After I had introduced Marco to the rest of the table, he was full of questions along the lines of 'who is he' and 'what does he do'. Here we go, I thought. He's a great friend of mine but he does get rather tedious as he has a one-track mind. Business. He runs an online recruitment company in Dublin and, on discovering there were four Irish businessmen at the table, and even better, one that was in the hospitality industry, his eyes lit up.

'Give it a rest, Marco; they're on holiday and so are you.'

'OK, who's that guy then?'

'His name's Tarquin.'

'Tarquin?' he scoffed. 'What sort of name is that?'

'A polo player's. And Jodie Kidd's boyfriend.'

'Boyfriend?' he scoffed louder. 'Bollocks, they don't look very close. You should have a crack, mate.'

'Don't be ridiculous, that's her boyfriend, and I hardly think they've come on the Gumball together so she can cop it off with somebody else,' I replied, as Tarquin and Jodie exchanged a frosty look. 'Apart from anything else, Marco, she's a bit horsey for my tastes.'

At the party, Marco conducted himself with the vim and vigour that might be expected of someone who has enjoyed recent long and interrupted nights of sleep. Richard and I, on the other hand, went into auto-party mode, careering around with little sense of aim or intention. After seeing Richard forget himself, and his ability, and venture on to the dance floor, I was lucid enough to grab a photographer thinking that such hilarity needed to be captured for posterity. It is true to say that we all have an instinctive level of self-preservation. This applies equally to life and death situations as it does to the consequences of having a few drinks. For instance, I have often woken in the morning with a serious headache and no recollection of having got home, but the fact that I am home can be attributed to that sixth sense that lets you know you've had enough, it's time to go home and more often than not even gets you there. Similarly, Richard has such levels of self-awareness that he is under no illusion just how ridiculous he looks when he struts his stuff on the dance floor and, while from time to time, as in this case, he forgets himself sufficiently to be tempted to throw some shapes, his subconscious instinctively picked up the presence of a camera and he ran for cover immediately. I might have given the game away by madly pointing and laughing, but nonetheless, if there was to be any doubt of just how hilarious Richard's dancing is, his turn of speed to avoid being photographed speaks volumes.

My own sixth sense obviously kicked in because without any warning at all it was eight o'clock and Richard was barking at me to get up. Richard is a morning person without a doubt. He likes to get up early in the morning, regardless of how early in the morning he has gone to bed. On this particular morning, he was shouting at me, all action stations and 'gung ho, sergeant major, get up, we've got work to do'. The work involved ringing Volvo and explaining our predicament. Since the office had been shut over the weekend, this was our first opportunity. My reluctance to get out of the bed was not because I was scared of ringing Volvo, which incidentally I was, but because it was actually 7 a.m. in England and the office would not be open for another couple of hours anyway.

We had breakfast in silence, bar regular outbursts of 'Ring Volvo now, ring Volvo now,' making the time drag, like watching paint dry, until it was sensible to call. As it turned out, ringing at the earliest opportunity was a blessing in disguise, offering a brief respite since there was only an office junior to take my call. A bit wet behind the ears, and having been trained well in the 'customer's always right' vein, she was reluctant to bollock me, concentrating only on being helpful.

'Hi, my name is Clement Wilson. I have one of your press cars and I crashed it in Morocco. But it's in Barcelona now,' I said, thinking it best to get it all out.

'Sorry, slow down, you crashed in Morocco, but now you're in Barcelona. Is the car in Barcelona?'

'Yes, we managed to drive it here, good work eh?'

'Whatever. Is anyone hurt?'

'No. Thank god we were in a Volvo,' I said, laying it on pretty thick.

'Of course. Is the car all right?'

'Well, no, not really, hence my call. It could do with a new wing for a start.'

'Is it driveable?'

'Well we've driven it eleven hundred miles on the spacesaver and there are all sorts of ominous-sounding messages emanating from the dashboard concerning the brakes and such like. To be honest, we're reluctant to drive it any further.'

'What happened? How did you crash?'

'We swerved to miss a donkey.' Technically true, I justified matters to myself.

'Right, leave it with me. You need another car, yes? I'll try and sort something out.'

'Great. Many thanks.'

I tossed the phone back to Richard, and said, 'Right, they're sorting it, calling back with details of a replacement car.' All we could do now was wait. I was quite pleased that the tricky business of telling them about the damage was over, and they seemed to have taken it remarkably well. Perhaps this sort of thing was all in a day's work for them. We waited some twenty minutes and the phone rang again. The onscreen display announced the good news, flashing up 'Volvo press office'.

'Hi, Clement, it's Andrea.' Oops, not quite so good news. Andrea was no office junior and was the person who had been responsible for taking the decision to give us the car in the first place.

'Oh, hi, Andrea, how's tricks?' I asked nervously.

'Not great, now you mention it. I have just spent all night on a plane from the States, and I've arrived in the office to discover you've crashed our car.'

Unfortunately, an argument ensued. From a combination of stress and lack of sleep, I got on my high horse and began to make outrageous demands that a replacement car simply had to be a Volvo, and I could not get my head around why that was not possible. Being jet-lagged, Andrea was herself suffering from lack of sleep and stress, caused by my actions in crashing the car, and now I was adding insult to injury by expecting prima donna treatment. It was not a productive conversation, and it achieved nothing. I threw the phone back to Richard.

'What's the story?' he asked.

'Well, we need another Volvo, but of course they can't give us one.'

'Any more progress than that?'

'Not really.'

'You're unbelievable,' he said, shaking his head. 'For the last two days, you've been worried about breaking the news to Volvo, and then you lambast them for being unhelpful. I can't believe you spoke to her like that.'

He was right. It must have been my guilty conscience that caused me to lash out like a wounded animal. I had presented Volvo with a bit of a problem to say the least, not to mention a large bill, and I was hardly showing the levels of contrition that might have been expected of someone in my position. I went for a wander to clear my head from the chaos of the foyer and take a phone call from Marco, who had disappeared at some stage unbeknown to us.

'What happened to you, Marco? Where did you get to?' I asked.

'A bloody great night. You two were in some state so I abandoned you towards the end of the party. Although I did not think much of the Grand Prix itself, I knew there was bound to be some fun on the back of it in central Barcelona. What I did not expect was to become a Gumball VIP, with the freedom of the city. I still had the Chevrolet's Gumball pass and everyone had heard about your antics and, thinking I was a bona fide Gumballer, bought me drinks all night. The Grand Prix groupies were well pissed off.'

Back in the hotel, this started to make sense. The Gumball was big news and people were poring over the papers checking out the headlines: UN RALLY DE RICOS Y FAMOSAS ACABA CON CINCO PARTICIPANTES ENTER RAJAS. 'Rally of the rich and famous ends with five participants behind bars' as translated by the concierge. The papers and the police had taken matters very seriously, reporting speeds in excess of 190 mph. Although they had not got specific evidence of any speeding, they had been checking the tolls and found one car to have covered a distance of 116 miles in 50 minutes. That is an *average* speed of 140 mph. Average! No wonder they were disgruntled.

The foyer itself was chaotic because it was difficult to tell whether the Gumballers were coming or going. As a steady stream left, there seemed to be a similar amount arriving either fresh from jail or from Morocco. Neither group had got much sleep and there were a few angry scenes as they checked in, only to be told that they would have to check out again in an hour. There was at least one Gumballer with no such worries. Chris was just beginning to wake up having spent the night in the back of the taxi.

'Morning, Chris, good night's sleep?' I asked sarcastically.

'Bloody marvellous,' he enthused, 'the best I've had all week. I'm sick of being dragged out of bed every morning at the crack of dawn, so last night instead of the room I simply headed straight for the taxi. That way, if they wanted to leave early, they could just drive off. Nobody needed to wake me and I could sleep as long as I wanted. Which is exactly what I've done.' He engaged in a bit of a stretch with the satisfied groans of a man who has enjoyed a full five hours' sleep instead of his regular two. It would have been cruel to point out that, although his plan was sound in theory and presumably seemed an excellent idea when he crashed out in the small hours, 'they' had also chosen that particular morning to enjoy a lie-in and were still in a bed in a five-star hotel.

Aidan was in the bar, taking it easy and enjoying a coffee.

'How come you're still here?' I asked him.

'I'm just relaxing after a heavy night. The police are going to be all over the shop so I might as well chill out here, and proceed at a leisurely pace to Cannes.'

'Quite right too. So a big night then? What happened to your forehead?' He had a bit scratch above his eye.

'I got hit by a club sandwich. Fifty or so people headed back to my room after the party. It got well out of hand. Room service was summoned and sent off with a fat order, not because anyone was hungry, but because they were planning a food fight. I woke up this morning and went to put my shoes on – some git had filled them with prawn cocktail.'

'Holy shit, much damage?'

'Dunno yet, but they've got my credit card.'

'Bad luck.'

'Yeah, God knows what it will cost. I've trashed a few hotel rooms in my time and they're never cheap.'

Aidan's tales of defending his hotel room with a cocktail stick were a welcome diversion from my own woes, but, although I didn't know it at that stage, I had a few more of them to look forward to.

Amid the hanging around in the hotel waiting for a plan of action, I had the first opportunity in a week to check my email. Naïvely I had brought my laptop with me as well as the greatest of intentions to get some work done along the way. To date, the laptop had only been opened once, and that was to retrieve the emergency number for Volvo.

Like all modern and classy hotels, the Hotel Rey Juan Carlos sported an ambitiously titled 'business centre', which was basically a room with a couple of computers, a fax and a pretty secretary to add to the personal touch. The atmosphere was more jovial than businesslike but that was all about to change when I checked my email.

Another of my day jobs at the time involved working for *Les Routiers*, the hotel, restaurant and pub guide. My responsibilities were to visit and inspect existing members, and recruit new ones, a role which obviously required the personal touch. I had not actually told my employers that I was off on the Gumball, and consequently they understood me to be pressing the flesh in London SW whatever at that precise moment in time. My cunning plan had been to get around this by firing off a daily email review of places I had visited prior to departing for Paris. I had misjudged the Gumball to such an extent that I had envisaged myself typing away on my laptop as Richard drove, and simply plugging in at the nightly hotel stop to attend to my correspondence. That was now looking to be a pretty stupid assessment of affairs.

Opening my Inbox revealed my absence had not gone unnoticed. Amazingly, there were more emails from Imogen, my direct boss, than there was spam and I was fairly confident that she was not emailing with offers to increase my wealth in three easy steps. On reading the missives, it was obvious that there was going to be some difficulty explaining why I was in Barcelona and not Battersea.

Under the circumstances, these were difficulties that could wait for another day, and I sent a quick reply to reassure her that I was alive and well, apologising for not being in touch and explaining that I had just experienced the most hectic week of my life, culminating in a car crash, or 'road-traffic incident' as I put it. Although it all sounded a bit like 'the dog ate my homework', it was true, even if I did omit to mention that, rather than doing the rounds of suburban London, my busy week had seen me pass through three countries in two continents. Covering this sort of ground in seven days would normally have earned me a bonus, though as I pressed 'send' I knew the Moroccan factor was going to be a stickler.

'I think I might have lost my job,' I said to Richard, when I rejoined him still looking fairly forlorn in the foyer.

'Oh yeah, *Les Routiers* have caught up with you, have they? It's about time and you can't say you didn't have it coming. Spare a thought for poor Andrea; she might well lose hers too. She's back on the phone so you can apologise to her,' he said, passing me the phone.

Suitably chastened, I now conducted my conversation with a more appropriately meek demeanour, which unsurprisingly was more helpful for all involved. Andrea had been playing a blinder and offered to fly us to Nice, where we could then hire a car and proceed to Cannes, or, failing that, Volvo would pick up the tab for a rental car. As tempting as the flight was, we reckoned, with all the luggage that we had accumulated, it was probably simpler to do the drive. A further factor was that we had somehow gathered up Jim the cameraman and offered him a lift to Cannes.

We arranged that we would leave our car in a Volvo dealership in Barcelona, and then pick up a hire car. Since we had spent most of the morning faffing about, it was now shortly after one o'clock. After a short but fraught journey to the Volvo garage, we were dismayed to find it was shut.

'Bollocks!' said Richard, with feeling. 'Shut for lunch.'

I looked at the opening times information on the door. 'Lunch, my tits! The lazy Spanish bastards are having a siesta. Sod it; we'll have to leave it at the hotel.'

Back at the hotel, I tried to explain the dilemma to the concierge. Could they look after the car since the Volvo people were having a siesta? He was not amused at all. Not because it was a burden to cope with our car, but because I had inflicted a racial slur on Spain. Siesta? Don't be ridiculous; they're not asleep; that's just the way we do things in Spain. Exactly, they sleep all afternoon. That's what they're famous for – siestas. Well, siestas and bull fighting. Personally, being a lazy, antivegetarianist, I think they're marvellous, and it was only on this occasion that I found their habits irritating. Unfortunately, particularly as we were pressed for time, the concierge was hell bent on getting me to admit that Spaniards did not indulge in a bit of daytime kippage before he would consider agreeing to house the car. The more I maintained I was very pro the practice, the more he convinced himself I was taking the piss. I blame the European Union. The boffins in Brussels are so hell bent on homogenising us that, just because the rest of Europe manages to work a forty-hour week, the Spaniards have a complex about doing two mornings a week and partying all night. Live and let live, I say. Or work and let sleep. I did not expand on this theory as we were pressed for time. I looked at my watch and saw it was nearly two o'clock. Great, I thought, they'll all be asleep in about ten minutes or so. I'll just slip it in the underground car park then.

Meanwhile, Richard was unloading the car on to the pavement. We had to transfer all our stuff to a taxi and it was now strewn around the car while Pigalle the dog sat in a luxury taxi, watching the meter running. Over the course of the week, our belongings had permeated every nook and cranny of the car. An obvious advantage of travelling in a large estate car is the amount of gear you can pack into it, but this has its downsides when coming to retrieve it all again. We set about emptying it, periodically stressing just how important it was that nothing was left behind. It's most important, Clement. Couldn't agree more, Richard, stay alert. That sort of thing. Every door pocket, seat pocket, cup holder and even behind the sun visors was searched. I approached the glove box with particular care since it contained the 'Important Documents Folder'. This folder contained our passports and driving licences as well as the registration and insurance paperwork for the car. Such was its importance, since it had been placed in the glove box, it had only been removed on official business – for Immigration at Morocco and the Spanish police, for example.

My personal administration skills – or personal admin, as it had become known – had been something of an ongoing joke throughout the week. On numerous occasions, Richard looked on in astonishment as I lost my wallet or the car keys for the umpteenth time. The night before we left London, I had managed to lose the Important Documents Folder, only remembering at three o'clock that it was in a friend's apartment. Foolishly I let this information slip to Richard by way of explanation that I was a little late for our 5 a.m. departure. It wasn't a confidence-inspiring start and things did get worse. Luckily, it did not take long for him to be extra vigilant, so when we were driving out of Paris he took the sensible precaution to ask me whether I was aware of the folder's whereabouts. Well, when he mentioned it, of course, I knew where it was, or at least where I had last left it – on the street outside the hotel. Thankfully, it was still there when I returned, though Richard's sense of humour took a brief leave of absence.

Against this background, you can understand why I approached the task of sorting the folder's contents with extreme care. I needed to sort the items personal to us – passports and driving licences – while leaving behind the documents pertaining to the car. One can also have a certain amount of sympathy for Richard keeping a close eye on me and wanting to double-check matters.

'Have you sorted this?' he asked, waving the folder.

'It's done,' I answered curtly.

'Perhaps I'll just double-check, what do you think?'

'Bloody hell, Richard, I've said it's taken care of. I'm not a complete fucking imbecile and we don't have time for your anal neuroticism.'

'All the same, I'd feel better.'

'Fine, suit yourself.'

After a quick rummage, Richard unearthed a rather official-looking pink-and-green piece of paper. He held it up and said, 'Listen, mate, this is my driving licence; it might come in handy, don't you think?'

Fair point, but luckily we did not have time to discuss it, and proceeded to load up the taxi. Driving off, of course, we noticed that Pigalle's stay had cost us the princely sum of €12. The taxi driver was unrepentant at this blatant rip-off, and suggested that it was not his fault if we felt that the pavement was not good enough for a stuffed dog. We gave instructions to go to the Avis car-hire depot in the city. Or rather I gave him instructions while Richard gave him directions. He was at it again, and this time with no excuse. He had repeatedly maintained that his habit of instantly assuming control of navigational duties was a long-standing one that stemmed from experiences of driving with clueless jockeys and ex-girlfriends. But this time we were in a taxi. It is a taxi driver's job to know the best route around a city and to offer him alternative directions would be rather like telling your dentist which teeth to remove. It might have been understandable had we been on Richard's turf in Fulham, but we were in the vast metropolis of Barcelona. Initially, I gave Richard the benefit of the doubt, suggesting that he was concerned that the driver was ripping us off, playing us for the dumb tourists that we clearly were. No, was the answer, he had simply thought that he knew a better way.

After some negotiating of the route and the price with the taxi driver, he dropped us off at Avis, glad to see the back of us. Here we discovered the shocking news that a bog-standard Volkswagen Passat was going to cost €800 for four days, since we would be dropping it back in another country. Volvo had offered to pay the bill, but I was not looking forward to telling them the size of it. In the meantime, we coughed up the readies, thinking that we must be the only Gumballers to have spent their speeding fine budget on a hire car.

14. BARCELONA TO CANNES

When we finally got out of Barcelona, the drive to Cannes was a relaxing one. Most of the police presence had calmed down and what little there was took no notice of us in our Spanish hire car. It was also a particularly novel experience not to be refuelling every couple of hours.

We were so far behind the pack that we only came across two Gumballers on this leg. The first was a Ferrari 575 that had been stripped of its stickers for subtlety. Jim the cameraman had a job to do, however, that was not quite so subtle. He was contracted to film Gumballers and, as we pulled alongside the Ferrari at the tollbooth, he was struggling to scramble out of the window with his massive camera. This was not so subtle and attracted the police attention, not to us but to the Ferrari drivers. They were last seen engrossed in a heated debate. The only other car we passed was Chris Eubank's Bentley and we noticed that he himself was not among the occupants. We were on a high-speed autoroute and that ruled out the possibility of him scooting along behind, so the obvious assumption was that he was travelling in somebody else's car.

The decreased pace and relaxed ambience also seemed to encourage some meaningful and intelligent discussion about the pressing issues of the day. First on the agenda was the obligatory post-mortem of the night before.

'So how did you guys enjoy last night, then?' asked Jim.

'Dunno,' we replied, almost in unison.

'What time did you hit the sack?'

'Dunno.'

'Well, do you think you had a good night?'

'Oh fantastic, undoubtedly.'

'But I think my drink was spiked. I can't work out how I got so merry,' Richard said, in all seriousness. I was glad I was not driving at the time or I would have had another crash as I collapsed into uncontrollable laughter. 'It's not funny, mate. John told me he saw me swaying in the doorways, having difficulty negotiating them.'

'John told me he saw you dancing,' I said, laughing.

'I'm seriously going to stay off the drink tonight,' Richard continued his fantasies.

From there, the supposedly intelligent discussion deteriorated. Pub chat is one thing, but three blokes in a car on a long journey are capable of talking some real rubbish. No matter how good the intentions, invariably somebody drags the conversation down to a lavatorial level. It is almost instinctive. As an example, a conversation about the varying sizes of a man's penis was traced directly back to a craving for Starbucks coffee.

I was on a bit of a rant and for once not about horses, but about Starbucks, and not your usual hippy anti-capitalist-style rant. Something I missed on the Gumball was my Starbucks coffee of the day. I had never put any stock in hippie conspiracy theories against Starbucks' aim for total world domination by lacing their coffee with addictive substances but I began to think twice. It was not any old coffee I was craving; it was specifically Starbucks. Despite my enthusiasm for the beverage, my normal daily routine of buying the coffee was somewhat tainted by having to visit the Clapham branch on the Northcote Road.

From now on, if I move house, one of the tests I will apply to an area is to check out the Starbucks clientele as it is quite revealing about your potential neighbours. For instance in St John's Wood, where I used to live, it was all terribly civilised with a diverse crowd of people taking a break from a variety of jobs and pastimes. In Clapham, the place is full to the brim of breastfeeding mothers calmly discussing the colour of their children's faeces, and other such worries. I am certainly not against breastfeeding in public but not en masse like milking cattle. It is even worse when their elder toddlers are off school because they career around, oblivious to the quantities of scalding coffee on the premises, and playing strange spitting games with the milk jug.

I was ranting along these lines when Jim joined in. What really annoyed him about Starbucks was the ridiculous naming system they employed. The Mochichoccy Whatsits were bad enough, but he reserved a particular venom for the practice of offering sizes in *Tall*, *Grande* and something like *Venti*. I had to agree he had a point and evidently so did Richard.

'Yeah, you're right, that is annoying. I mean *Tall* is small whatever way you look at it. Maybe I have an enormous todger but I don't go round calling it a *Venti*. Though it might make more sense for you, Clement, you could be a *Tall*.' He laughed, at his own (unfunny) joke.

'Piss off, short arse, or tall arse as it would be in the circumstances,' I replied.

Jim intervened and tried to raise the conversational bar by telling us about his forthcoming nuptials. Privately, he was happy to admit that his week on the Gumball had been a welcome break from the incessant wedding planning he was suffering at home. I had some sympathy for him as I was relieved myself not to have heard anything about my sister's forthcoming wedding for an entire week. With no disrespect to my sister, as I have seen it happen with many brides-to-be, but the tiniest details are discussed ad nauseam, and major factors like guest lists cause almighty rows. There has to be a cut-off point and there is always somebody who takes offence. I was mouthing off along these lines, when I remembered Richard had been married; I had seen a photo of his wedding day. There was himself and his bride and, quite unbelievably, a horse!

'Richard, why did you have a horse at your wedding?' I asked, barely suppressing my giggles. 'It was in the photos like an honoured guest.'

'West Tip *was* an honoured guest. And I actually had two horses at my wedding – Charter Party, the '88 Gold Cup winner was there too.'

'You're taking the piss? I thought it was some shot for PR purposes, like Anthea Turner and her chocolate bars.'

'No, I'm serious. It's not that weird; it meant a lot to my mother that they were there so I agreed; it's what racing people do, and as a jockey it was not strange at all.'

Wow. What racing people do? I was gobsmacked. I knew racing people had some pretty odd idiosyncrasies and it was perfectly understandable why their social lives revolved around horses but this was taking it to a whole new level.

Sadly, this line in mickey-taking was interrupted by the telephone; a friend of mine called Bertie rang to say that he was in Cannes 'on business' and what were we up to. A bit of this and a bit of that, Bertie, why don't you come to the Gumball finish party; it should be a laugh. He thought that this was a great plan and volunteered to bring some of his 'stock'. His 'stock' should prove interesting, as I had heard that he had recently changed jobs.

Bertie is the brother of a very good friend of mine called Jamie, and he is a curious chap indeed. He had spent most of his twenties in the Highlands of Scotland, doing a variety of odd jobs – some a good deal odder than others – and then he opened a restaurant with his brother. Port-na-Craig enjoys an idyllic situation in Perthshire, and is affectionately known as Port-na-Posh, after a *Sunday Times* review mentioned that Bertie was 'posher than Bolly on the croquet lawn'.

Bertie had run the front of house, meeting and greeting, while Jamie worked his magic in the kitchen, each making the most of their respective talents. They are quite contrasting characters, and inevitably the partnership was not without incident. Jamie is your stereotypically angry, sweaty chef, with a tongue as sharp as his knife, and is not immune to the odd tantrum if things are not running smoothly in the kitchen. Thankfully, for the most part, the customers do not see this side of things and are left to marvel at Jamie's menu and Bertie's manners. I do stress 'for the most part'.

On one occasion, three American tourists arrived quite late, hoping to secure a table. As it was a fine summer's evening, they were waiting in the courtyard to be seated, while Bertie said he would just 'check with the chef'. There is a door to the kitchen that opens to the courtyard, which ordinarily is shut, but on account of the warmth of the evening the door was open and only protected by a very fine mesh, designed to keep out bugs but not sound.

The two brothers often communicate in a peculiar language called Appy Dappy, designed for situations just like this. It's essentially a simple concept, but at high speed is incomprehensible to the untrained ear. Aware of the open door, Bertie thought it best to speak in Appy Dappy.

'Japamapie, dapo wape hapave spapace fapor thrapee Yapanks?' Translated, this means 'Jamie, do we have space for three Yanks?' Under the stress of the kitchen, Jamie forgot the need for discretion and simply shouted loudly in tones as clear as his English, 'Three Yanks can suck my plums!'

Ever the professional, Bertie brought his manners back out into the courtyard and, banking on an American misunderstanding of British colloquialisms, simply said, 'I'm terribly sorry, ladies and gentlemen, it appears that the chef's plums are the only thing left on the menu.'

On reaching thirty, Bertie had suffered a premature mid-life crisis and decided that he needed to get out of the Highlands and move to London. Rumour had it he was looking for a wife, so I was surprised to hear that he had taken a job as a salesman for Mantric Marketing, purveyors of fine dildos and upmarket sex toys. Now he was in Cannes, flogging his wares, and planning to party with us that evening.

'That was Bertie, a friend of mine, who'll be joining us in Cannes. You'll like him,' I said to Richard, as I hung up the phone.

'Great, what's his story?'

'He sells sex toys.'

'Cool, will he give me a discount?'

Sadly, on this final leg of the Gumball, we had to miss out a checkpoint since the morning's delays had cost us dearly, and we needed to catch the rest of the pack. I pulled out a route card to see what we were missing. The destination was the Circuit Paul Ricard, a full-blown Formula 1 track, which had hosted fourteen Grand Prix races. This was unfortunate, since we would have had the opportunity to drive a few laps. I looked at the blurb:

> Today you get a real chance to drive your cars 'flat out' at the Paul Ricard Formula One Circuit.

We were a bit puzzled at the definition of 'flat out' as we were sure that we had covered some of that ground in Morocco.

Talking of Morocco, we reflected a little on the week's events as we approached the end of the journey. We were still in awe of the events and experiences in Morocco, which understandably dominated the conversation. We speculated on the fate of the crash victims of whom there was still no news bar the fact that no one had actually died, and we debated the moral issues of our behaviour and that of the Gumballers collectively.

There are those that are quick to condemn the Gumball and its participants on the grounds that such ostentatious wealth is in some way distasteful or indeed disrespectful. The Gumball has attracted these very criticisms while travelling through the USA, the world's richest country, so presumably there will be those who think the Moroccan antics were the epitome of ignorance. This is a predictable reaction, and indeed at times we were concerned that our own behaviour was in some way disrespectful, but witnessing the Moroccans' genuine delight at our presence reminded us that nothing could be further from the truth.

In reality, it is terribly patronising to the Moroccan people to feel somehow obligated to feign poverty as if it is a noble display of solidarity. Those who travel to Morocco and then complain that they are constantly pestered for money might find that the people were preying on their obvious sense of guilt, spotting them as easy targets. If they had brought a bit of flash money, they might have found some piece and quiet. Our approach to Morocco had been somewhat different and, having arrived with bells on, the reception was magnificent.

Richard was driving and seemed to have everything under control until he suddenly kicked off some car chat.

'This is an odd sensation after the Volvo. What make of car is this, anyway?'

'It's a Volkswagen, Richard, hence the big VW badge on the steering wheel that has been staring you in the face for the last five hours.'

Arriving in Cannes was predictably less relaxing, as Richard got back into Gumball mode. We stopped to stick a token Gumball sticker on the bonnet of our hire car, and approached the seafront with renewed vigour and intent. It had taken surprisingly little effort to persuade Richard to follow my directions and, after a brief flirtation with heading in completely the wrong direction, he recognised the logic of aiming for the sea.

At the seafront, or 'La Croisette', as it's known locally, there was a major Gumball traffic jam, the likes of which we had not seen since Paris. Cars were backed up for a couple of miles, as they crawled along La Croisette and then snaked around to approach the Inter Continental Carlton Hotel. Each car had to pass through the Gumball triumphal arch, then pose for photographs before unloading luggage and handing their car over to the valet parking attendants. As there were a hundred-odd cars in front of us, this looked like it would be a long wait.

Suddenly, Richard was inspired. After a week of going to pieces in every town, losing ground to fellow Gumballers at the last minute, he had spotted an opportunity to overtake the full hundred in one clean swoop. The road along the Cannes seafront is divided into four lanes, with a grass verge bisecting the two lanes of two-way traffic. Because of the Gumball parade, the two lanes on the hotel side of the street were closed but there seemed to be nobody in a position to stop us driving unhindered directly to the triumphal arch. All the other Gumballers were on the far side of the grass, doing a U-turn beyond the hotel and approaching from the other direction. We simply had to reverse for a couple of metres and proceed on the opposite side of the central island.

Like a man possessed, Richard slammed the car into reverse and gave it some welly. We lunged forwards, narrowly missing Joe French on a scooter. There had been no need to reverse this car as yet, and Richard was still not familiar with the layout of the gearbox. After another frantic stabbing at the gearstick, we were lucky to avoid a collision with a Gumballing Bentley. Third time lucky, he found reverse and narrowly missed the central island. In Gumball style, burning rubber and screeching tyres, we sped towards the finish, ignoring the disgruntled looks from those locked in the traffic. Richard slammed on the brakes as we reached the oncoming traffic and turned in towards the arch just ahead of a BMW M3. A job well done, and one that had saved us at least an hour and probably ensured a top-twenty finish.

A harassed-looking Gumball crew member was undergoing a heated discussion with the BMW behind us, and then came over to knock our window.

'Listen, lads, will you let this guy in ahead of you. He's doing his nut because he made it all the way here without a scratch on his car, and a local has just tipped into the back of him.'

'Sure, no problem.'

There was no problem, because it made no difference to us, but we were surprised at the level of self-absorption required to drive on the Gumball through three countries at insane speeds, blatantly disregarding local laws and limits, and then to object to a minor traffic incident caused by Joe French, who was a little frustrated at being delayed for a couple of hours for no better reason than our amusement.

Max was on hand to congratulate us. 'Welcome to Cannes, guys. What happened to the Volvo?'

'We left it in Barcelona.'

'Well, that was the Gumball; I told you you'd never forget it.' Understatement is not a word one instantly associates with the Gumball, but Max's assessment was taking the piss.

On checking into the hotel, the only unfinished business was for me to enjoy the party and for Richard to have his quiet night, off the drink.

'Will we kick off with a bottle of champagne then, Clement?' he asked, as he sauntered into the bar. Never mind about the ethics of Morocco, we were now in Cannes for the Film Festival where bad behaviour was positively *de rigueur*.

15. CANNES – 'THE MOTHER OF ALL FINISH PARTIES'

> Take a deep breath, you have just completed three
> thousand miles in just six days, and I hope you've had one
> of the best adventures of your life. Tonight's party is in the
> grand and very famous Ballroom of the Carlton Hotel. So
> wash, get changed and be ready for dinner, trophies and
> the mother of all finish parties.

'Take a deep breath?' Absolutely, and a deep swig of champagne. Having procured the necessaries, Richard disappeared to make an entrance on board the Hummer, which was still in the traffic, drowning out the bling-bling Gumball soundtrack with a rousing rendition of the 'Fields of Athenry', which was surely a Film Festival first in Cannes.

I went to look for Bertie, who predictably enough was to be found in the bar and equally predictably had already come across the American divorcees, who had flown up earlier from Barcelona. It is a cliché that you can tell a lot about a person from their friends, but I was slightly concerned that both my friends who had dropped in on the Gumball seemed to instinctively sniff out these two ladies. Despite my concerns, it did not take a man of Bertie's experience long to deduce that these two were a bit frisky, and he wisely chose to keep the contents of the cargo he was carrying to himself. There was no such luck now, though, as he could not wait to show off his stock, as excited as a kid in a toy shop. Or, more accurately, as a kid in a travelling toy shop. He opened up his sober-looking tartan satchel (you can take the Scotsman out of Scotland but

. . .) to reveal all manner of vibrators, dildos and assorted sex toys in a frightening range of sizes. I was stunned that he had been allowed to transport these monstrosities on to the plane, since any one of them had to be considered an offensive weapon particularly when compared to the matchstick your would-be terrorist could conceal in his shoe. If individually they were dangerous, the collection in its innocent-looking satchel had to be considered a veritable arsenal.

'What exactly are you doing in Cannes, Bert?' I asked as the range of stock sank in, though obviously not literally. While I was aware that he had gone into the sex-toys' business, I thought that he was at the discreet end of the market. Prior to leaving London, I had asked Jess to add his name to the guest list for the party, merely saying he was 'a colleague of mine in Cannes on business'. I had thought at the time that this sounded quite impressive; now I was afraid of being guilty of all manner of perversion by association.

'I'm on business here; I'm Mantric's man on the ground: "Mantric Marketing — where fetish meets fashion",' he said, trotting out the slogans while thrusting his business card into one hand and a twelve-inch 'Turbo Jack Rabbit' into the other. The Film Festival seemed an odd time to do his sort of business, though given the props on his person perhaps it would be a good idea to introduce him to the Irish boys. They could make a film together, though they would undoubtedly need a cast who were a little less fun size than the Gummi Bears.

'I have a meeting in the morning,' Bert explained, 'with some sex shops and have brought all this stock with me as demonstration models.'

'Is it all gigantic and obscene, or is there anything fun in there?' I asked, peering into his bag.

'I think you'll like this, it's a brand new model – the "Mantric Zing Finger".' He pulled out an intriguing-looking box, opening it to reveal some sort of toy that looked like a pair of mating computer mice, only smaller. 'You wrap that bit around your wrist like so, and strap that bit on to your finger like so. And then press that button to turn it on.'

Turn it on I did, and my finger began to vibrate at 3,500 rpm. On the wrist section there was a control dial, and I took it right up to the red line. My finger was going hammer and tongs, vibrating with such ferocity it could have measured on the Richter scale. Bertie smiled proudly, seeing his stock in action and sensing some customer satisfaction.

'I'm sure I don't need to teach you how to use it,' he said confidently. 'Let's just say it is from our "Dr Sands and his Sexy Hands" range.'

'This is wicked, Bert, can I hang on to it for the night?'

'Yeah, no problem but be very careful, I can't afford to lose any stock. I've already had to give the "Pulsa Dong" a surgical scrub.'

Bertie told me how he had unwisely left his bag of tricks unattended in his flat when he had gone to bed the night before he left London. On waking in the morning, he was alarmed to discover it had been tampered with and a quick roll call confirmed that the 'Pulsa Dong' was conspicuous by its absence, though the roll call was hardly necessary as I can confirm that the thing had a fairly conspicuous presence as well. Bert was understandably disturbed, as the obvious suspect was his flatmate and, although he had long suspected him to be a fairly keen masturbator, it was worrying to think that he might have resorted to Mantric's wares.

Scanning the room for further evidence, he spotted a guilty-looking handbag and then realised that the flatmate had met a girl the previous evening and had obviously been delighted to discover such a haul on their return. Bertie shuddered as he recalled making an apprehensive recovery of the 'Pulsa Dong' from the flatmate's bedroom floor.

'I tell you, mate, it was all a bit unpleasant.' He grimaced. 'But I suppose it could have been worse. If they had gone for one of the strap-ons, or the "Come Down Under" with its dual-pronged approach, I don't think I could have stomached it. Well, it's back in its box now, and I'll just have to hope our clients don't realise they are dealing with soiled goods.'

This sort of stuff might be all in a day's work for Bertie, but I couldn't stomach it just listening to him, and I suggested we get some fresh air and find Richard. We found Richard kicking off his quiet night on La Croisette, singing and sipping champagne on the roof of the Hummer. There was quite a crowd forming as they had also been joined by another friend from Dublin called Rob, who had flown out to enjoy the party and assist the long drive home.

I left them all to it and disappeared to go and clean myself up, agreeing that we would all rendezvous again at the party. On the way to the room I got involved in an angry and awkward conversation with an extreme skateboarder, who was far from 'stoked' and extremely 'pissed, man' at the lack of skateboards, which he had last seen in Paris being loaded into the back of our car. Amid all the shenanigans of Barcelona, we had offloaded their boards and associated paraphernalia, leaving them in what had turned out to be the less than capable care of a Gumball crew member. They did not seem to have survived the last leg to Cannes. His jiving and jargon were less comprehensible than even Richard asking for directions, but his exaggerated body language left me in no doubt that it was our fault his legion of fans were due to be sorely disappointed at his lack of aerial antics. I was too tired to really care; we had done our best for him and his skateboards and now I was just keen to get on and enjoy the party. I was even too tired to point out that we were in the Carlton Hotel in Cannes, on the eve of the Film Festival; his fans were likely to be pretty thin on the ground in this company, and, as it was after 9 p.m., it was past their bedtime anyway.

Some while later, I met up with Richard and Bertie as planned. In the meantime, Richard had also cleaned himself up and seemed to have washed away any fatigue and consequent desire for a quiet night, declaring himself fit and able for a party as if this was something unexpected.

I reached out, offering my hand and said, 'Well done, Richard, we made it in one piece, despite a few scary moments. Thanks for your excellent co-driving; it has been a real laugh.' Richard reached out to shake my hand, but, on doing so, snapped his hand away as quick as any freemason skateboarder could manage it.

'Christ almighty, what the hell was that?' he asked, staring at my hand.

'It's a "Mantric Zing Finger", Richard, courtesy of "Doctor Sands and his Sexy Hands",' I replied, nodding towards Bertie. Richard's eyes lit up, as I knew they would. Anybody with Richard's passion for operating at top speed could not resist a 'Zing Finger'.

'Here, let me have a go,' he said excitedly, as Bertie started muttering about the importance of merchandise and meetings, while we lectured him on learning to share his toys. Having wired himself up, Richard disappeared in a flash to try out his new toy, and Bertie began to accept the fact that it was unlikely any of his clients would be road testing the contraption in the morning.

Leaving Richard to play, Bert and I went to the bar. As we queued, we engaged in the completely non-original activity of talking about the various girls on the Gumball. Bertie pointed out a girl who Richard and I had noticed in Paris. She was with a guy in a Bentley Continental GT and was simply stunning.

'Yeah, Bert, she's gorgeous. But if you see the bloke she's with and the car she's in you'd instantly think easterneuropean brides.com.' This was an unfortunate comment as the bloke in front of us swung round to inform us that she was Lithuanian and the bloke she was with happened to be his best friend.

Thankfully, at this moment, before this line of debate could be continued, our photographer friend and fellow crash victim James made a timely interruption. I had asked him to take some final shots of us as we were both in our Cordings regalia for Cannes and I wanted some pictures for Noll Uloth, the managing director who had kindly supplied the suits. James stressed that this was not a problem as long as we did it right away, since he was weary from his week's work and keen to finally start partying. This was a problem though, since Richard was nowhere to be seen, having disappeared off to go 'Zing-Fingering' somewhere.

Thankfully, we found him relatively quickly, oddly enough chatting to Lucy and explained the need for immediate action. We wandered outside and posed for a few photographs on the steps of the hotel, but in the excitement and the urgency Richard forgot about his new appendage, hence the presence of a vibrating sex toy on his finger in our otherwise carefully planned pictures.

Back at the party, we noticed Torquenstein had arrived, minus his robot costume, which had been replaced by some pretty extensive bandaging. His appearance alone was commendable for someone we assumed might be dead less than 48 hours earlier. Holding up what little remained of his car he explained that he had felt it vital to make the party in Cannes and thus be considered as a finisher. He had arrived just in time for the awards ceremony, which was fortuitous as appropriately enough he won the Gumball Road Safety Award, although a little tongue-in-cheek.

Max and his wife, Julie, presented the trophies, with Max adding the quips as he called out the characters. All participants received a limited-edition bronze of the original Gumballer Burt Reynolds wearing a Fez in recognition of our African adventure. Predictably enough, when it came to our turn there was a Volvo gag.

'And Richard Dunwoody and Clement Wilson in the Volvo . . . former champion jockey Dunwoody presumably is used to a little more horse power.'

We got a great cheer, though it was difficult to ascertain whether it was from the converted for the Volvo's pace or for

Richard's partying power. The partying of the rest of the Gumballers had noticeably been raised a notch or two, notwithstanding the fact the previous shindigs had been fairly hard-core affairs. The atmosphere was clearly shaping up to be 'the mother of all finishing parties' and Max's final administrative announcement confirmed at least one Gumballer's rush to get going. He held up a large set of keys to display to the packed room.

'Would the owner of these keys please claim them; somebody just chucked them at a parking attendant without telling him the make or model of car, or indeed where it was parked.'

Sheepishly, Steve from the Hummer went to collect the keys.

Apart from the increased appetite for the party, secure in the knowledge that there was no more driving to be done, there were also a lot more people around. Previous Gumballers, wives and girlfriends and assorted celebs in town for the Film Festival swelled the ranks. Everyone was getting on famously and there was a considerably flirtatious atmosphere in the air. At the bar I bumped into Sarah again, the browsing Brazilian camerawoman who had spotted our website and landed me in it in Paris.

'I might like to dance a little later on,' she said suggestively.

I was a little taken aback and could only muster a 'Well, I might like to ask you' before wandering off wondering about the directness of her approach. I know I had suffered some communication problems in Marrakech but there was no doubt here. It was like being back in Iceland.

Icelandic girls are the most staggeringly direct in the world, with a confidence arising from the absolute belief that they are the most beautiful in the world. Which they are. There is no arrogance either; they enjoy a collective confidence in the beauty of all Icelanders, and are not uppity about the whole thing on an individual level. On one trip to Iceland, I met an author and a photographer who pointed out a girl working behind the bar, and told me that she was Iceland's top model.

Really, why then was she pulling pints? Look around you, they said; it's not so well paid here. Sure enough, practically any one of the girls in the bar could have been Iceland's top model, or any country's. The incontrovertible economic principles of supply and demand ensured that she needed a supplemental income. This was all very well in Iceland, and you get used to their directness there after a while, adjusting to it like time zones and jet lag; you quickly realise that it is just another national characteristic like fog, rain and woolly jumpers but encountering it elsewhere was a bit strange.

Sarah, albeit half-Brazilian, had been brought up in London and this sort of direct approach, while undeniably sassy and attractive, surely was not terribly normal. It was not rocket science to work out in Iceland it was a nationality thing but it took the social scientist in me to identify the 'Gumball' factor. There are proper, learned social scientists that undertake all sorts of studies on human interactions and rituals, and I had come across one in particular whose findings might have been relevant in this situation. Social science boffins are not very Gumball but Kate Fox is a little different, choosing to study areas like interaction in pubs and nightclubs with a specific interest in the science of flirting. She has a personal 'league table' of the most sociable environments and the whole horsey racecourse scene tops the table. It is a highly effective flirting environment as well apparently.

I was trying to identify the factors that make a particular environment conducive to flirting, and eventually came up with three key factors: alcohol, sociability (particularly the acceptability of conversation with strangers) and a shared focus of interest. Race meetings turned out to be among the very few settings that offered all three factors.

Parties and bars, generally regarded as appropriate flirting environments lack the important shared-interest factor – and many of the settings that do have this factor

(such as hobby-clubs, gyms, evening classes, other spectator
sports/events) lack either the social lubricant of alcohol or
the necessary degree of sociability . . . Racing is the only
setting however, that not only is open to anyone but also has
the advantage of a ritual conversation-starter including the
word 'fancy', as in 'What do you fancy in the 3.30?'

Kate Fox, The Racing Tribe; *Metro* 2002.

Fancying myself as a bit of an amateur social scientist, I'd like
to put the Gumball party in Cannes up there above race
meetings. For a start, racecourses are always full of horsey girls
who ought to cost a couple of points immediately; it is difficult
to properly flirt with a girl you suspect of having rosettes and
pony posters on her bedroom wall comparatively recently. And
by the time it can be no longer considered recent they're just
plain scary, which is even less conducive to flirtatious banter.
Secondly, presumably Richard Dunwoody has spent more time
than most at race meetings and, if his flirting technique on the
Gumball was anything to go by, he did not learn a damn thing.
If anyone asked Richard, 'What do you fancy?' his hot tip was
to 'Go ugly early.' This questionable advice was apparently
delivered by another well-known Irish sporting figure.

The Gumball party had lashings of drink, total acceptability
of sociability and an enormous amount of acceptable ritual
conversation-starters concerning any number of the insane
happenings of the previous week. I believe it to be a sound
theory and one that explains Sarah's flirtatious banter but
perhaps quick-witted social-scientist types might point out that,
while the stock Gumball conversation-starter of 'What are you
driving?' was a legitimate opening gambit, our response of 'a
Volvo estate' was not as sexy as it could have been in the present
company. Indeed, Ms Fox would probably laugh and back up
her argument by telling me that with those sorts of lines I'd have
more luck at Plumpton than in Cannes.

Back in the throng I noticed Aidan was taking full advantage of the interaction opportunities and clearly had ignored any advice Richard might have offered, presumably believing in the adage that it is ultimately the bookies that win every time. If I had been a gambling man, I would have put my shirt on what was looking to be a racing certainty. Aidan, in a display Kate Fox would have been proud of, had the drink and the sociability angle well and truly covered, and presumably had got the shared interest factor off to a flying start. 'Mine's a Lamborghini, what do you drive? Oh a Maserati, good stuff. Italian cars, eh? You've got to love 'em, goodness me, what a lot we have in common.' If flirting was the order of the day, Aidan was playing a blinder with Jodie Kidd.

With all this mischief kicking off, it did not surprise me to see that Roberto di Milano – Bertie's alter ego when not brandishing dildos – had made an appearance. The nickname di Milano was coined when somebody noticed his occasional ability to come over all Italian, delivering his well-rehearsed chat-up lines, irrespective of any acceptable social conditions. Surprisingly enough, this performance seemed to be fruitful for him more often than not and his unfortunate victim on this particular occasion was Tish, one of the Gumball press girls. This was a particularly disappointing development as earlier I had been engaged in some fairly energetic flirting of my own in that particular department, but I knew better than to go and exchange cheesy lines with Roberto.

I was perfectly prepared to interrupt Richard, on the other hand, though I got a bit of a surprise to discover that he was chatting up a girl who was asleep. He seemed pretty surprised himself when I pointed it out to him, but at least it clarified matters why she was not contributing to his conversation. He swore that he had not been talking about horses again, but the deep snores of his friend suggested otherwise.

I had found him in the foyer with the Irish lads who somehow or other had bumped into another pile of people from

Dublin. They were friends of Bob's apparently who were on a girls' weekend in Cannes. I know the world is a small place but these lads were taking the piss. Everywhere we went, parties of people holidaying in the locality were coming out of the woodwork. Rob, who had actually flown out deliberately to meet them, appeared to have taken Richard's advice some time ago, and was now locked in a passionate embrace that was threatening the stability of the antique chair they were in.

Things were definitely beginning to get out of hand in the 'Spirit of the Gumball'. The word was going around that there was a party in Room 403, although nobody seemed to know who our generous host was. I went to find Emma, the ersatz porn star, to persuade her to join the party, though sadly she declined. She did seem touched though by my gift of a red rose that had taken some performance to extract from the clutches of the concierge.

As I was leaving the lift on the fourth floor, the girls from the foyer were getting back in. Apparently, they did not find the party to their liking since somebody had switched the pay-per-view channels on. Perhaps Emma would be making an appearance after all.

Room 403 was a suite, with all the trimmings and a balcony with a sea view over the yachts. By this stage, it was dawn and I took a few moments to admire the surroundings. On the floor below, I noticed a couple doing much the same thing, but as Aidan would later put it more poetically: 'Dawn, in Cannes with a view over Croisette, on a balcony of the Carlton Hotel with Jodie Kidd. It doesn't get much better than this.'

Back in the room, Tim Roth, of *Pulp Fiction* fame, had appeared from nowhere and was now pontificating with an enthusiasm more usually associated with Chris Eubank. The striking thing about him was his scruffiness, as his T-shirt was peppered with rips, tears and holes. Nobody seemed to know where he had come from and his presence caused some comment, though perhaps not the celebrity worship that he might have expected. Tish, who had since abandoned Bertie somewhere, took one look at him and dismissed him with a withering 'Tim Roth? Look at that shirt – Tim Moth is more like it.'

The highlight of the party in Room 403 was the food. Our makeshift hostess, who ought to remain nameless, decided to order some food. Unable to make a choice from such a lavish room-service menu she sportingly ordered the whole lot. Minutes later the waiters arrived and wheeled a trolley in which was transformed into a table for ten. This was your upmarket version of meals on wheels and was a positive banquet.

After the meal, Richard had fallen asleep on the bed and someone was just making the beginnings of an indelible-marker moustache on his face. The Irish lads were passed out in front of the porn, except Mark who was talking toe-jobs with Jess. Tim Roth was still chatting away, and, after surveying the scene, satisfied with a job well done, I headed for bed.

Tuesday, 11 May, our first post-Gumball day was my birthday. I had been woken intermittently throughout the morning by an irritatingly repetitive telephone call but decided to sleep on, thinking my birthday greetings could wait. When I eventually answered it at about 2.30 p.m., I found yet another angry concierge on the other end of the line. In a scene repeated throughout the hotel that morning I was lambasted for not obeying the official check-out times since there were some pretty irate A-list Hollywood stars waiting to take up occupancy. They had arrived for the Film Festival and much to their annoyance found their favourite hotel full of Gumballers who were too tired and drunk to stir from their beds.

Richard had already risen but even he had slept until after midday. I caught up with him downstairs and was touched to see he had bought a bottle of champagne for me as a birthday present. I was also amused to see that his marker moustache was still faintly visible. We had lunch with the Irish crowd and discussed the many variations on the events of the night before, filling in the blanks as it were.

One thing we were all agreed on was that Richard's technique had reached new lows in trying to chat up a girl who was asleep, as John raised a toast and officially declared, 'Your days of riding winners are over.'

Steven was somewhat distressed by the memory of going to bed to be greeted by the sight of Rob's companion's backside. As they were squeezed into a single bed, space and sheets were at a premium with Rob emerging the better off. His companion was understandably concerned for her modesty.

'Rob, can we swap sides please,' she asked.

'Why?'

'Because Steve can see my bum,' came the reply.

'Well, there's no point in swapping because you can guarantee he doesn't want to see mine.'

Apparently, Tim Roth eventually shut up, crashed out and received the marker pen treatment, with even more thoroughness than Richard had.

John told how he had woken up in Room 403, a little disorientated and was disturbed to discover he was not only surrounded by sleeping men in front of a porn film, but one of them had his arm around him. He did not name names, but promised to keep an eye on the culprit in the future. Steve piped up, admitting that he was the culprit in question, but made the fair point that John's hairstyle made it a little difficult to tell the difference after a few drinks.

But, above all, everyone who had lasted the distance in Room 403 wanted to know the same thing. What had happened to Richard? He was last seen disappearing into a lift with a guy who was widely believed to be bisexual at best, having asked him did he 'want to go downstairs?'

EPILOGUE – RECOVERY IN MONACO

'Honestly, how many times do I have to tell you? I asked him to go downstairs looking for some more partying as everybody in the room was asleep,' Richard said, getting increasingly exasperated as I continued to wind him up. 'And then I realised that it sounded odd. To make sure he realised I DEFINITELY wasn't looking for that sort of thing, I marched out the front of the hotel and got into a taxi. When Benny Bisexual, as you call him, got in, I started urging the driver to take us to a bar with lots of women to stress the point. The taxi driver drove us about five yards to the front door, told us all the women were asleep, and then charged €15.00 for the journey.'

I knew that this was exactly what happened, not least because his 'companion' had told me so. Nonetheless, two days later, it was still too good a joke to let go of that easily.

'I know, Richard, of course I believe you but you've got to admit it might look odd,' I said, tossing a copy of *The Times* with a story headlined 'SECRET CLUB FOR GO-GETTERS WHO GO FASTER'. A *Times* correspondent was in Cannes to cover the Film Festival and had stumbled upon the Gumball party and found it to make good copy. 'Don't they own the *News of the World*? Sunday's papers might make interesting reading – "DAWN DALLIANCE FOR DICK DUNWOODY".'

We were in Monaco recuperating. Volvo had booked us flights home from Nice on Friday, which had worked out rather nicely as it gave us an extra couple of days' rest instead of driving the car all the way home. We had the use of a luxury flat that had kindly been lent to us by a friend of mine, and we were enjoying the sun on the balcony reflecting on our adventure.

We both agreed that we would do the Gumball again, although it would be wise to take a holiday beforehand. I reckoned that I would be happy even to do it with Richard again, though I would like to bring a translator with us. For his part, Richard said that he would do it again with me if he could install a better speed limiter, which I thought was a bit rich. I doubted if either of us would be Gumballing with Volvo again.

In the two days that we had been in Monaco, the rest of the Gumballers dispersed. Aidan and Jodie headed off to play on a yacht and cement their blossoming relationship. The Irish lads had headed for Dublin via an extra night in Cannes and a €2,500 drinks bill, except Mark who had returned for a holiday in Marbella. Rumour had it that Jess was spotted holidaying in Marbella as well. Chris and Graham had gone back to London in the taxi with the meter running. We spotted quite a few familiar cars on the streets of Monaco that week. We never discovered if Emma was, in fact, a porn star, though we agreed that it was highly unlikely.

My personal admin had also made a complete disappearance with the discovery that my passport had not been seen since Barcelona, and was unlikely to be seen again, much to Richard's amusement. Things went from bad to worse when I managed to get our hire car towed away, only to be recovered at vast expense. For all my slagging of him and his eccentricities, he had to put up with a lot, and found my complete lack of organisational skills an ongoing nightmare. With the journey over he was able to laugh about it, and found the passport loss unsurprising as well as amusing. Richard was not above losing things himself though; the whereabouts of the 'Mantric Zing Finger' remains completely unknown, much to Bertie's fury.

The bottle of champagne that he had so kindly given me for my birthday also made a suspicious disappearance in the company of Richard and two German girls the night we went out on the town in Monaco. He was uncharacteristically tight-lipped about the details, beyond promising to replace it.

Richard left on the Friday, as he had to be back to run a mini-marathon on the Sunday. I still had to discuss my citizenship with the consulate in Marseilles, so I stayed for the weekend. The Grand Prix Historique was on in Monaco and, as our lodgings enjoyed the finest view of the circuit in the principality, I was not too distressed at the inconvenience. I was enjoying the break. I dropped Richard off at Nice Airport, and we were having a drink in the bar as he waited for his flight. I looked longingly at the destinations on the departures board.

'I need a holiday, Richard.'

'You need a passport first,' he replied, showing a working knowledge of international-travel regulations.

'Well, yes, but the first thing I will do when I replace my passport is book a relaxing holiday.'

'Excellent, sort it out then and we'll go to Iceland.'

Hmm, Iceland? Some of my enthusiasm for the place seemed to have rubbed off on Richard. Reykjavik with Richard Dunwoody was not exactly my idea of relaxing. I considered it for about a nanosecond.

'Absolutely, Richard, you're on,' I replied before I realised that airport pub chat is the most dangerous of all.

INDEX

WIN A Supercar Driving Experience courtesy of Virgin Books and Virgin Experience Days

Discover the passion and power of driving a Ferrari or Porsche. Alternatively, enjoy a full day learning handling skills in an off-road vehicle, rally car or single seater. With a Virgin Experience Days premium Supercar Driving Voucher you can test your driving ability to the limit.

What's included:
- Training from a qualified instructor
- Safety briefing and initial group instruction
- Track familiarisation
- Hands-on experience of driving your chosen vehicle
- Course duration varies from 2–3 hours to max 7 hours
- Over 18 locations to choose from
- Personal accident cover to a value of £50,000 plus cancellation indemnity

To enter the competition simply send your name, address and a daytime telephone number on a postcard to:

GUMBALL RALLY competition
Marketing Department
Virgin Books
Thames Wharf Studios
Rainville Road
London, W6 9HA

Closing date for entries: 31 December 2005
See overleaf for terms and conditions

Inspirational Gifts

www.virgin.com/experiencedays

www.virgin.com/books

TERMS AND CONDITIONS

1. The competition is open to residents of the UK and Ireland only, excluding Virgin employees and their families.

2. To take part in the Supercar Driving Experience you need to meet the following criteria: Minimum age 17–21 depending on location (under 18's need parental/guardian consent). Participants should hold a full UK driving licence: Ferrari and Porsche drivers should have held a full licence for min 2–3 years depending on location; single seater, rally and off-road drivers for min 1 year at some locations. You should be in reasonable health and agile enough to climb into a vehicle fitted with a roll cage. Minimum height 5'–5'4" (152–162 cm), max height 6'2"–6'4" (188–193 cm) depending on location. Maximum weight 16–18 stone (102–114 kg) depending on location.

3. Closing date for receipt of entries is 31 December 2005.

4. The first entry drawn on 9 January 2006 will be declared the winner and notified by post.

5. The decision of the judges is final. No correspondence will be entered into.

6. No purchase necessary. Entries restricted to one per household.

7. The prize consists of a Supercar Driving Experience gift box including smart wallet, personalised voucher, message card and single use camera. Not included in the prize: travel to and from location, food, drinks, insurance (other than that provided by Virgin Experience Days within the gift package).

8. Full terms and conditions for Virgin Experience Days will be included in the prize pack sent to the winner. A copy of the terms and conditions can be found at www.virgin.com/experiencedays or by calling 0845 330 5115

9. The prize is non-transferable and non-refundable and no alternatives can be substituted.

10. Responsibility cannot be accepted for damaged, illegible or incomplete entries, or those arriving after the closing date.

11. The winner's name will be available from the address overleaf from 9 January 2006.

12. Winners may be required to participate in publicity events.

Inspirational Gifts